I0900944

IMAGES
of America

BRADFORD AND WARNER

On the Cover: The Simonds Free High School class of 1906 stands in a hayrack in front of Hardy's studio. Members of the class are bound for a picnic at French's Brook on Mount Kearsarge in May 1906. The high school was free for Warner students, but pupils attending from surrounding towns paid tuition ($5 per semester). This class had students from Bradford, Dunbarton, Newbury, Sunapee, and Warner in its ranks. (Courtesy of Warner Historical Society; photograph by Hardy.)

IMAGES
of America

BRADFORD AND WARNER

Laurie Buchar and Rebecca Courser

ARCADIA
PUBLISHING

Copyright © 2012 by Laurie Buchar and Rebecca Courser
ISBN 978-0-7385-9261-9

Published by Arcadia Publishing
Charleston, South Carolina

Printed in the United States of America

Library of Congress Control Number: 2011945926

For all general information, please contact Arcadia Publishing:
Telephone 843-853-2070
Fax 843-853-0044
E-mail sales@arcadiapublishing.com
For customer service and orders:
Toll-Free 1-888-313-2665

Visit us on the Internet at www.arcadiapublishing.com

To Milly (Ingalls) Kittredge (1934–2010), archivist and soul of the Bradford Historical Society. To Warner photographers Ralph Pratt and husband-and-wife team Charles and Alice Hardy.

Contents

ACKNOWLEDGMENTS

The authors drew heavily from the Bradford Historical Society's *Two Hundred Plus: Bradford, New Hampshire in Retrospect 1771–1976*, published by the Bradford History Committee and Bicentennial Committee in 1976 and *Looking Back* by Allene Hamilton, published in 1987. Information was drawn from the *Kearsarge Independent* and earlier research was by Annie Cogswell, Orton Hill, and Roxanne Smith. The following people offered excellent editorial and/or scholarly assistance: George Cilley, Gary Clark, Louise Clark, Richard Cook, Harriet Douglas, J. Ann Eldridge, Sonny Harris, Rick Hedrick, Everett Kittredge, Alan Lord, Dick McLeod, and Rachel Parsons.

Many of the Bradford photographs seen here are courtesy of Steven Hansen, who shared his extensive personal collection. Individual images are courtesy of John Belanger, Connie Dayton, Everett Kittredge, and Brackett Scheffy. The photograph of the scythe stuck in the tree is courtesy of Ray Steiger. The archives of the Warner Historical Society abound with photographs donated to the collections over the past 40 years that have been used for this publication. The images in this volume appear courtesy of the Bradford Historical Society (BHS) and the Warner Historical Society (WHS). Several images courtesy of the Warner Historical Society were taken by Ralph Pratt (WHS–Pratt) and Charles and Alice Hardy (WHS–Hardy).

The authors are also grateful for the support of their individual historical society boards for encouraging them to undertake this rewarding project. They urge others to be a part of the ongoing story of Bradford and Warner by becoming members of the local historical societies. For more information, visit warnerhistorical.org or bradfordnhhistorical.org.

Introduction

When Dorcas Presbury fell gravely ill in her log cabin in Bradford, her husband climbed Goodwin Hill and fired his musket. Their nearest neighbor, Israel Morrill, heard the shot in Warner, and his wife, Sarah, went on foot through the forest to offer help. Such was the scope of community and communication in the 1770s.

Early New Hampshire settlements followed major rivers, where water and land routes had been established by Native Americans. Bradford and Warner, however, lay in a vast frontier between the Merrimack and Connecticut Rivers, navigable only on foot. They belonged with a line of towns granted and laid out by the General Court of Massachusetts in 1736 to act as a buffer against Native American attacks, as well as gain dominion for the British crown. The Penacook tribe had abided here for generations living in close harmony with nature, but the settlers sought to impose European "lines on the land."

Industrious Francis and Betsy Davis built a mill and broke ground in the 1760s in Davisville with their stalwart children. Intrepid souls like William Presbury and his wife, Dorcas, as well as Isaac Davis and his wife, Keturah, brought their families from neighboring settlements to Bradford around 1770. Although we have no photographs of this period, the stories we know from diaries and historical records paint a vivid picture to fuel our imagination. What made these people endure the rigors of this challenge? We can only speculate, but a sense of adventure can still be found here, where opportunity and natural beauty still reside.

These chapters show the progression of our town's development. In the beginning, early settlers swarmed to stake their claim on the landscape. Thus began the dance with the pervasive forest forces. They cut, cleared, planted, and defined their homesteads in order to live off the land. Within several generations, the forests would once again dominate the landscape. After the establishment of gristmills and sawmills, people converted their crude log cabins into some of the frame buildings that still exist today. All of these efforts, plus human nature, led to the need for gathering places where people found fellowship and support. Communities required meetinghouses, churches, taverns, and schools as populations increased. Footpaths were expanded into roadways that provided connections for communication and commerce. Businesses grew to serve the needs of citizens and visitors alike. Development of the railroad system, combined with the natural beauty of the area, led entrepreneurs to accommodate the tourist trade by building hotels and boardinghouses. Recreational pastimes blossomed as people had more leisure time.

Both Bradford and Warner reflect New Hampshire's historical population patterns. Bradford, settled in 1771, had 130 residents by 1787 when it was incorporated. It had been called New Bradford and Bradfordton, named by settlers from Bradford, Massachusetts, honoring their ancestral home, Broadforth, England, which means "broad ford." Settlers came to Warner (New Almsbury) in the 1730s, only to be burnt out by the Native Americans. At the end of the French and Indian War in the 1760s, men from Amesbury, Massachusetts, returned to the waterfalls in what is now Davisville to establish their foothold in the wilderness. In 1774, the population of 230 inhabitants petitioned for township under the name New Almsbury, but the area was renamed Warner by Royal Governor John Wentworth.

During the next few decades, the populations of Bradford and Warner expanded as families established their roots and industry flourished. In the 1820s, Warner's population peaked at 2,246, followed by Bradford's boom of 1,341 in 1850. There ensued a slow decline in both communities as farmers moved west seeking better farmland. Others went to cities seeking employment in the burgeoning industrial arena. Eventually, the same railroads that made the area prosperous served as a vehicle for further change. Many of the "old folks" were left at home on the farm to manage as best they could. Some hardscrabble farms were abandoned and reclaimed by the forest. Other farmers found ways to adapt to new scientific agricultural trends and increased their production of hay, milk, meat, and orchard products. Mills and businesses adapted similarly to developing technology. Over the years, our communities continued to develop and flourish, eventually forming the towns we live in today.

Thankfully, every New Hampshire town can boast a white steeple, a public library, notorious characters, and prominent landmarks; Bradford and Warner are no exception. Despite each town's unique features, we share a common history of the rugged life that defined New Hampshire. This book offers a composite story told through select images of Bradford and Warner. We recognize and cherish the images of our towns and, thus, fortify a vital sense of community. These images, of course, can only tell part of the story; the rest is for you to discover.

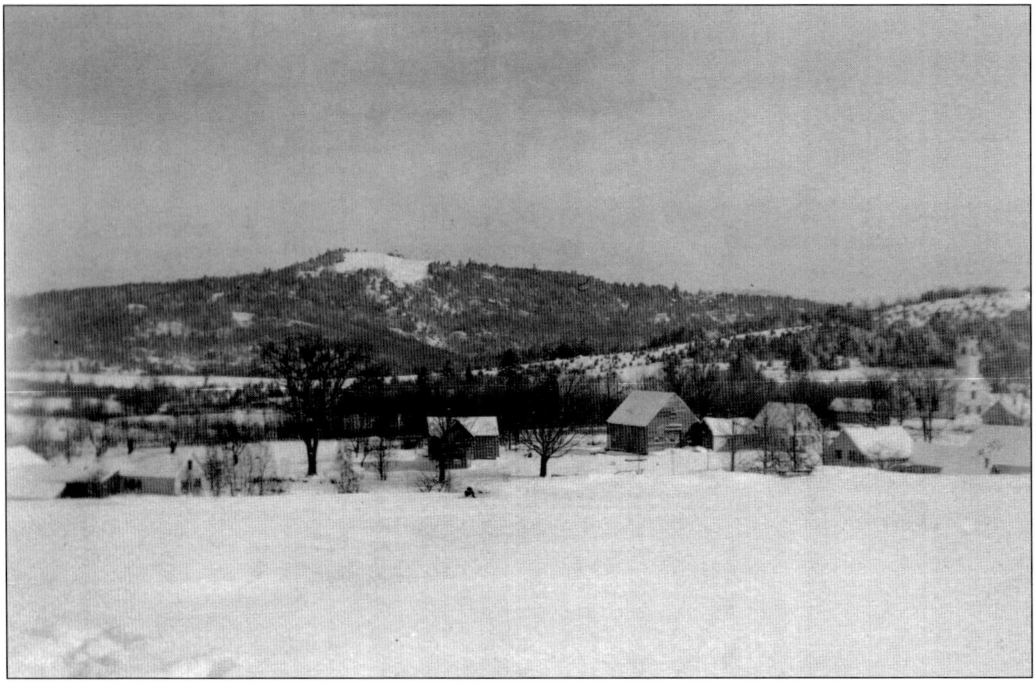

Although Bradford's first two families settled near Lake Massasecum and the Warner River, the first town developed at the geographical heart, Bradford Center. In the early 1800s, dozens of families would convene there to worship, post mail, trade at the general store, have their animals shod at the blacksmith's shop, or talk politics at the tavern. Only the schoolhouse flag, the meetinghouse steeple, and Goodwin Hill still preside over the center. (BHS.)

One

Our Landscape

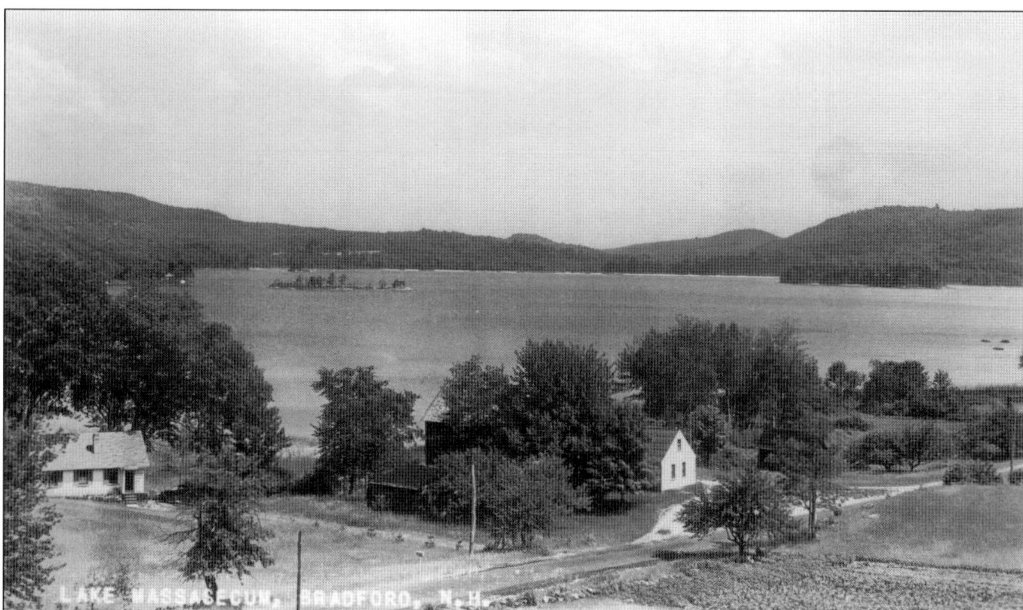

According to legend, Lake Massasecum (Bradford Pond) was named in the 1850s for a Penacook sachem that lived on its wild shores for many years. He was buried at Massasecum Rock by a passing pioneer named Eastman. The lake boasts rocky outcrops, sandy shores, and Massasoit, Spruce, and Loon Islands. The lake connects at its northern outlet to the Warner River. Guild Hill can be seen rising on the left. (BHS.)

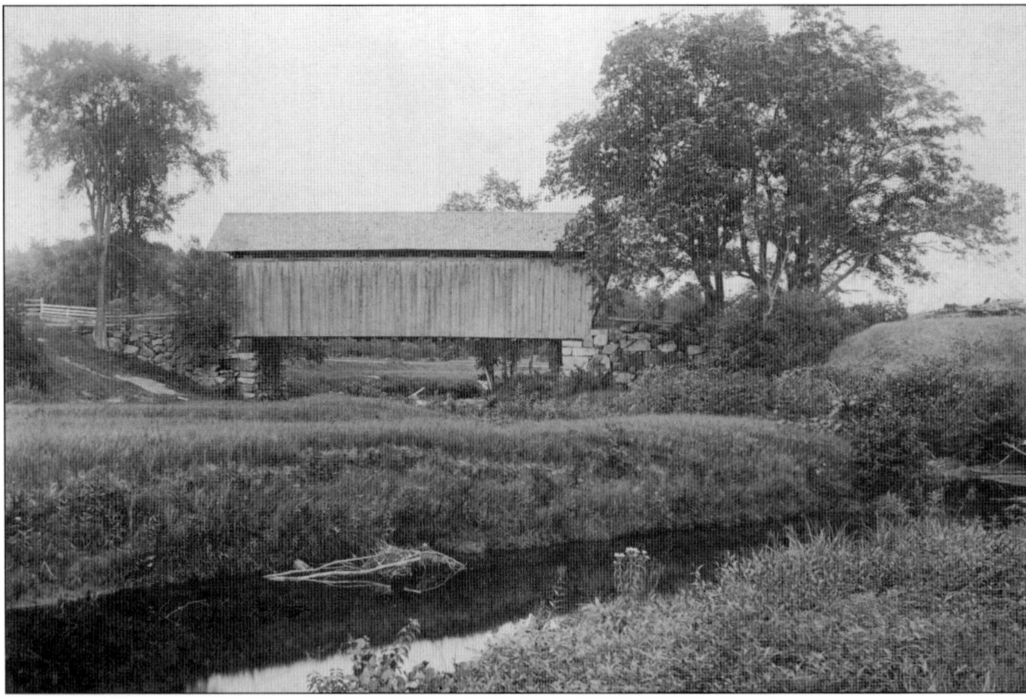

The Bement Bridge was built in 1854, after a vote decided that labor would be rewarded with rum. It is one of the last Long truss bridges in the country, and it spans the Warner River. Bridges were covered to protect the trusses, not the travelers. Signs for Fletcher's Castoria, Smith Brothers' Cough Drops, and Lydia Pinkham's Pink Pills used to adorn the wooden walls, while Blueberry Joe hunkered down puffing his pipe. (BHS.)

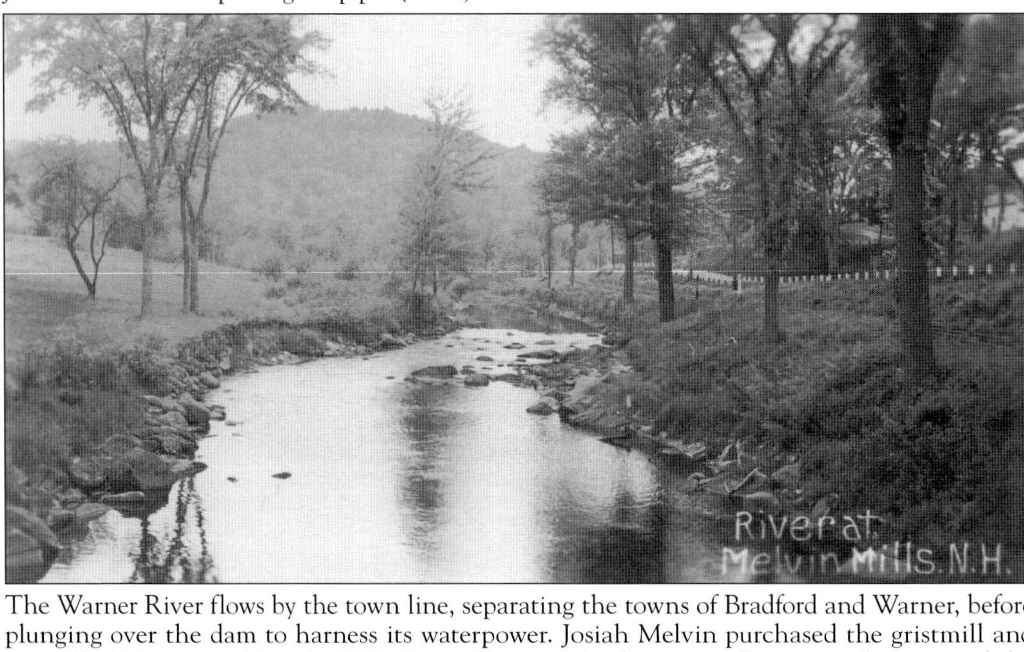

The Warner River flows by the town line, separating the towns of Bradford and Warner, before plunging over the dam to harness its waterpower. Josiah Melvin purchased the gristmill and sawmill of Lieutenant Hoyt in 1798. Five of his sons also became millers or mechanics, and the village was named Melvin's Mills in their honor. (WHS–Pratt.)

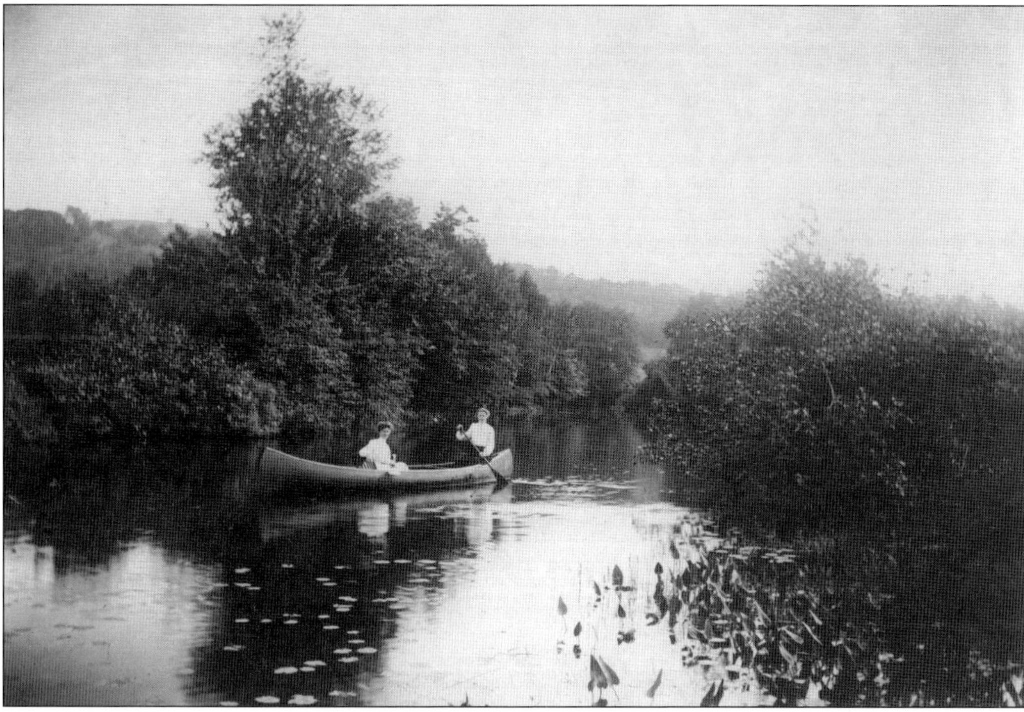

These women are leisurely canoeing down the Warner River on a hot, lazy summer afternoon. The inns and hotels located along the river advertised that guests would be able to enjoy boating, fishing, and swimming along its banks. (WHS.)

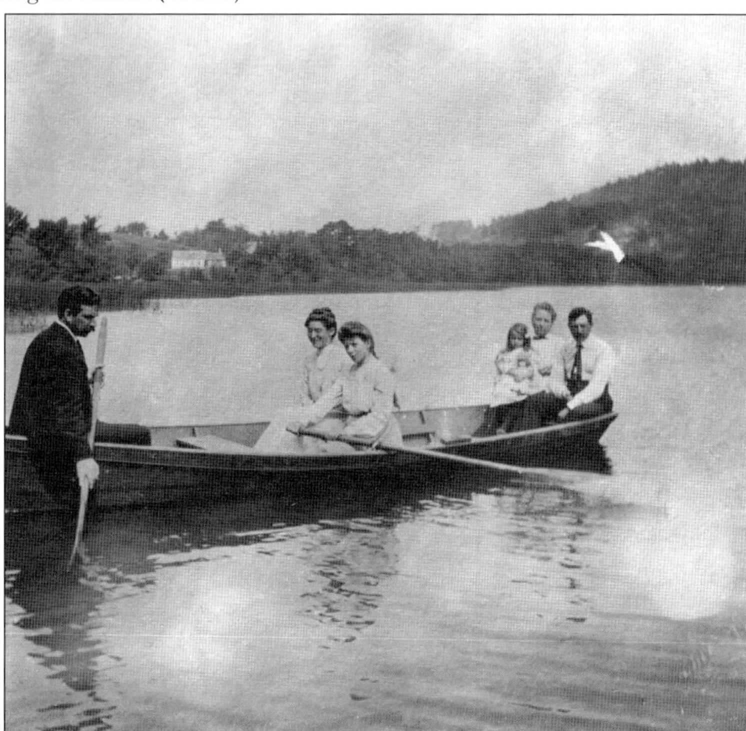

Cottage settlements began here in the late 1800s on land adjacent to the Jameson and Cheney farms. Clark "Del" Stevens established a summer resort called Oakdale, which included six cottages, a store, an icehouse, and garages with boats to rent. By 1916, there were 39 pioneer cottages on Lake Massasecum. Over the years, many cottages have been called colorful names like Kalorama, Redwing, and Pretticute. (BHS.)

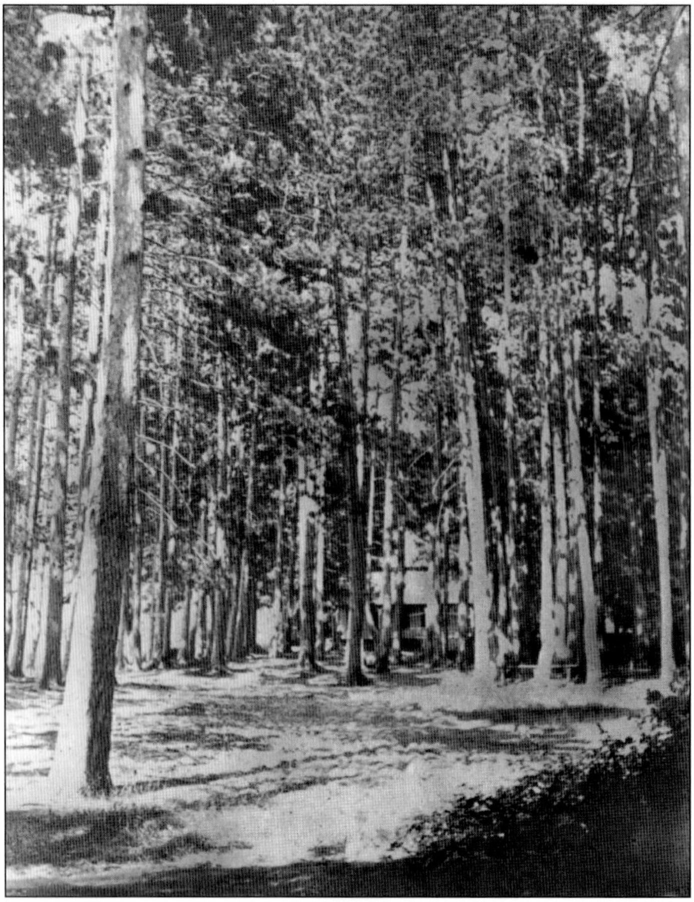

Sand Shore on Lake Massasecum was bordered by this Norway (red) pine grove as it appeared before the 1938 hurricane. Bradford is also home to Tall Pines State Park, where a dozen 100-foot-tall pines with 10-foot circumferences have been placed under the protection of the New Hampshire Division of Forests and Lands. Tall pines like these, once reserved for British masts, are older than the United States. (BHS.)

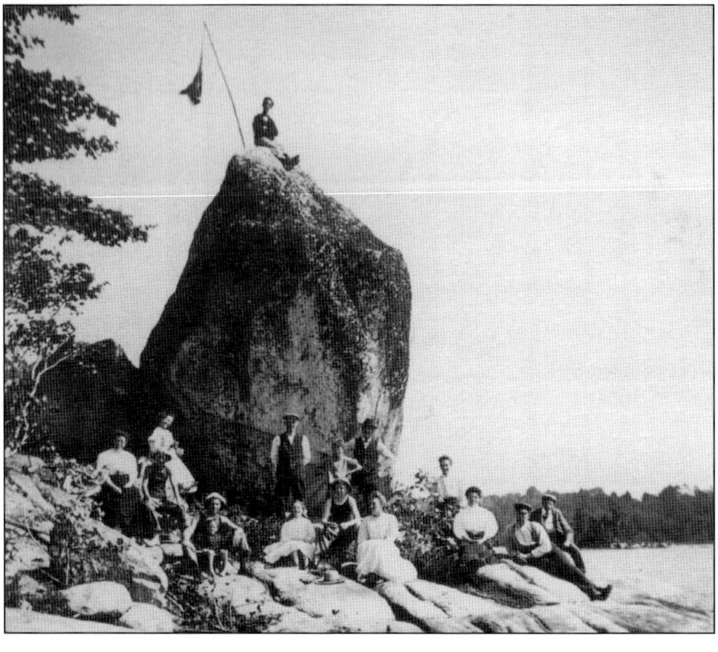

Haystack Rock was a popular spot for summer visitors and campers at Lake Massasecum. This impressive boulder, situated on the eastern shore, nods to the glaciers that once formed the rocky terrain. It was once a challenge to climbers but has since broken into several pieces. Lake Massasecum is unusual because it has a fluctuating water level and is not dependent on man-made dams. (BHS.)

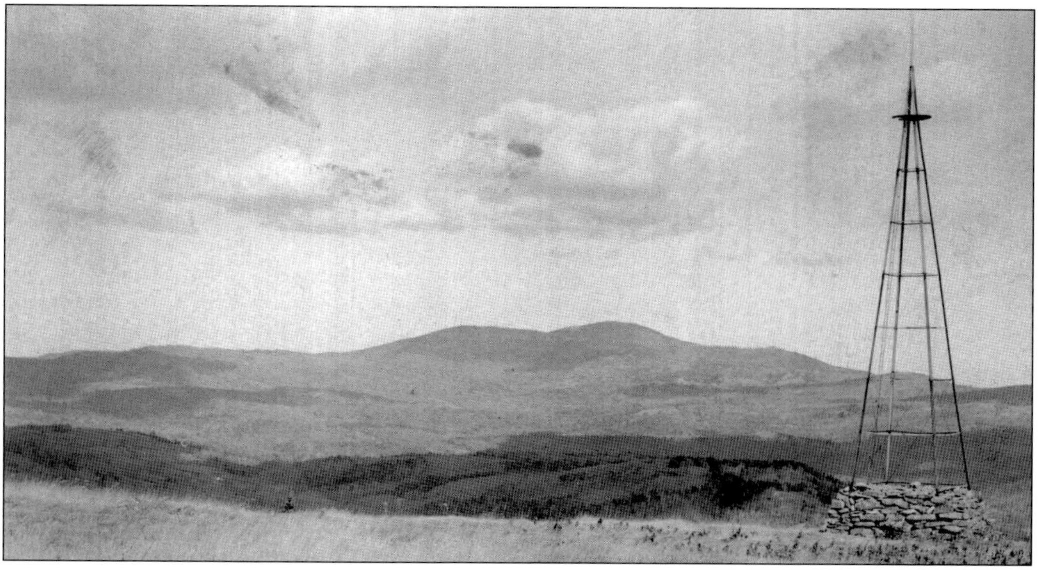

The picnic area located on Chandler Mink afforded expansive views of surrounding peaks. Towering to the north are the broad shoulders of Mount Kearsarge, welcoming visitors to climb its granite dome. Sen. William E. Chandler purchased many of the hardscrabble farms in the Minks and built this tower in 1909. Later, his family donated the land to the Town of Warner, and it is known as the Chandler Reservation. (WHS.)

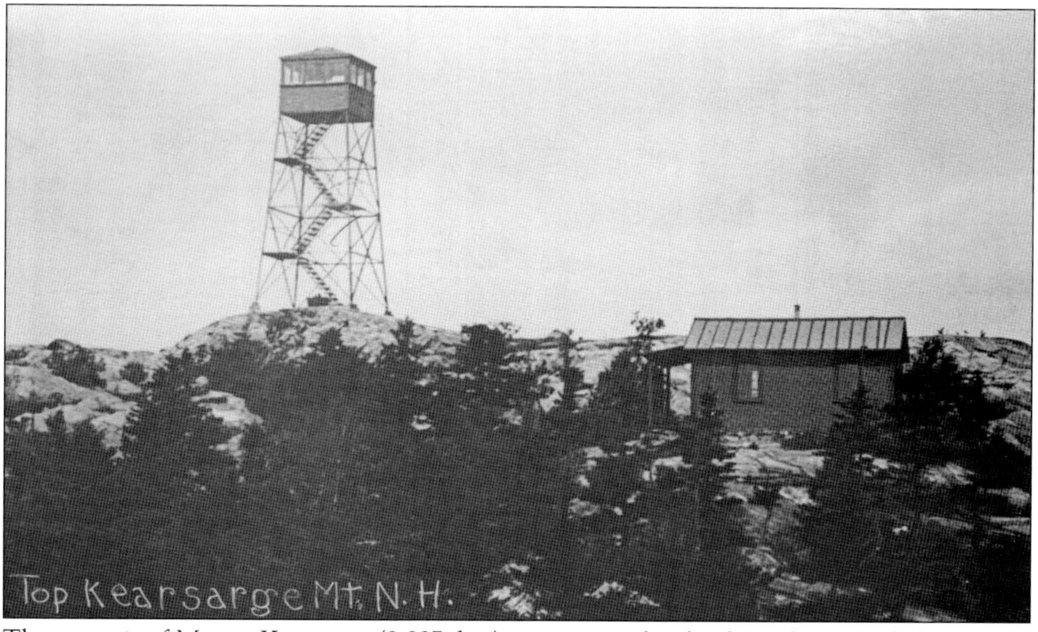

The summit of Mount Kearsarge (2,937 feet) is a granite knob of weatherworn ledges. Local legend says the peak was burned in the Colonial period to rid it of panthers. Today, it is a popular destination for hikers and picnickers, as they are rewarded with a 360-degree view. The fire tower was built in 1924, and the fire warden stayed in the cabin below the summit when on duty. (WHS–Pratt.)

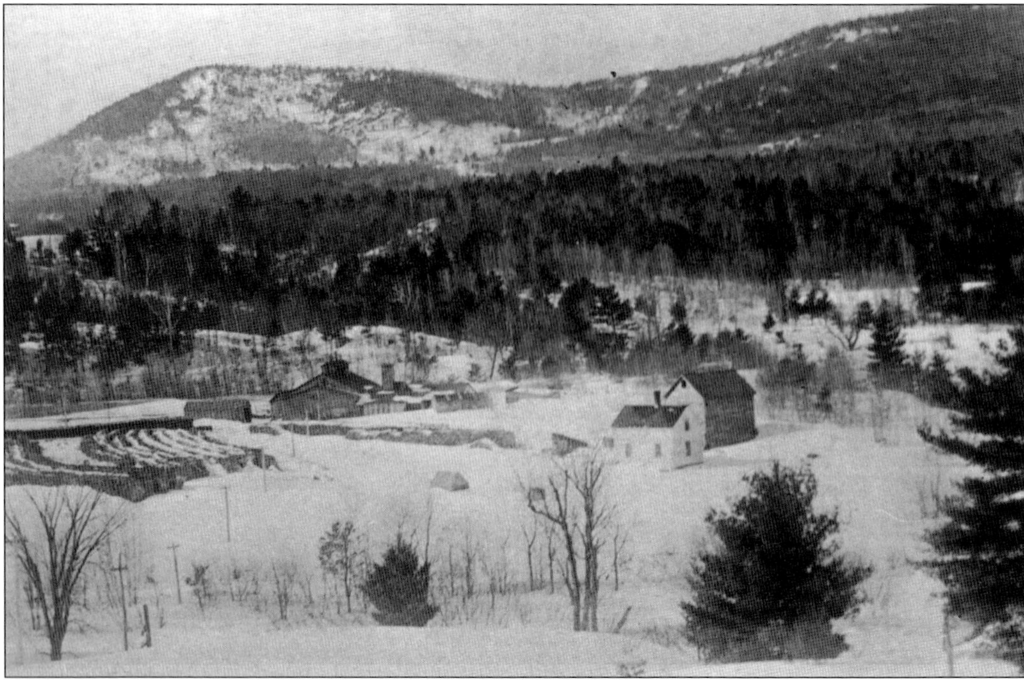

Bradford and Warner both enjoy views of the Minks Hills, although the views are different. The hills were named for the large number and size of the minks found here by the early settlers who trapped them for their pelts. There are 22 hilltops over 1,000 feet in elevation and three over 1,500 feet. Many parcels have conservation easements protecting them from future development. (WHS.)

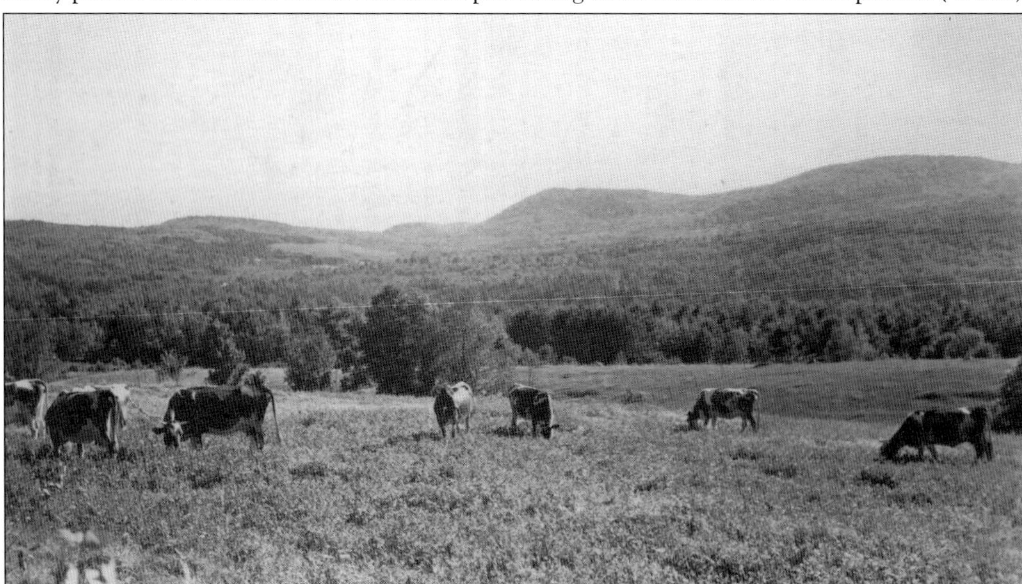

This photograph of the Minks Hills was taken descending Tory Hill with cattle grazing on a lush field of grass. This pasture was probably owned by Stephen Pattee, a successful farmer and educator, whose farm was known as Maple Grange. Hardscrabble farms in the Minks were the first to succumb to westward expansion, as better agricultural and industrial opportunities became available. (WHS–Pratt.)

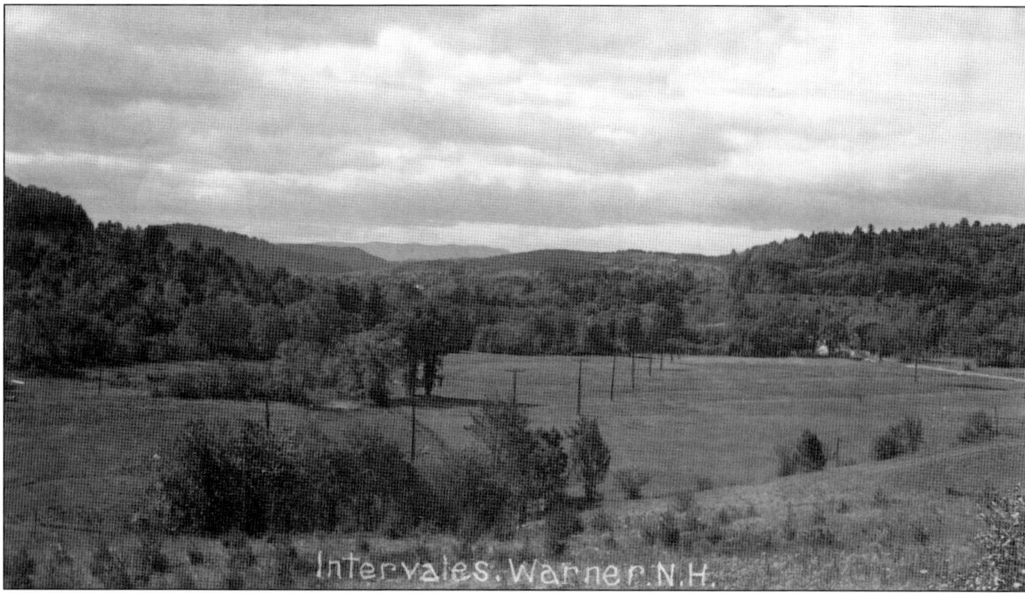

An intervale is a low-lying piece of land located along a river. During the early settlement period, these meadows would have provided sustenance for the cattle of several families. This field catches the high waters of the Warner River during flooding and is currently the location of Exit 9 off I-89. (WHS–Pratt.)

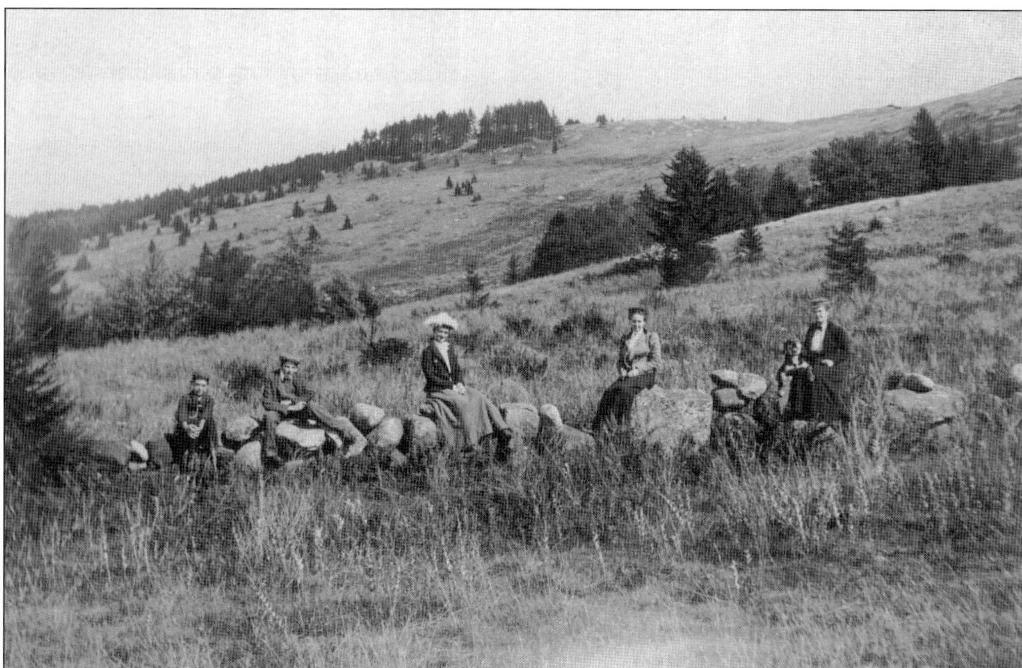

All are dressed in their Sunday best for this portrait on a stone wall near the Ring of Spruce. Spruce trees have low-hanging limbs that will re-root and create a ring of smaller trees around the parent tree. New Hampshire is rockier now than when it was settled. The duff layer was reduced once the heavy forests were cut and the subsequent deeper frost loosened the rocks. (Courtesy of Sonny Harris.)

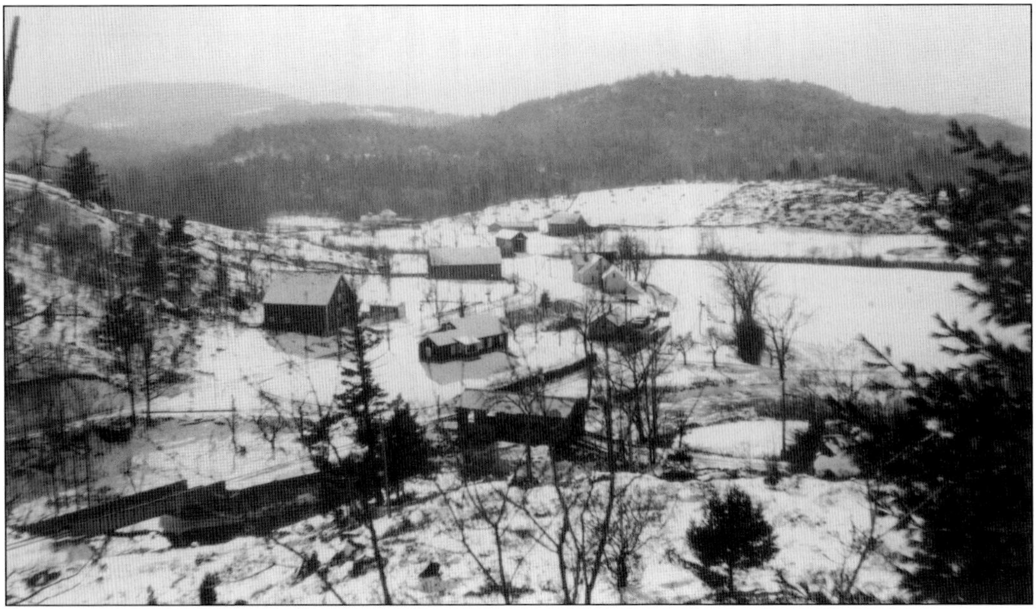

This aerial photograph of the Roby District shows the covered bridge in the foreground spanning the river on the road to South Sutton. The Roby Railroad Station, freight yard, and railroad covered bridge are in the background. Notice how the hills have been cleared for pasture and orchards. The old Route 103 ran along the river, and the new route would not be established until the 1930s. (WHS.)

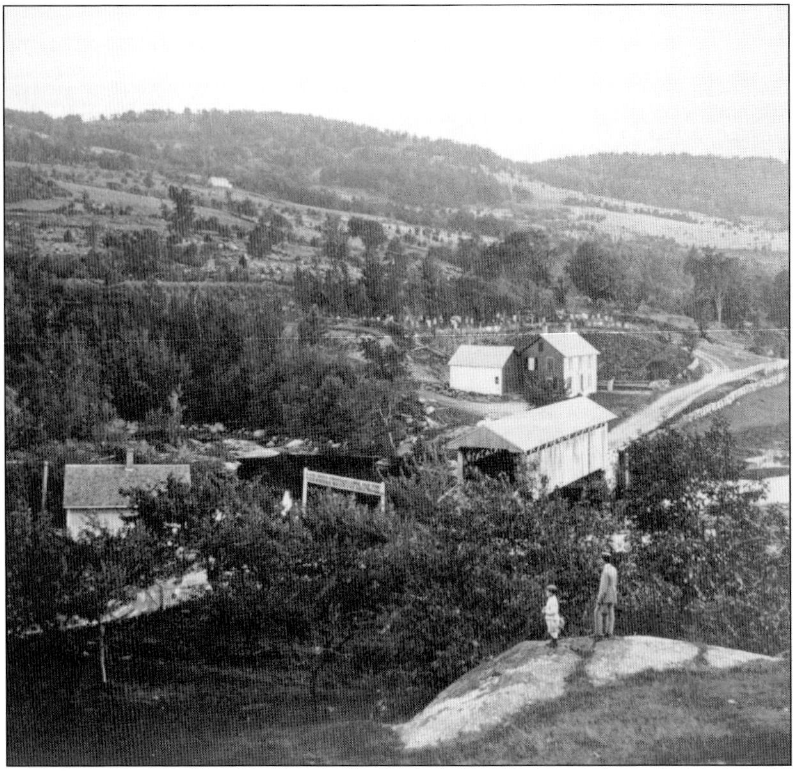

Warner is home to several villages located along the Warner River, springing up to take advantage of the drops, which provided a place to build the first sawmill and gristmills. The people in the foreground are viewing the railroad depot, covered bridge, the stationmaster's home, and the Old Waterloo Cemetery. The sign says, "Railroad Crossing. Look out for the engine while the bell rings." (WHS.)

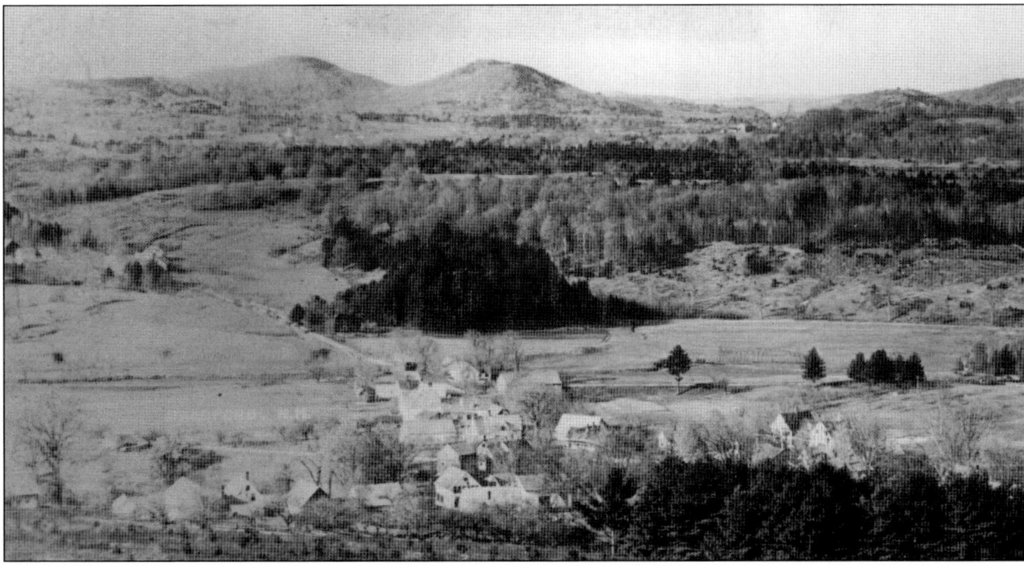

This photograph, taken from Ring Hill, shows the village in the foreground. The Bradford Center Meetinghouse and Twin Hills (Jericho and Pickett) are in the background. Burial Hill (center) was so called because it contains the oldest of Bradford's 17 cemeteries. On an adjacent knoll, youths built a 20-foot ski jump and careened down to the farming flats where a golf course would later be located. (BHS.)

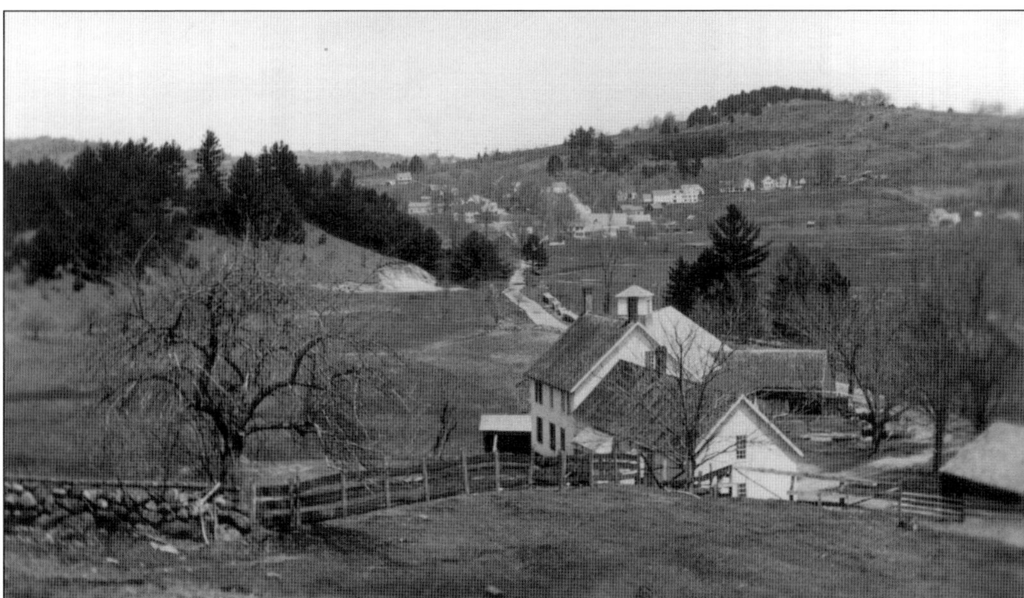

The house in the foreground stands on the site of the first frame house in Bradford. Later, this was the scene of wild sled rides. "Clear the track!" would echo up and down the frosty roads all over town, as children would ride their runners, sparks flying on the dry spots. One time, George Morse went straight through a front door, coming to a stop by the woodstove. (Courtesy of Steven Hansen.)

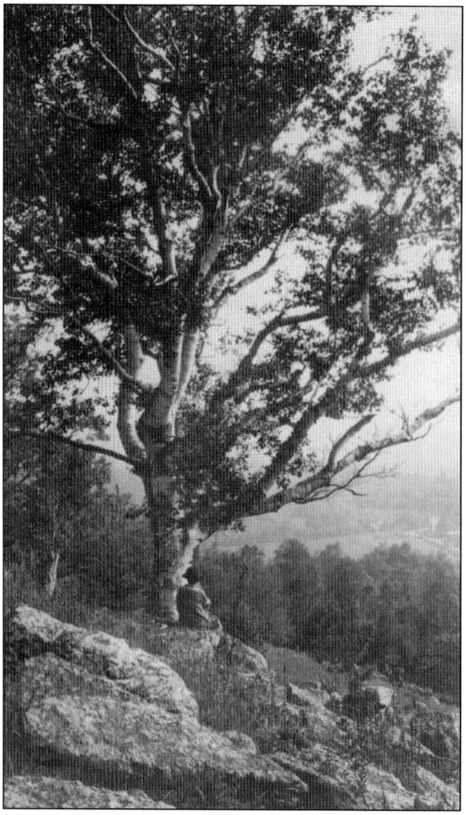

A man enjoys a moment of respite as he lingers by a stately birch on Silver Hill. Bradford has a dozen peaks surpassing 1,000 feet, the highest being spruce-covered Durrell (or Moon) Mountain (2,096 feet), near the border of East Washington. (Courtesy of Connie Dayton.)

Piles of stone can be found throughout area forests, attesting to the gargantuan task of clearing this soil for farming. This particular site on Piper Farm became a granite quarry. The oldest remaining structure in Bradford Center is the stone pound, which housed stray animals at the keeper's expense until they were claimed by their owners. This unpopular job was often assigned to political hopefuls as a rite of passage. (Courtesy of Steven Hansen.)

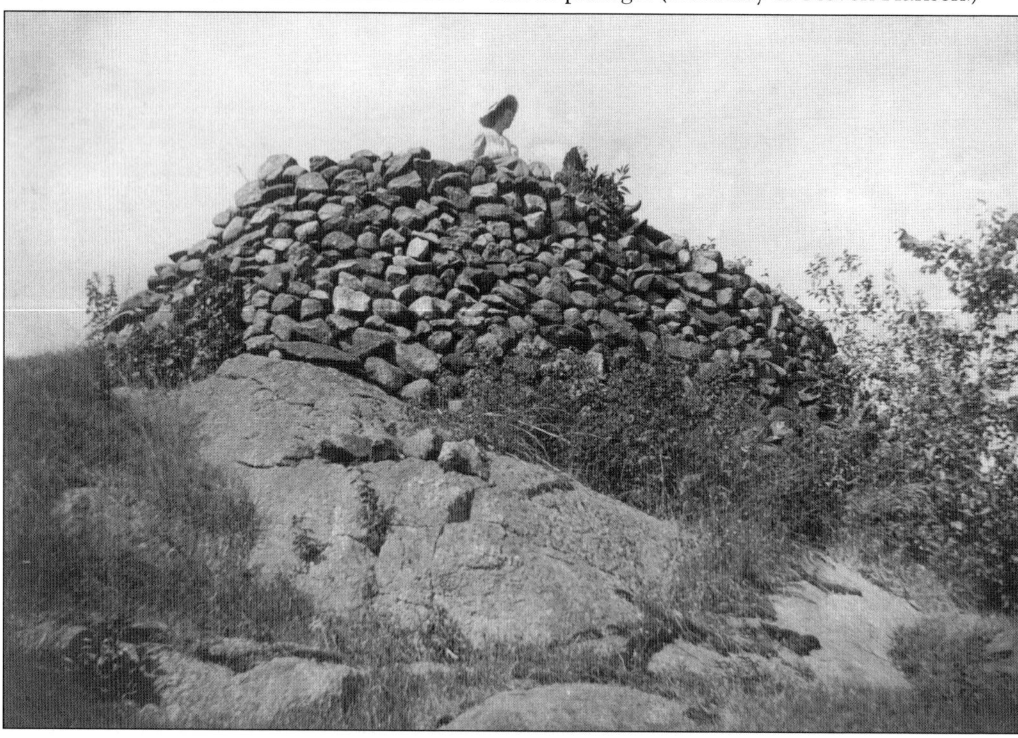

Two

From Forest to Farm and Back Again

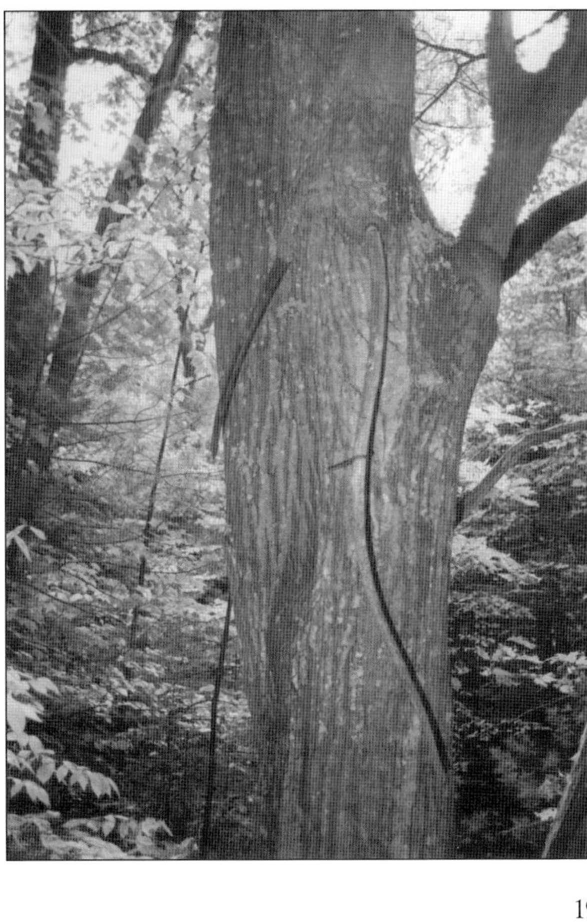

A farmer left his scythe behind in this tree on Mount Kearsarge. Land was cleared to establish farms during the sheep craze of the early 1800s. When farms were abandoned, pastureland gradually reverted to forest. (Courtesy of Ray Steiger.)

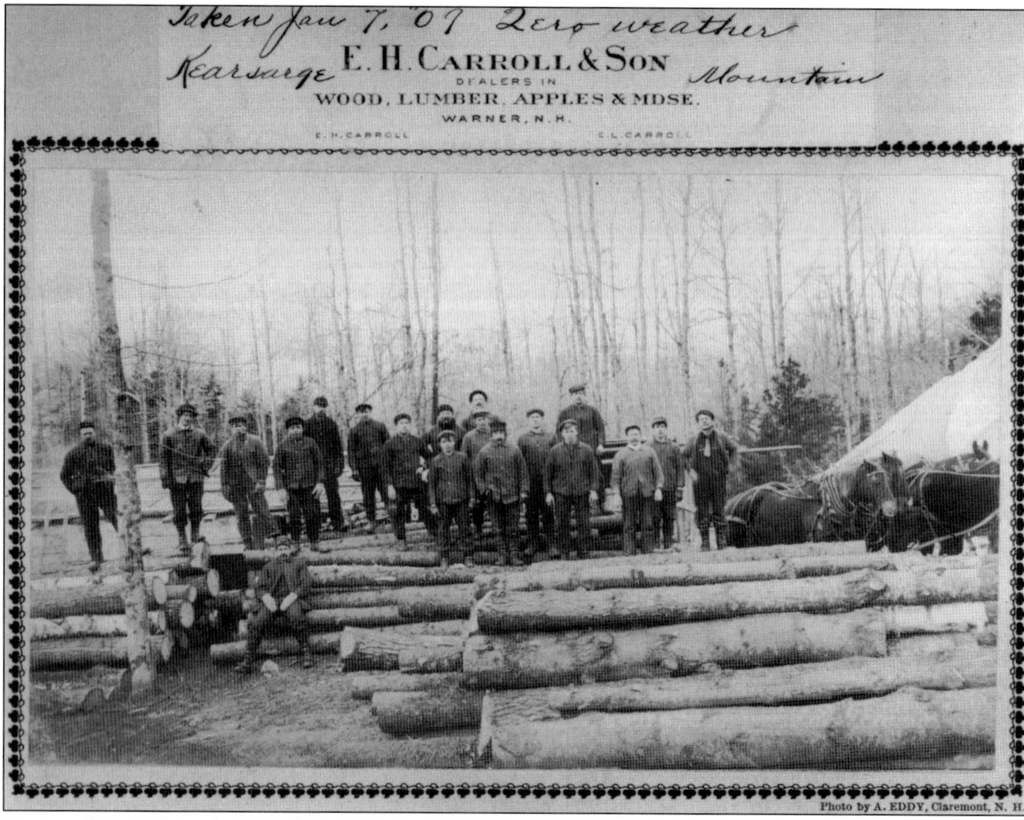

Engaged by Edward Carroll & Son, French Canadian lumbermen harvest timber on Mount Kearsarge on a cold, clear morning. Teams hauled this harvest six miles down to the railroad depot in Warner for shipment. To stay warm, men were dressed in high leather boots, long underwear, flannel shirts, and wool pants, coats, mittens, and hats. (WHS.)

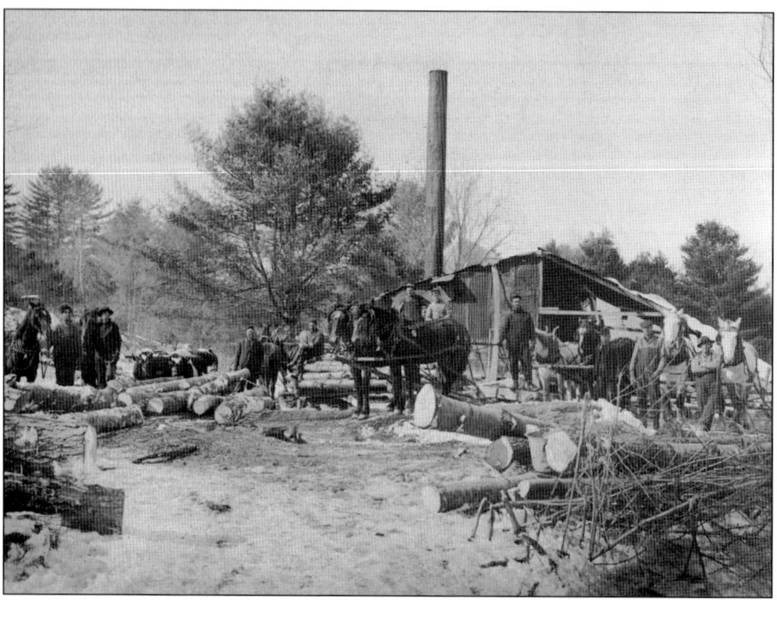

Five teams of horses and a team of oxen haul logs to Ben Adams's portable steam mill, located near a water source to operate the steam engine. Sawdust generated from the operation was blown into a large pile and would take years to decompose. (WHS.)

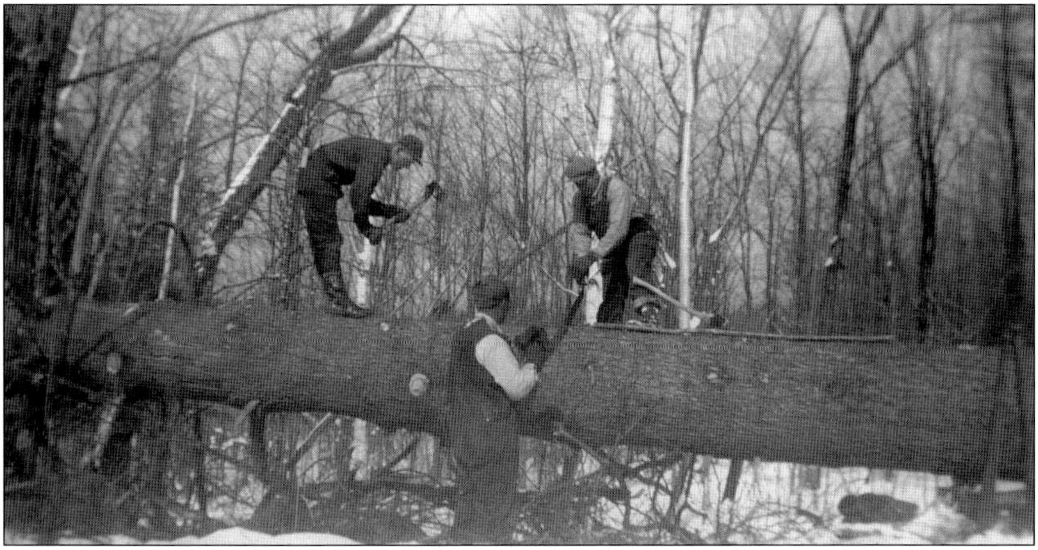

Logger Howard Bagley wields an ax while Earl and Walter Heselton Sr. work a crosscut saw. Two-man saws were designed to allow for cutting on both the pull and the push strokes, working at a right angle to the grain. Teeth were sharpened and set differently according to the type of wood to be cut. After a tree was felled, it had to be bucked and hauled to a landing. (Courtesy of Sonny Harris.)

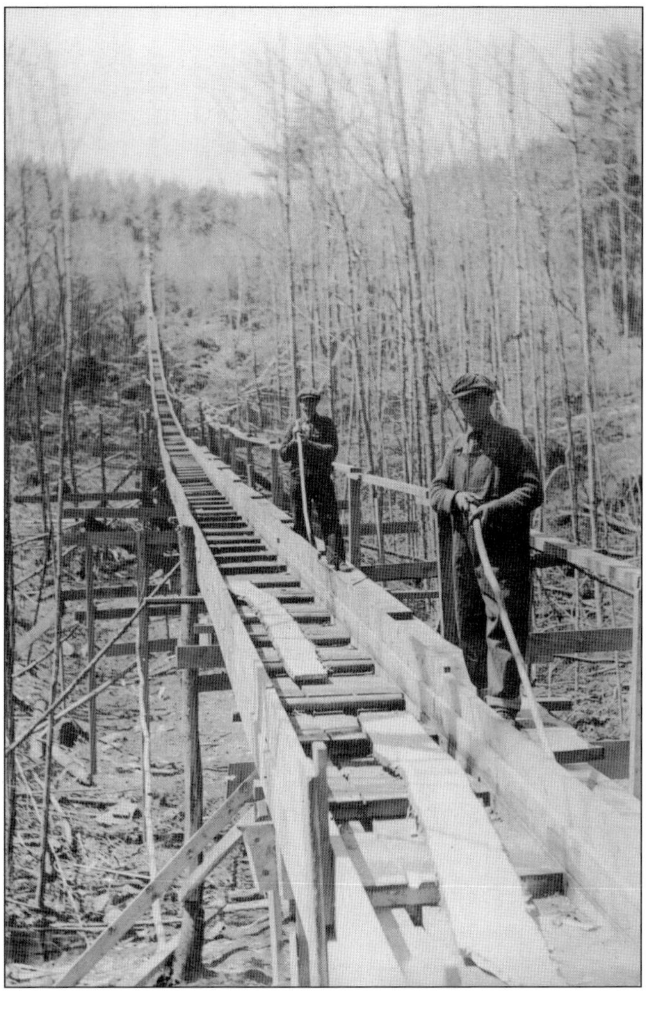

This lumber slide was built in the Minks Hills in 1917. Because of the steep terrain, it was easier to locate the mill at the top and slide the sawn pieces to the landing. Divie Downs and Roy Burbank kept the lumber moving by walking along the edge and pushing with their poles. The rough-sawn lumber was stacked onto wagons and hauled to the Main Depot for shipment. (WHS.)

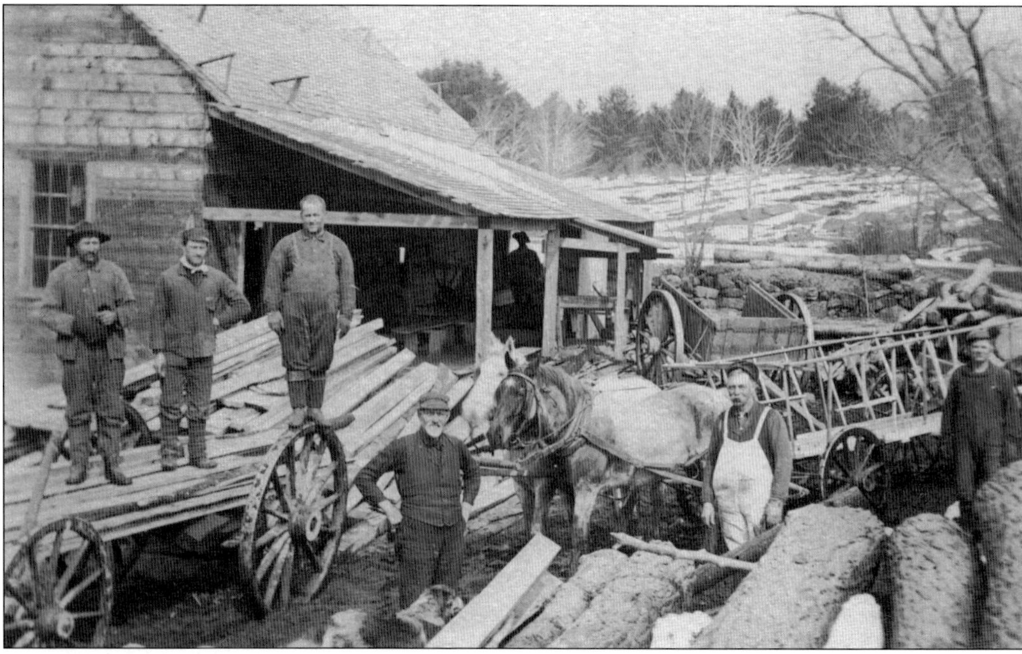

Sawyers from the Stevens and Cressy families pause in their work at Sullivan Stevens's Saw Mill in Bradford Center. Trees furnished the backbone of the economy, first to supply logs and lumber for local homes and businesses, then for the manufacture of furniture, bobbins, clothespins, picker sticks, and boxes. In the early 1800s, wood ash mills produced tons of potash each year to be used for fertilizer. (BHS.)

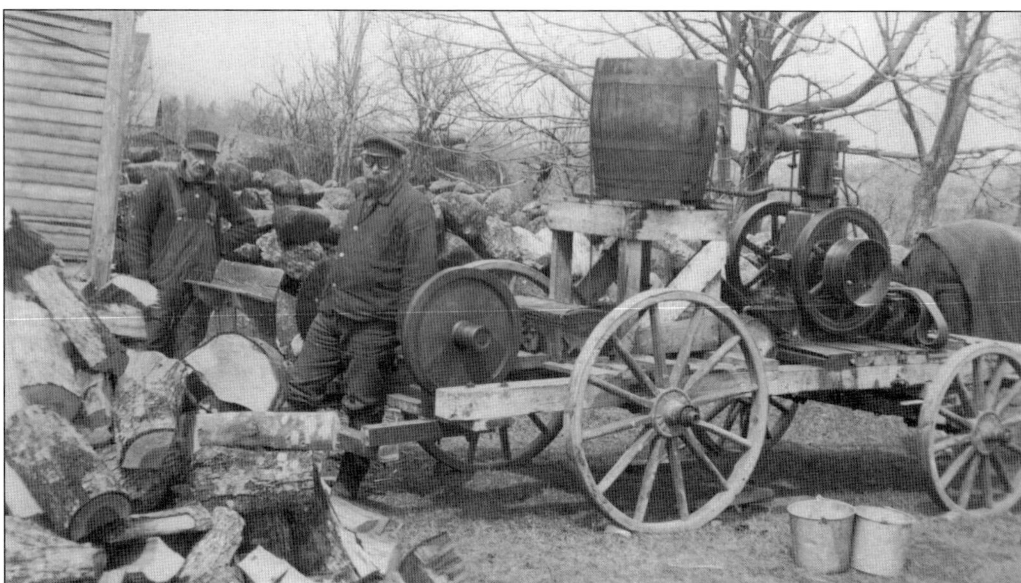

This horse-drawn saw rig cut stove wood on site. It features a gasoline-powered "make and break" one-lung engine with a water tank for cooling. The arm at the front of the machine would rotate the log into the blade's path. Households required huge amounts of wood for heat and cooking. Following the sheep boom of the 1800s, wood actually became scarce until the forests reclaimed the open spaces. (BHS.)

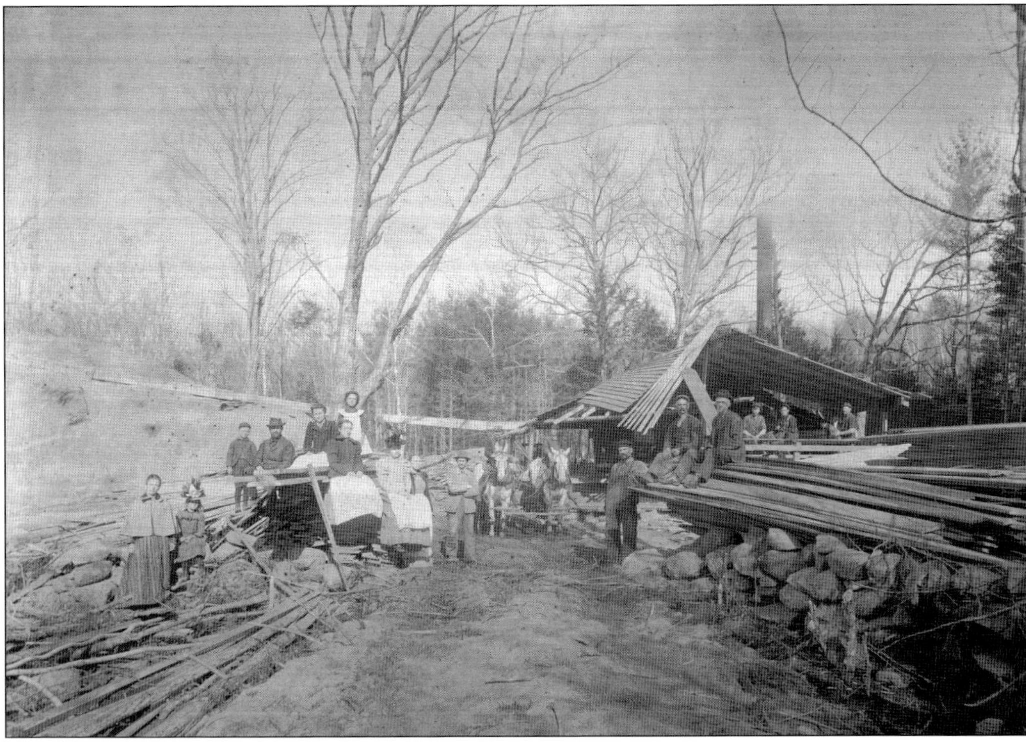

Women and children are visiting this mill site. The three women sitting on the board pile are wearing aprons; they may have brought their husbands a hearty lunch. Sometimes the mill worker families would travel from camp to camp with them. Mill owners would house single men or their families in abandoned farmhouses or build temporary camps. (WHS.)

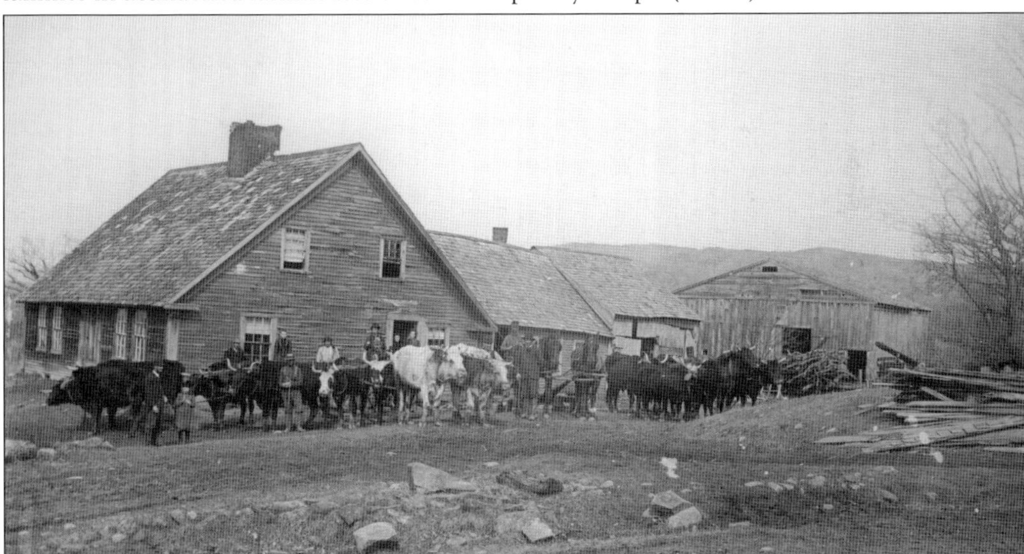

Capt. Bill Flanders's place in the Kearsarge Gore was owned by his son George at the time of this photograph. Eight teams of oxen and a team of horses are hauling logs to Warner's first steam sawmill set up in 1892 by John P. Hill. The paper reported that there were 10 steam mills in operation on the mountain in 1902. (WHS.)

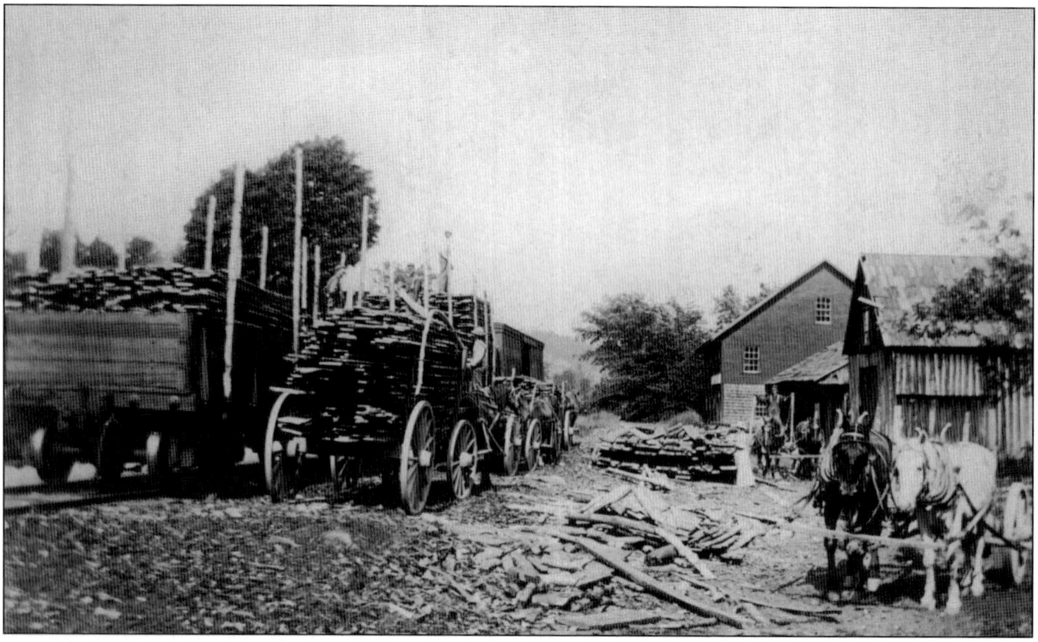

Lumber is being carefully loaded from the wagons onto railroad cars located at the siding in Waterloo. Several of the railroad stations and mills along the river had sidings where empty rail cars could be dropped off and picked up once full. In the 1870s, Stephen Pattee felled a 150-year-old hemlock measuring three feet at the base, and two 40-foot logs were sawn from the trunk. (WHS.)

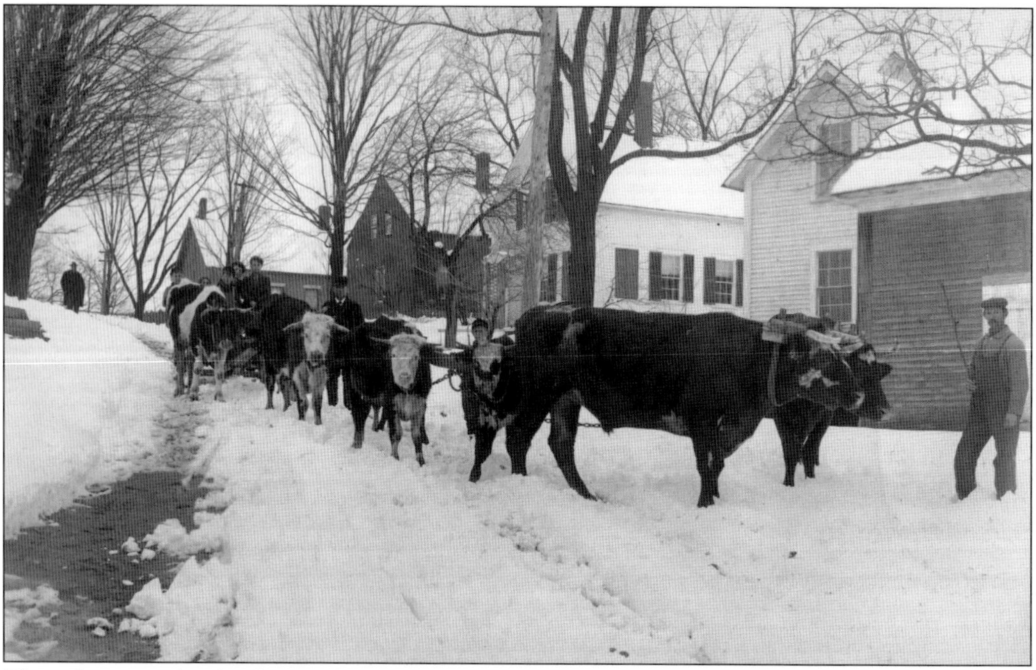

This photograph of a four-ox hitch was taken in front of the Hardy studio. Starting in the background, from left to right, are George Edmunds, a scoot full of children, George and Horace Martin, and Bert Mason. The scoot is used to carry wood down to the Ela Mill to be converted to lumber, as the Martin family was putting an addition onto their store. (WHS–Hardy.)

The Benjamin Nichols farm was built in the early 1800s on the road to East Washington. Haystack Mountain stands tall behind this example of a typical farm of the era. The rugged soil, sparse track, sturdy stone walls, and purposeful buildings all testify to the supreme tenacity that fueled early settlers in their quest for opportunity, sustenance, and often, survival. (BHS.)

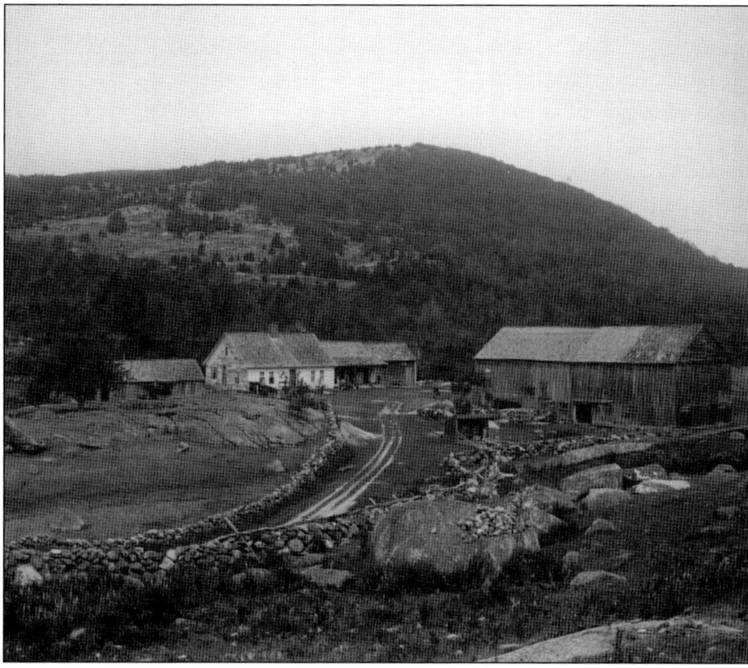

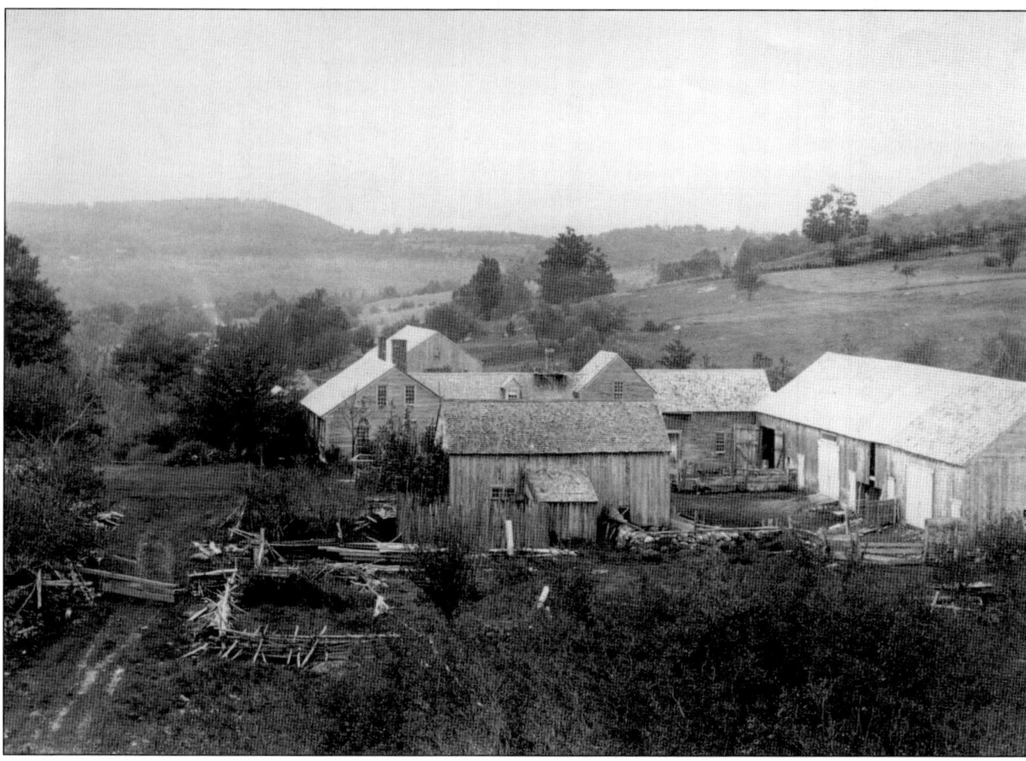

Three generations of the Badger family lived on this prosperous farm in the Minks Hills. It is a great example of the children's nursery rhyme, "big house, little house, back house, barn." The barns were English in style, separated from the main house with three doors located under the side eaves. The platform on the roof indicates they were repairing a chimney. (WHS.)

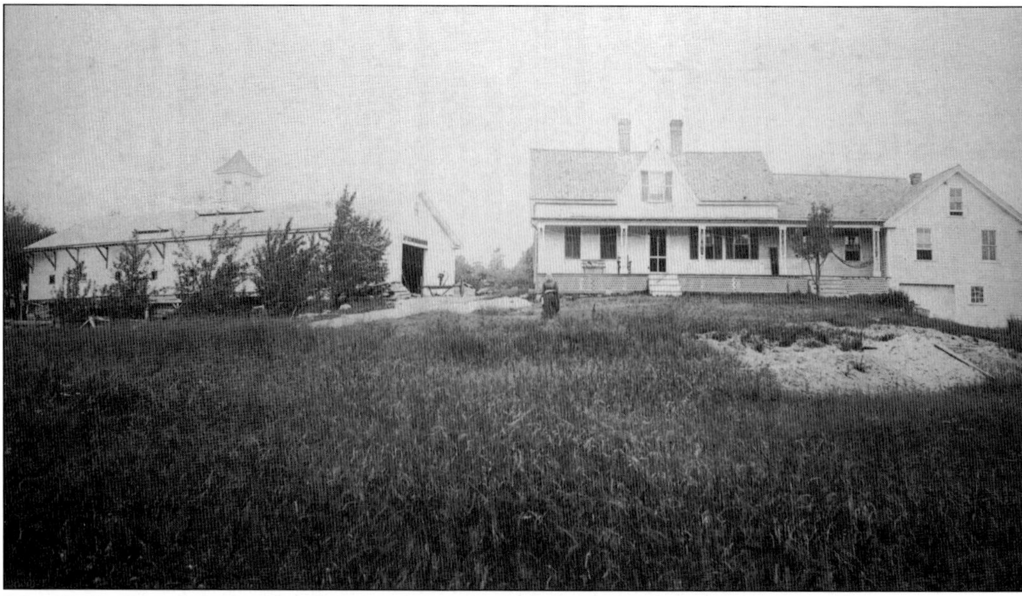

The Hollis Blood Farm (later known as Dodge Farm) was built in the early 1800s on Fairgrounds Road. The exceptionally long barn housed cattle and horses for many years. The milk room in the house was supplied with gravity-fed water. During the war years, chicken coops were added to host a large, government-subsidized egg operation. Estella Dodge was known to give bushels of tomatoes as gifts to her egg customers. (Courtesy of Steven Hansen.)

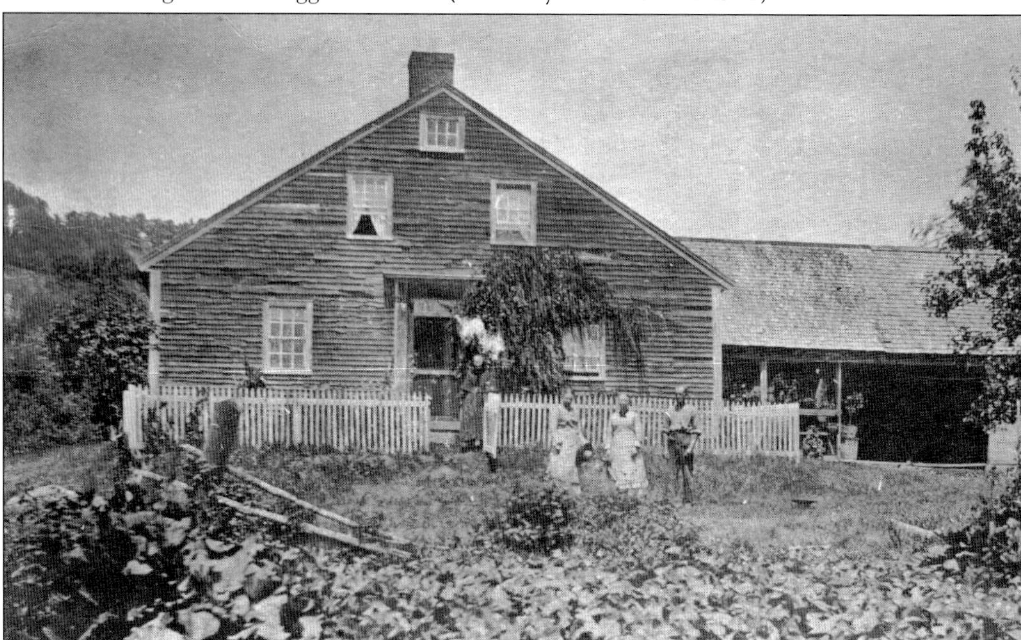

Built on the south side of Stewart's Peak in the Minks Hills, the Barnard and Maria Colby farm housed three generations. Their grandson Irving Colby shared his memories about growing up on this hillside farm, including hearty meals, barn chores, cutting wood, sugaring, haying, walking a mile to school, and ending the day with evening prayer. The ledge in front of the house was carved with family names and dates on its smooth surface. (WHS.)

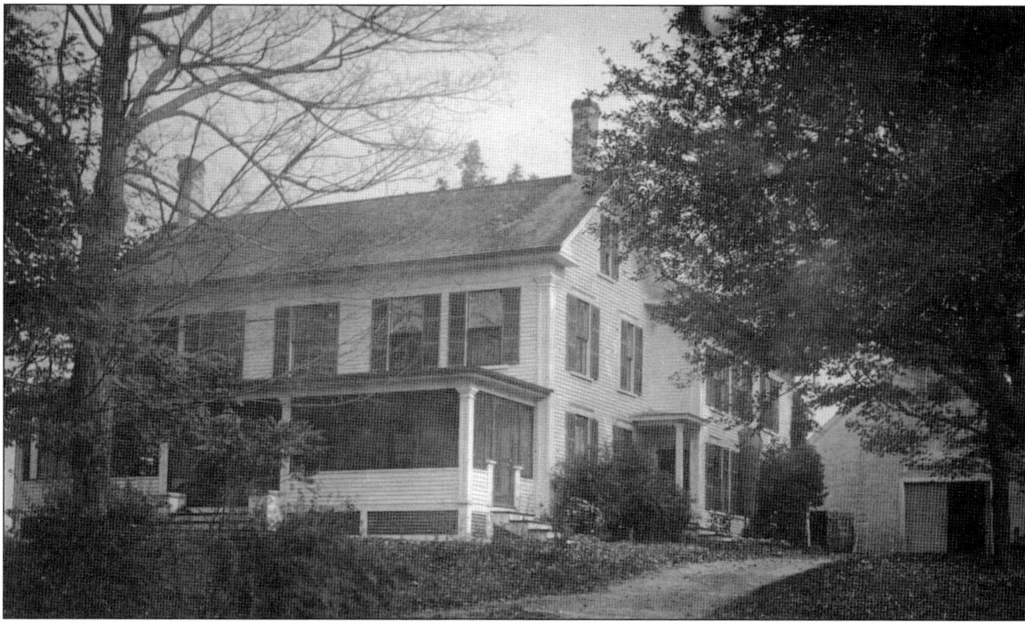

Blacksmith Richard Cressy fought with Col. John Stark's Regiment at the Battle of Bunker Hill. One cold February day in 1794, he brought his family here to settle in a log cabin. This Greek Revival home, called Sunnyside, replaced the cabin in the 1860s. The site is now operated as Stoneridge Farm, a Community Supported Agriculture (CSA) operation that sells certified organic produce, fruits, herbs, flowers, and maple syrup. (Courtesy of Steven Hansen.)

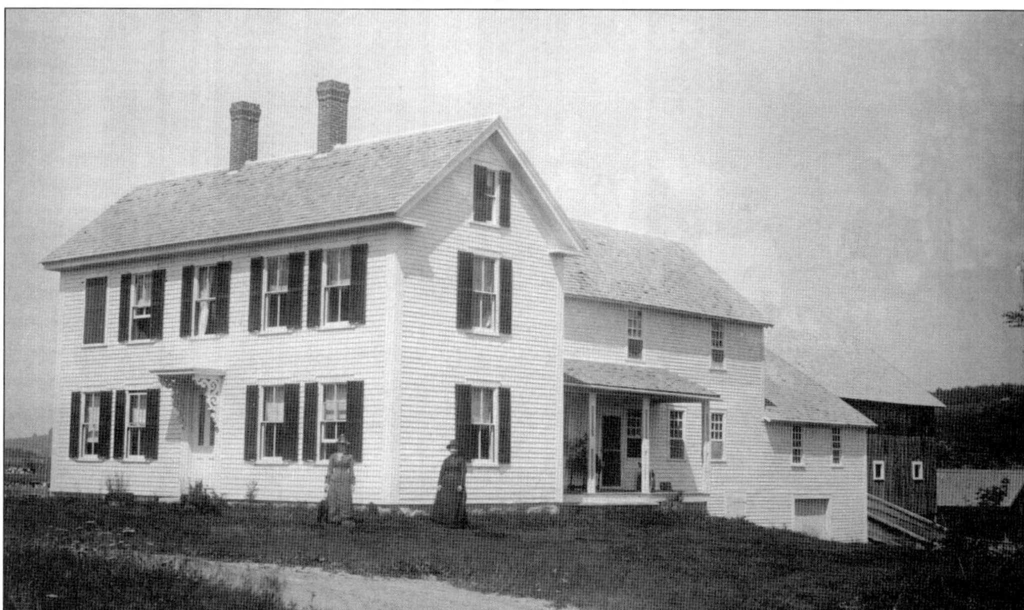

Col. Richard Straw moved his family here in the late 1700s. Straw was one of the largest landowners, served as a selectman, was a colonel in the state militia, and operated a tavern. The Courser family has owned this farm for over 100 years and currently raises sweet corn, tomatoes, squashes, pumpkins, and produces maple syrup, markets cordwood, and trains steers. The farm and adjoining acreage has been placed under conservation easement. (WHS.)

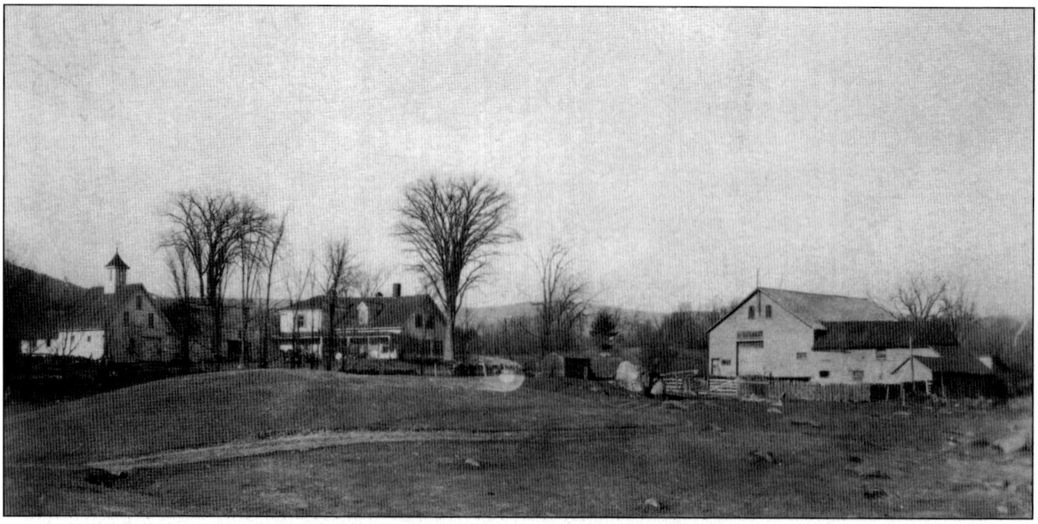

Although Nicholas Durrell was unschooled and illiterate, he became a model farmer with his wife, Polly Bachelder. It was said that, "No one raised such good produce . . . such fine horses . . . nor owned such broad lands as Nicholas Durrell." His son David raised up to 73 head of blooded cattle. The Durrells owned several hundred acres in Bradford and East Washington and became generous benefactors to the poor. (Courtesy of Steven Hansen.)

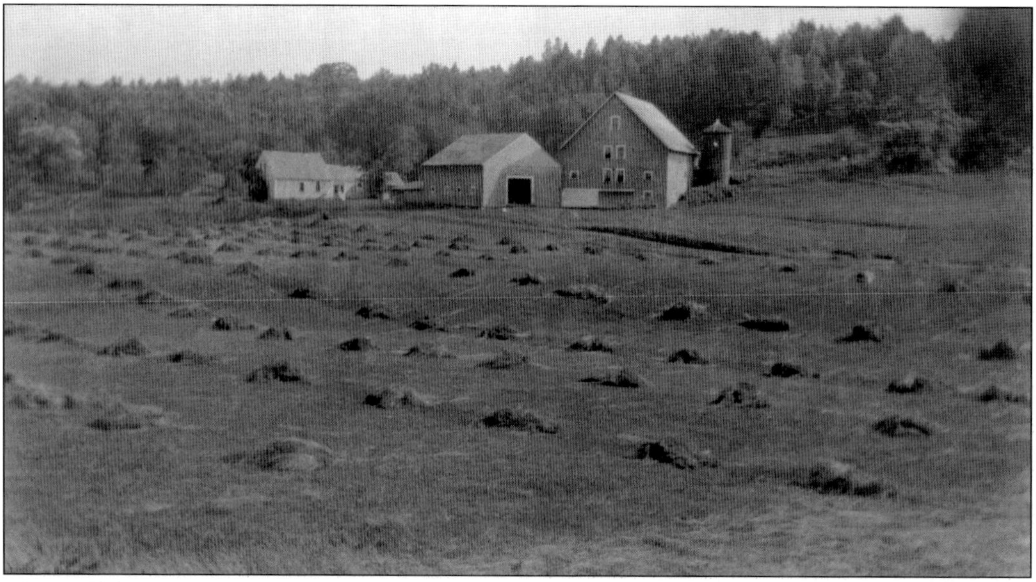

The Willaby Colby farm lies across the windrows of hay, located on the intervale next to the Warner River. George Martin owned the farm in 1905 and had the large, 40-by-60-foot barn built in June. Both barns succumbed to fire on a cold winter night in 1940. Many barns in town were lost to fire due to tipped over kerosene lanterns, lightning, or green hay overheating and igniting. (WHS.)

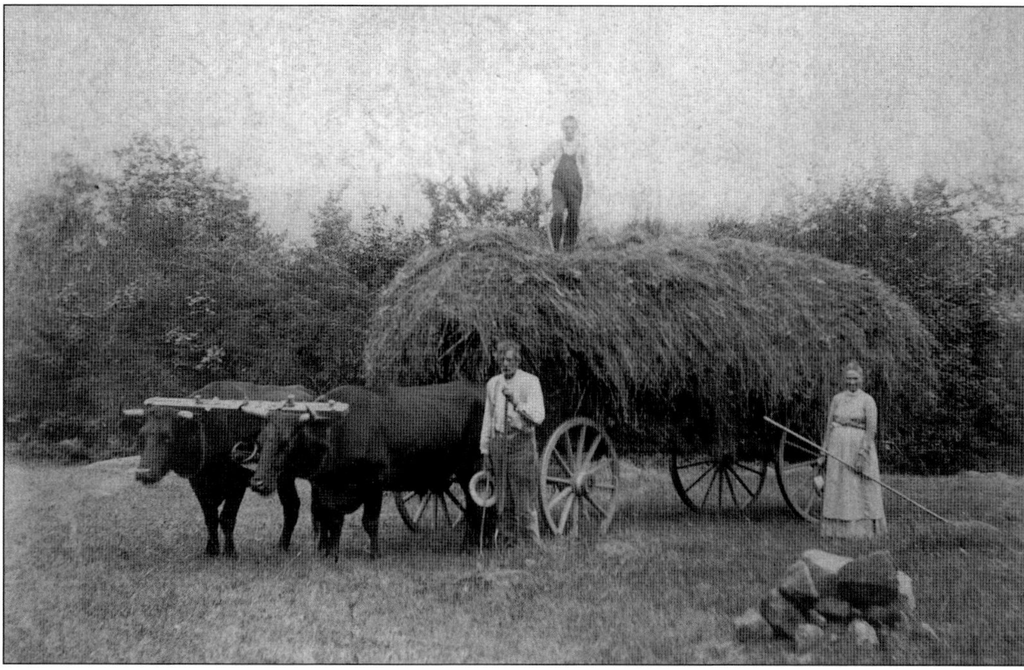

Adonirum Jameson's farm was on the shores of Lake Massasecum. The Jamesons drove beef cattle to Boston on foot and delivered wares in a peddler's cart. At haying time, women left their constant household chores to "rake after." Hay was pitched precisely onto the wagon so that the load would not be lost on the way to the barn, where the dusty chore of unloading took place. (BHS.)

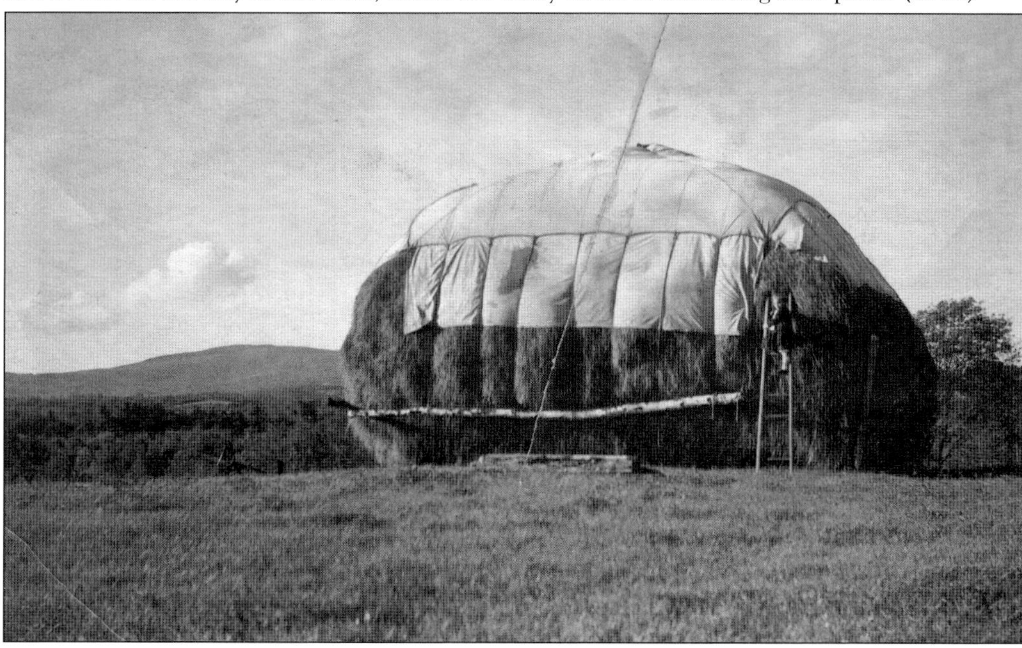

Believe it or not, this is a 40-ton stack of hay on Waldron Hill. The man on the ladder is tying ropes laid over tarps to protect the pile from the elements and from blowing away in the wind. The ropes are attached to a length of tree limb to hold it down. Pitching hay from a wagon and treading down the load was quite a feat at this height. (WHS–Pratt.)

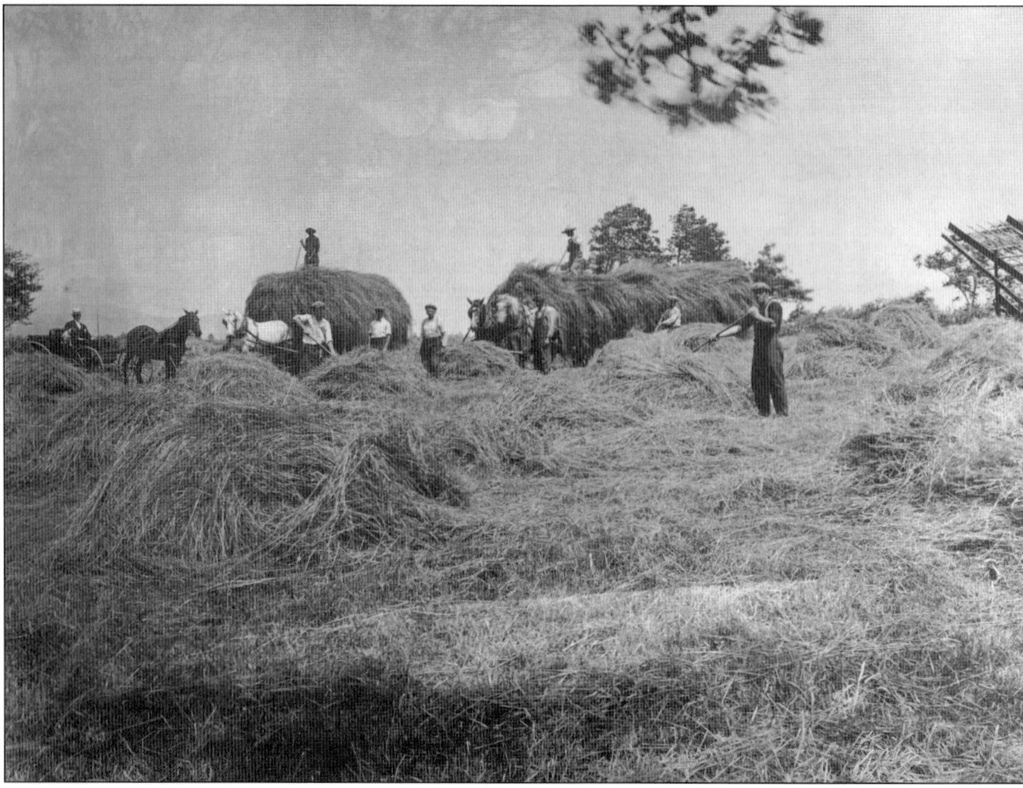

Edward Carroll and his son Lee were interested in scientific forestry and agriculture. They purchased this 40-acre property on Denny Hill and reclaimed the field by picking rock, fertilizing, and cultivating. The field yielded crops of timothy and redtop grass, averaging about three tons of well-cured hay per acre. Edward Carroll and his dog sit in the carriage surveying his men loading the hayracks. (WHS.)

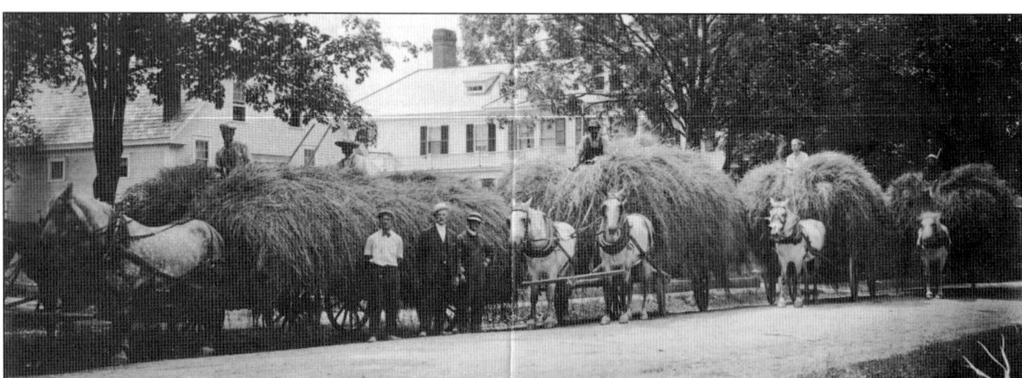

These loads of hay are lined up in front of the Carroll residence on Main Street. Carroll's hay field production caught the attention of the commissioner of agriculture Andrew L. Felkner, who proclaimed their agricultural technique a success. This field of grass was written up in an illustrated article in the *Boston Transcript*. The Carroll family raised cattle for milk and meat, as well as Morgan horses. (WHS.)

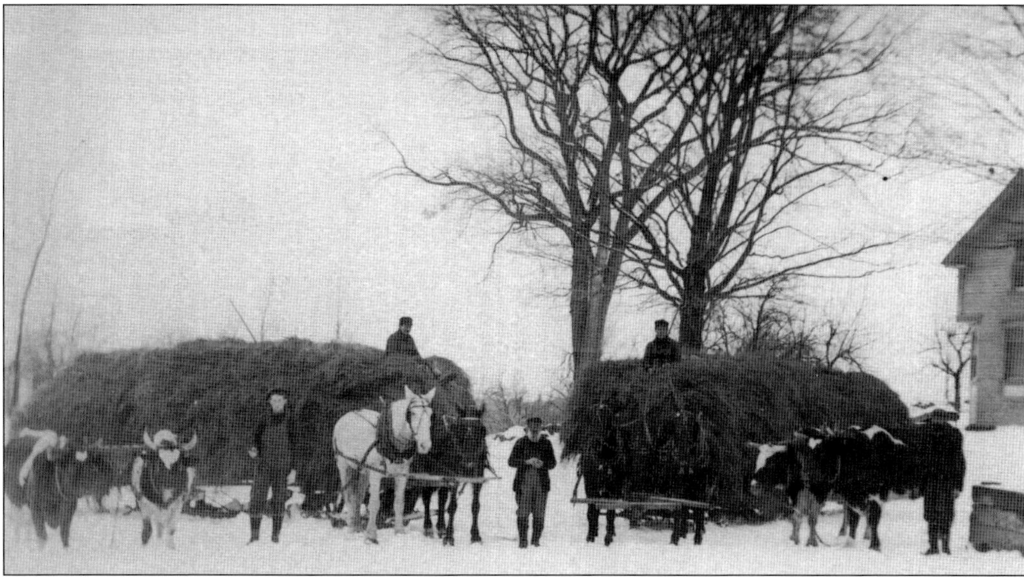

In this photograph, two loads of hay pass through Bradford Center, most likely to be sold to folks who had no storage space for feed. Both oxen and horses were used to haul loads, the former known for their durability and steadiness, the latter for their speed. Oxen also provided meat and hides to the subsistence farmer. At one time, the area's chief agricultural products were sheep and cattle. (BHS.)

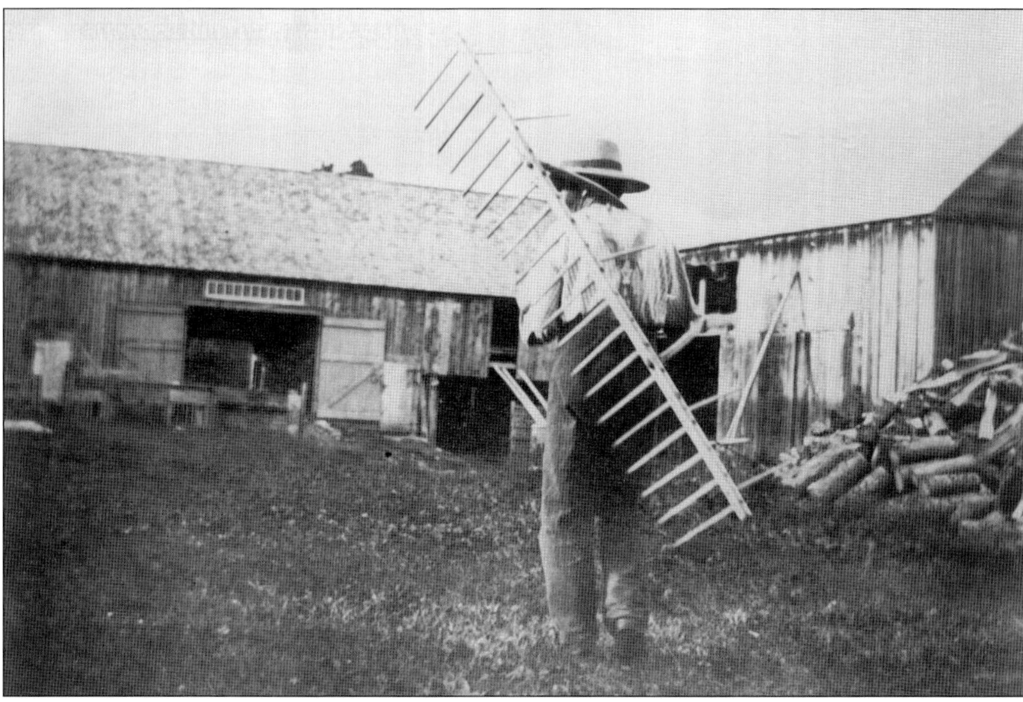

Herman Badger limps back to the barn with a hay rake slung over his shoulder in 1893. Nearly 20 years earlier, Badger was felling trees when the ax nearly severed the muscles in his left foot. Farming and lumbering were dangerous occupations because the risk of injury or death meant individuals had to cope with life-threatening injuries without the support of insurance. (WHS.)

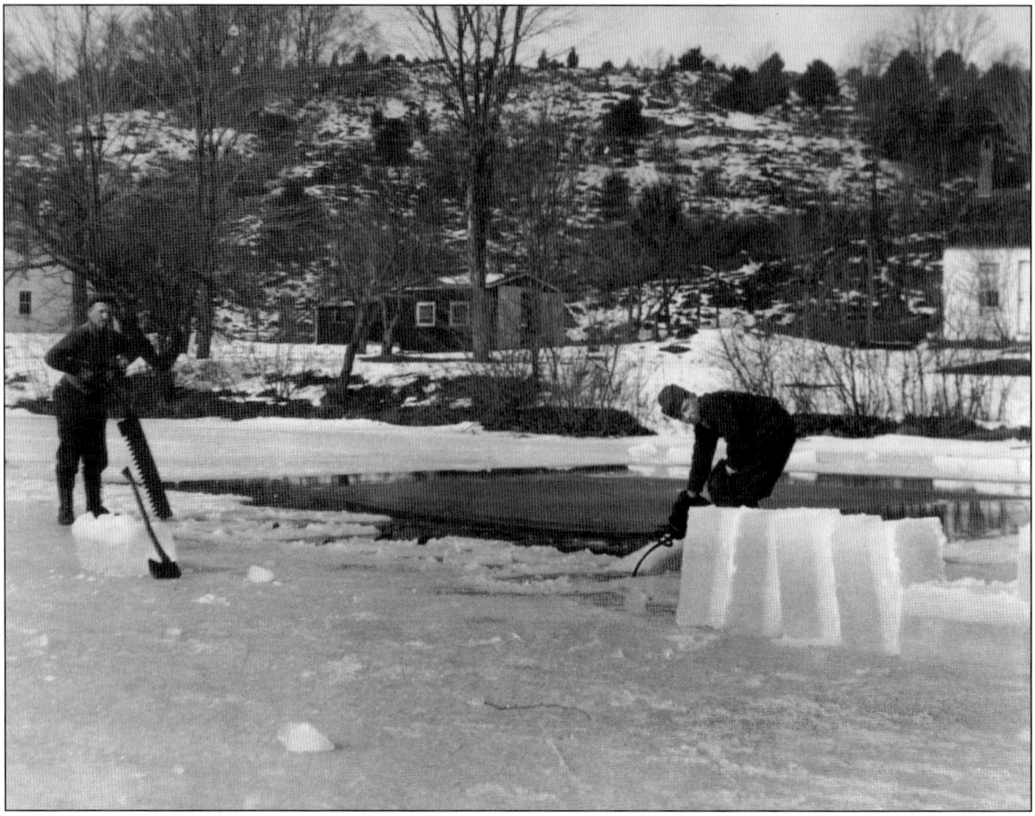

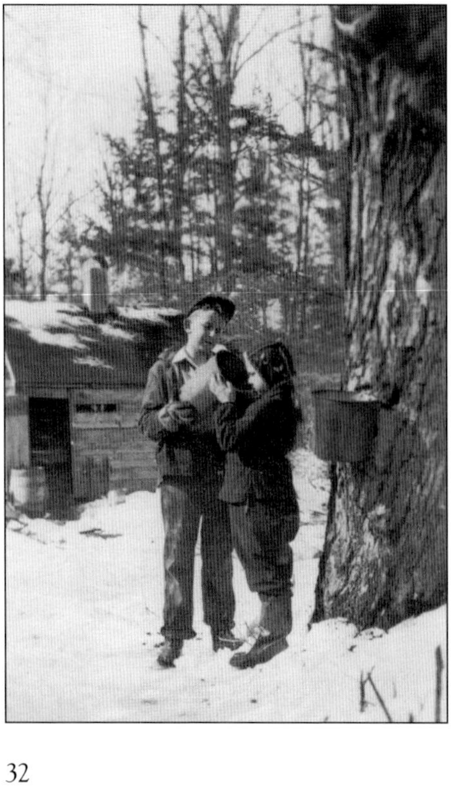

Cutting ice from ponds and rivers was a winter chore. Walter Webster and his son Kim are cutting ice in Roby on the Warner River in 1920. It was usually a group activity; many hands were needed to cut, float, and transport the blocks of ice for storage. Ice was stacked in specially built icehouses and packed with sawdust to slow the melting process. (WHS.)

Maple sugar was often the first cash crop of the season. It was cheaper than cane sugar shipped from the Caribbean. Maple molasses (maple syrup) was finished off into pound blocks. With the advent of railroad transportation after 1849, farmers shipped the "sugar of their labor" to cities more easily. Here, Herman and Cynthia Dow enjoy a sip of sweet maple sap. (WHS–Pratt.)

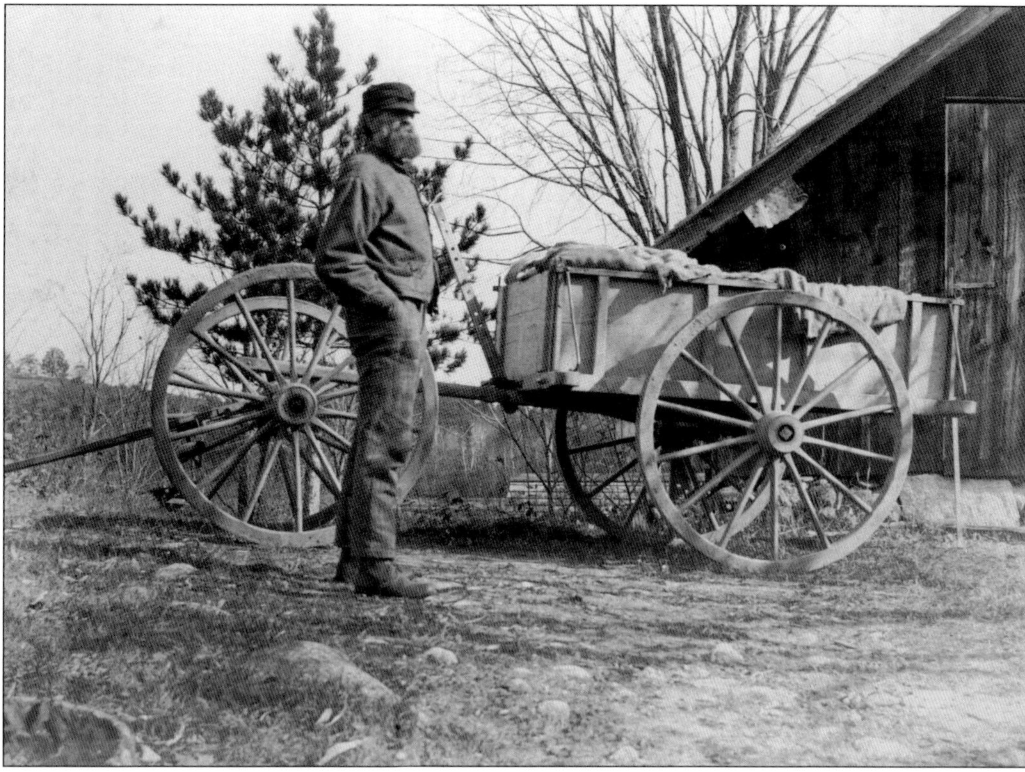

Charles Morse, with his dump cart, surveys his yard near Hoyt Brook. He operated an apple cider mill that processed the yields from neighboring orchards, where "drops" were collected and ground in the mill. Next, the "pummy" was pressed and strained to yield the sweet juice beloved by hornets and humans alike. Hard cider and vinegar were standard commodities in every household's cellar. (Courtesy of Steven Hansen.)

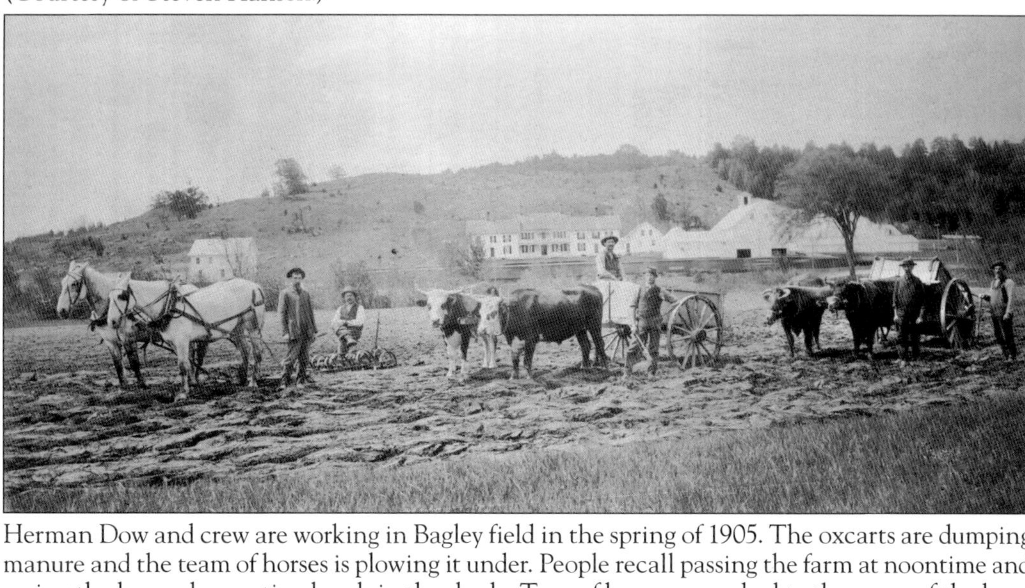

Herman Dow and crew are working in Bagley field in the spring of 1905. The oxcarts are dumping manure and the team of horses is plowing it under. People recall passing the farm at noontime and seeing the haymakers eating lunch in the shade. Tons of hay were packed to the eaves of the barn loft, which sheltered over 100 head of cattle and several teams of horses and oxen. (WHS.)

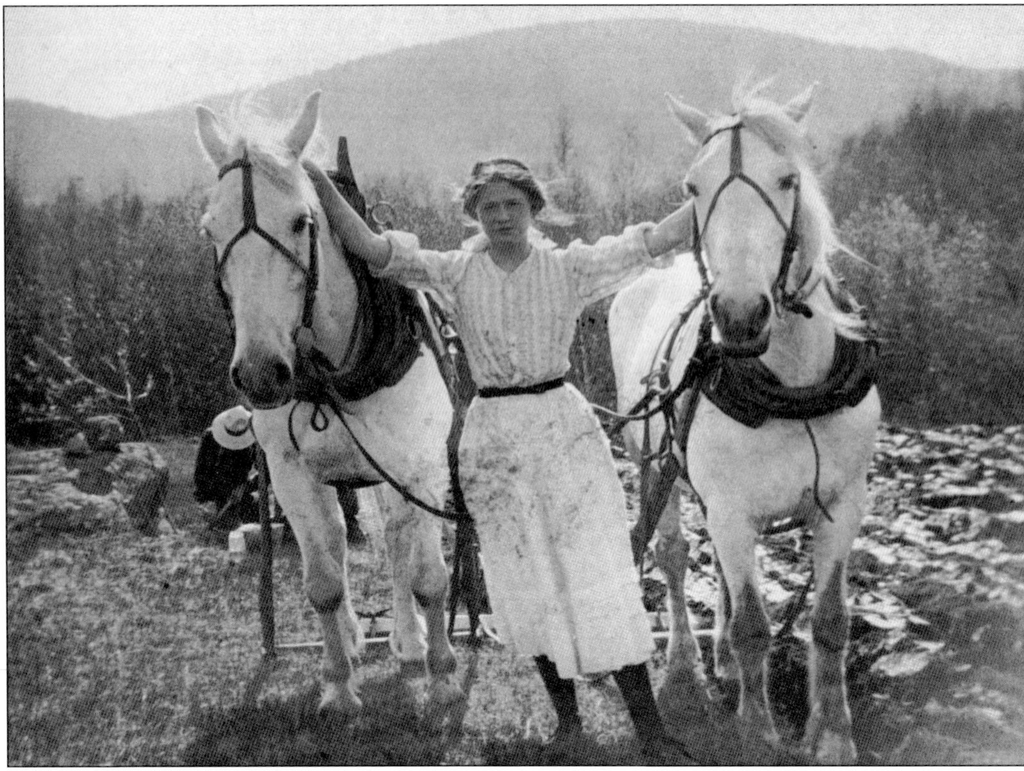

Charles Graves, a farmer on Waldron Hill, kneels in his freshly plowed field. His daughter Ella holds the finely matched team of horses bathed in the dappled spring light. The field behind them had been harrowed, and Graves is picking rocks, otherwise known as the annual crop of "field potatoes," which was a tedious spring chore. All hands were needed for preparing and planting the fields in spring. (WHS.)

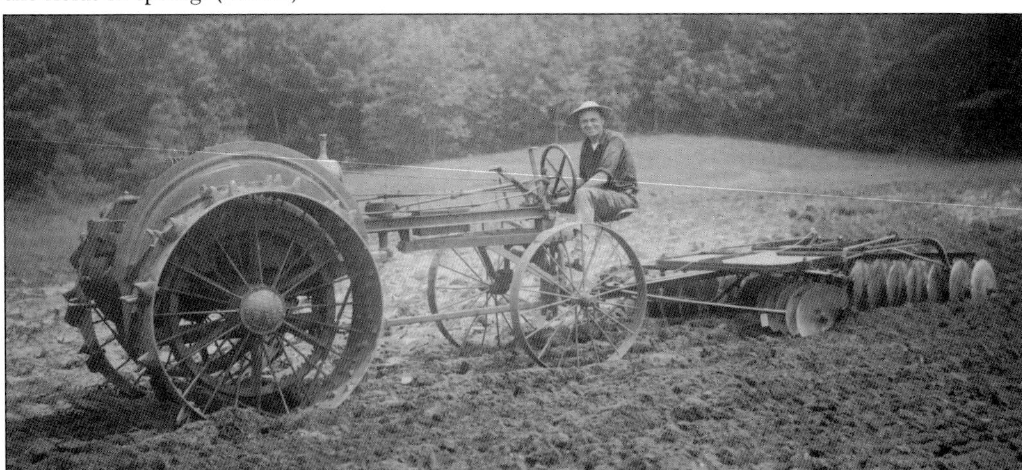

On a family field in the early 1900s, Roy Messer operates an early tractor with a disc harrow to mix and smooth the soil he had previously broken up with a spring harrow. With his wife, Marion, he produced milk, butter, eggs, fruits, and vegetables to serve at their popular Pleasant View resort. Early farmers had endless seasonal chores such as thrashing, winnowing, binding rye, and drawing muck. (BHS.)

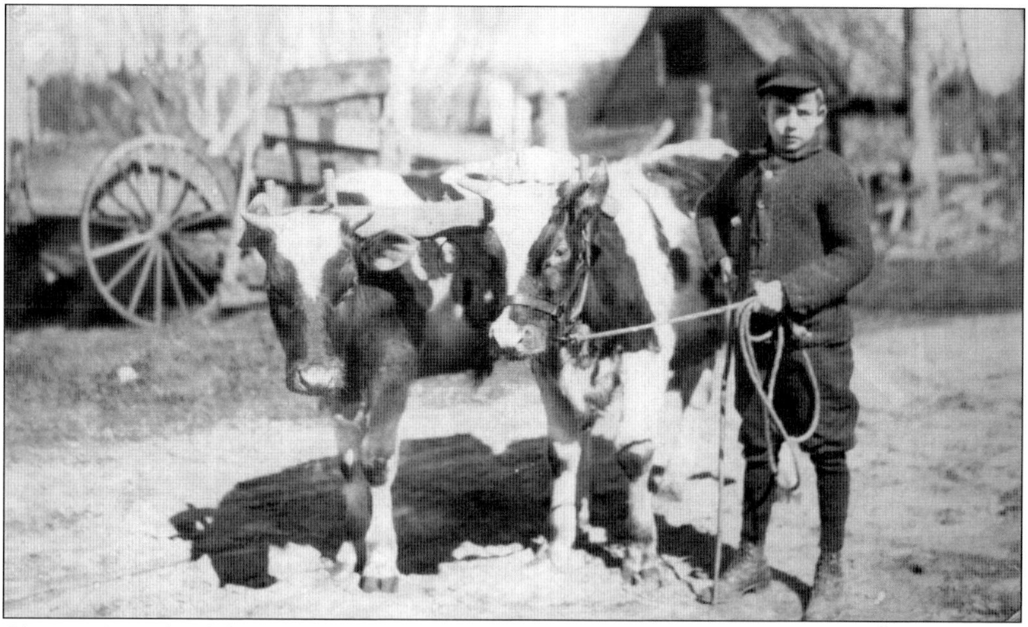

Clayton Craig leads his prize team in the 1920s. Children worked hard on early farms, often forgoing days of school to help their families survive, and gaining self-respect in the bargain. Oxen were the bulldozers of the day, moving logs, produce, and stones. Craig's family built four houses at the intersection of Center and Rowe Mountain Roads and owned acreage that spread well into the town of Hillborough. (Courtesy of Steven Hansen.)

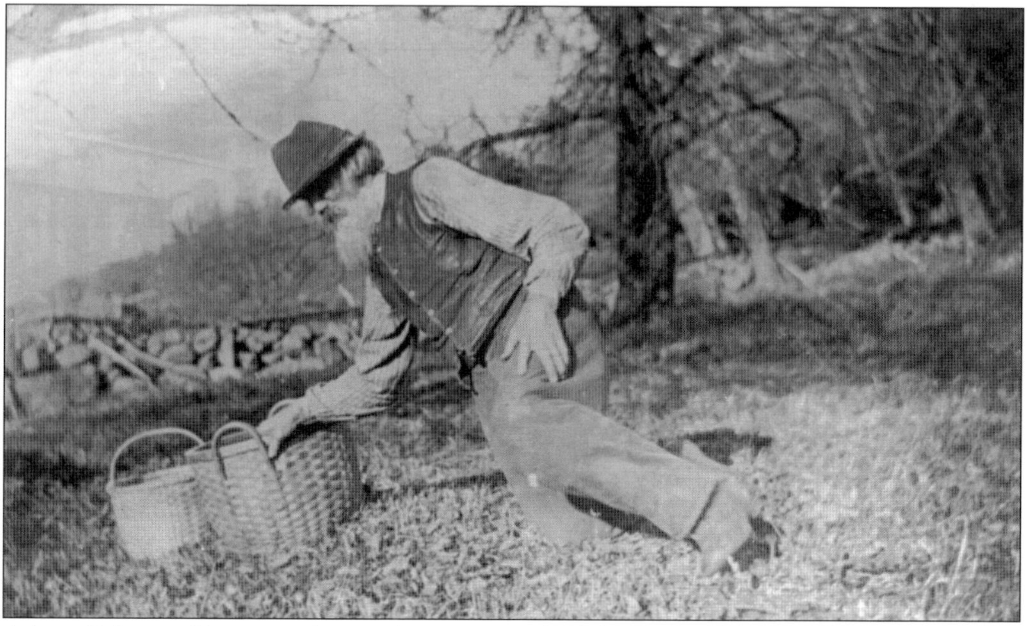

A lame Sylvester Hoyt rises from picking nuts in the field on an Indian summer day. Fall was a time to harvest potatoes, pick apples, dry beans, pickle cabbage, brine meat, and can anything left from the garden. Wood needed to be cut and stacked in the woodshed, the foundations of homes were banked with leaves or hay, and loose farm implements were corralled and stored for the winter. (WHS.)

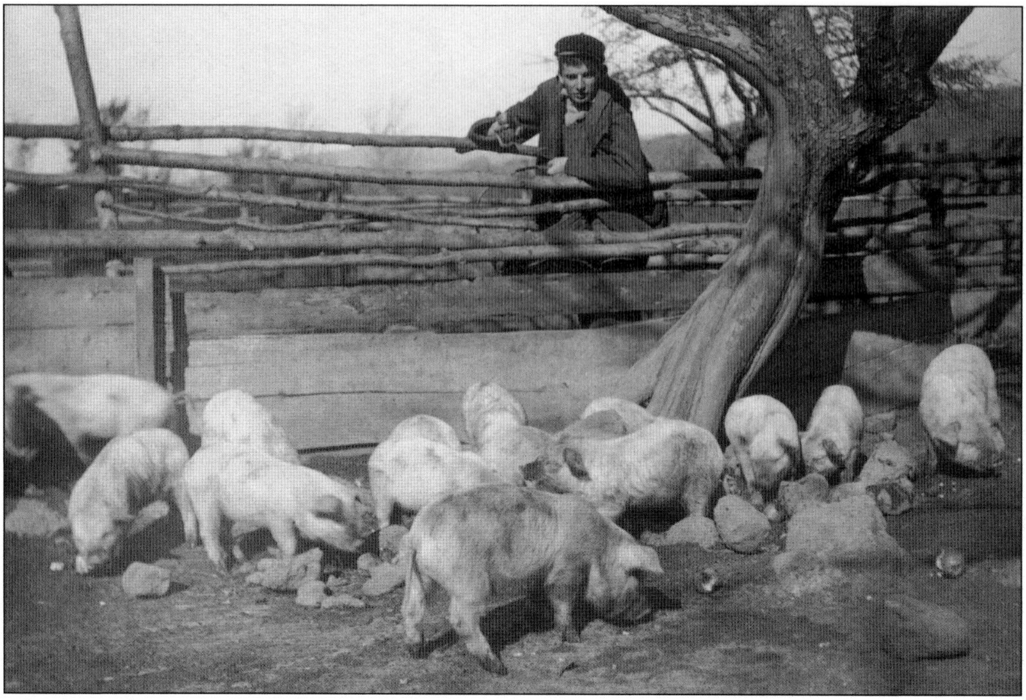

Charles Wilson sizes up his piglets. Pork was an important meat for early farmers because it lent itself well to the preserving techniques of the day. Meat was cured in brine, then smoked and hung in the rafters or cellar. Mold was scraped off the rind before consumption. Charles raised lambs as well for the growing tourist trade. (BHS.)

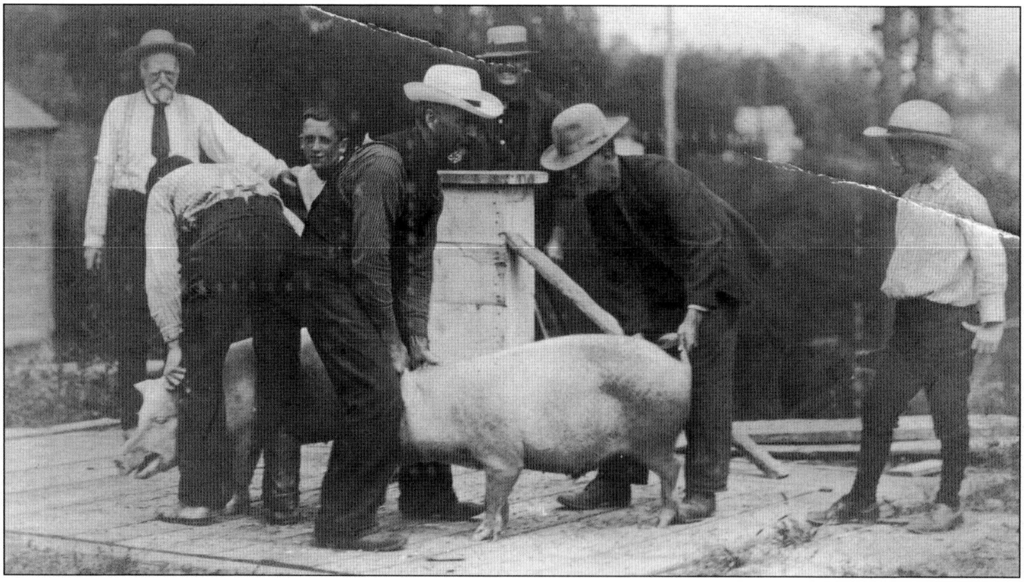

Elderly gentleman Charles Gillis and youngster Rodney Underwood look on with equal concern as merchants wrestle hogs onto the public scale. These animals are no doubt headed for the nearby slaughterhouse. The scale was large enough to hold Delbert Nelson's wagonloads carrying coal. The railroad had smaller scales used for measuring freight, providing a source of amusement to all who wanted to weigh themselves. (BHS.)

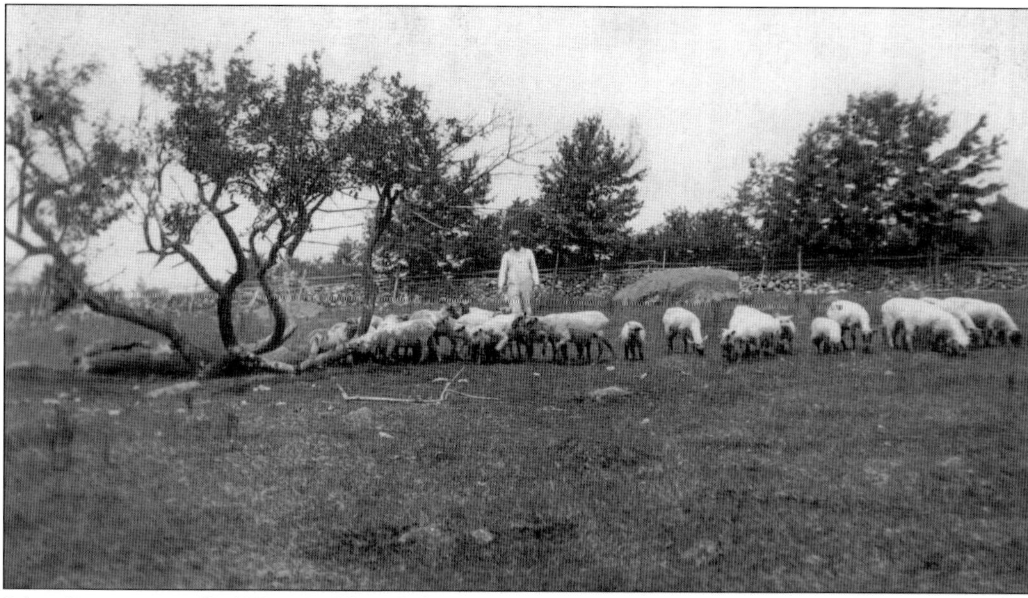

John Cressy was called "Doc," although he was not a man of medicine. He is seen here shepherding in his customary dapper attire. He and his wife, Esther, ran a summer guesthouse at Meadow Brook Farm and raised many children (including twins), prize-winning Morgan horses, and sheep, providing meat and wool to use or sell. In 1883, there were more than 1,900 sheep in Bradford. (Courtesy of Steven Hansen.)

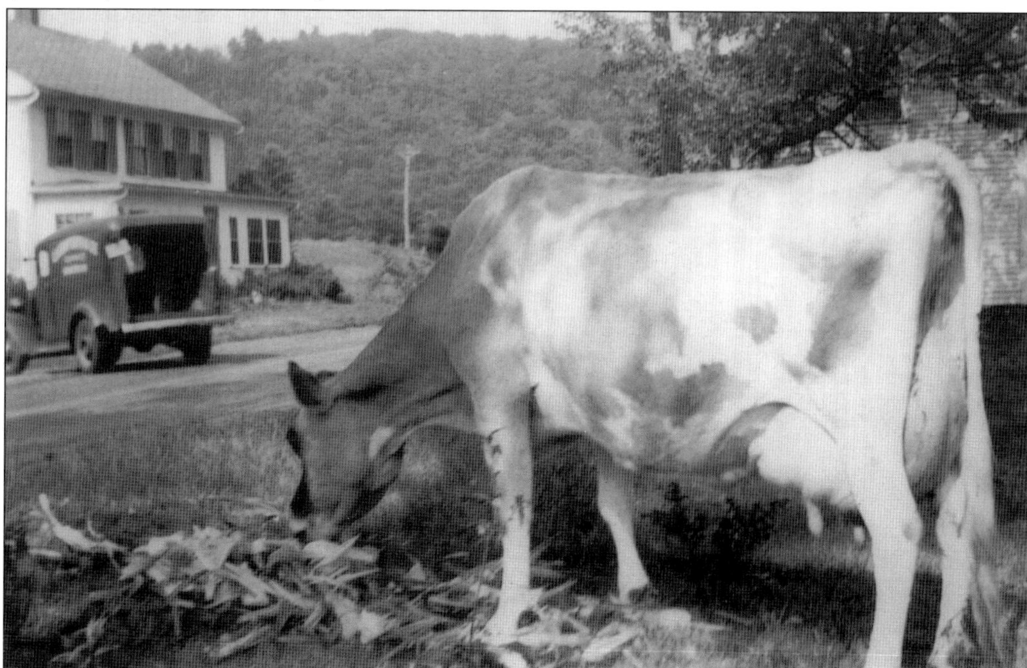

Esmeralda was a prime dairy cow at Sunshine Farm. In the early days, even village families owned a cow, which would give enough milk to sell for 5¢ a quart. Outlying farms with larger herds transported their milk in 20- or 40-quart cans to a special loading dock. The cans were then placed in the refrigerated car on the morning train to Boston. (BHS.)

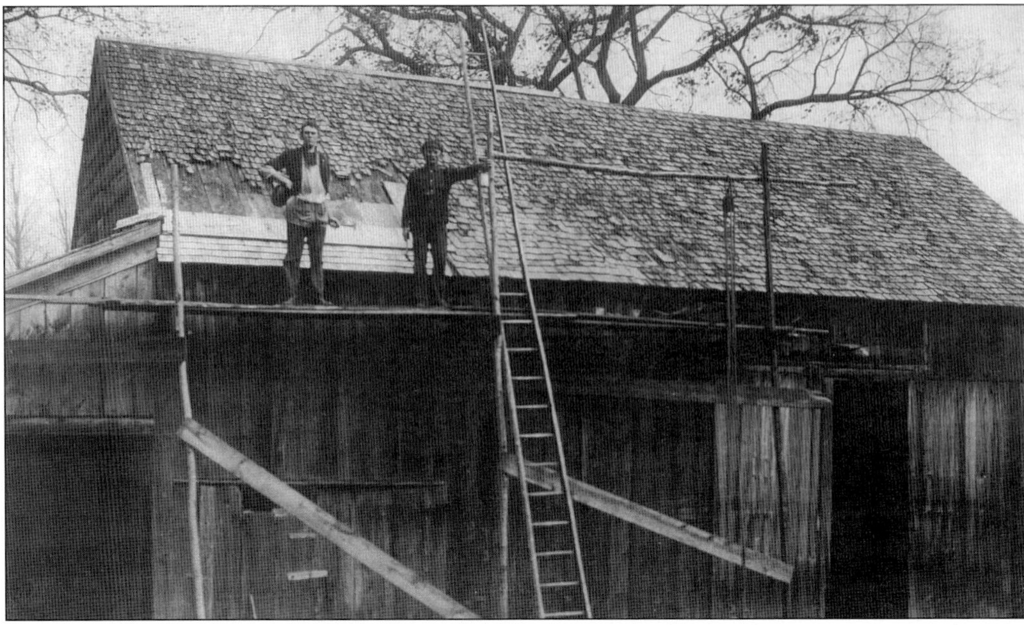

Horace Bagley, a barn builder, repairs this barn on West Road around 1920. It is situated near a mill, built in the late 1700s by Stephen Hoyt, Bradford's first schoolteacher. Husking bees were held in barns such as this to entertain the young people and complete the harvest. Whoever found a red ear of corn could claim a kiss from a sweetheart. (Courtesy of John Belanger.)

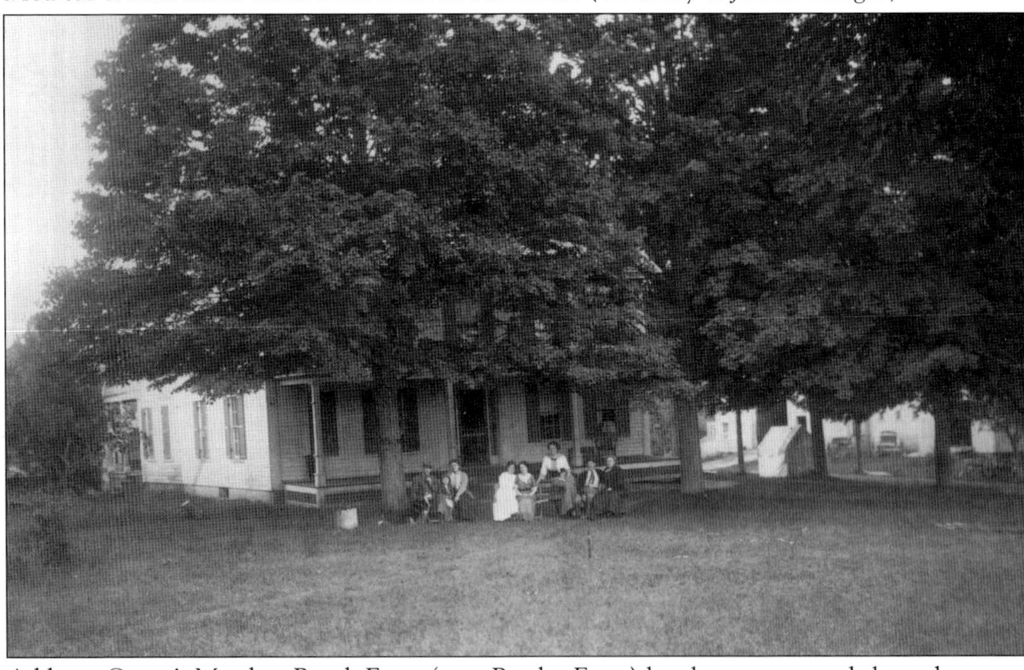

Addison Cressy's Meadow Brook Farm (now Battles Farm) has been preserved through a grant from the Land and Community Heritage Investment Program, recognizing it as an important natural, cultural, and historic site. In 1897, *New Hampshire Agriculture* said Cressy "brought in 70 tons of hay, put in 75 tons ensilage, raised several hundred bushels corn, plenty of fruit and vegetables, five horses, and twenty-five head cattle." (Courtesy of Steven Hansen.)

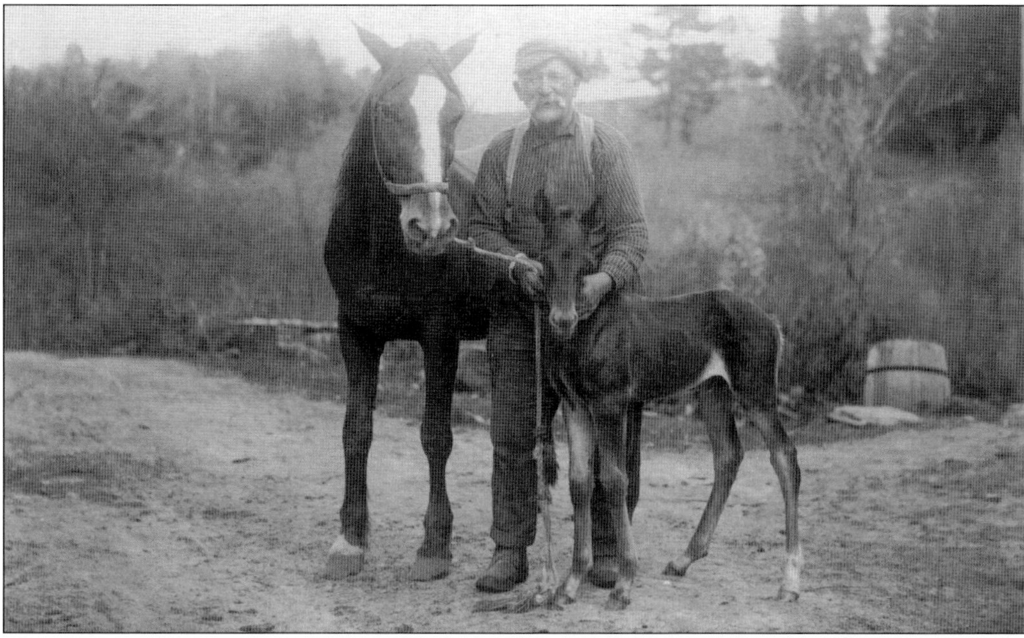

Ed Ring shows off a mare and her foal that grazed on his beautiful Ring Hill pasture. Larger draft horses were also valued here beginning in the late 1700s. Morgan horses were popular because of their strength, speed, and endurance. Their compact bodies made them suitable for a variety of tasks, especially pulling stumps or carriages. They were prized for their steady gait and work ethic. (Courtesy of Steven Hansen.)

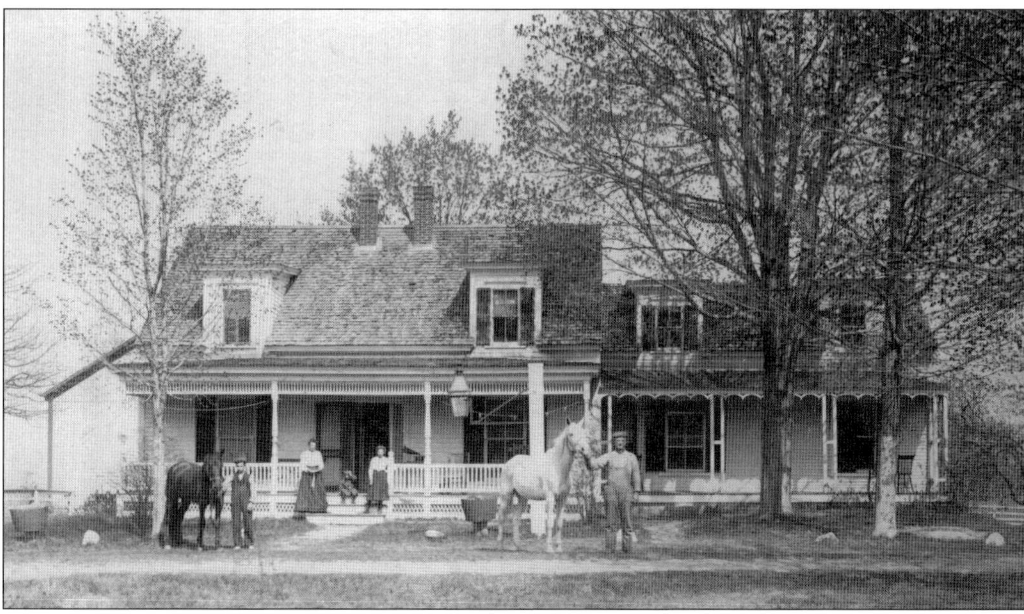

This farm on Hogg Hill was restored by the Brown family. Once, when Norman Brown fired at a crow, the bullet traveled across the open pasture to Main Street, where it flew clean through a parlor window without hurting a soul. Ethel Brown raised horses, cows, and chickens and shipped produce to Boston. Many other farms have been restored in Bradford to preserve the historical character of the landscape. (BHS.)

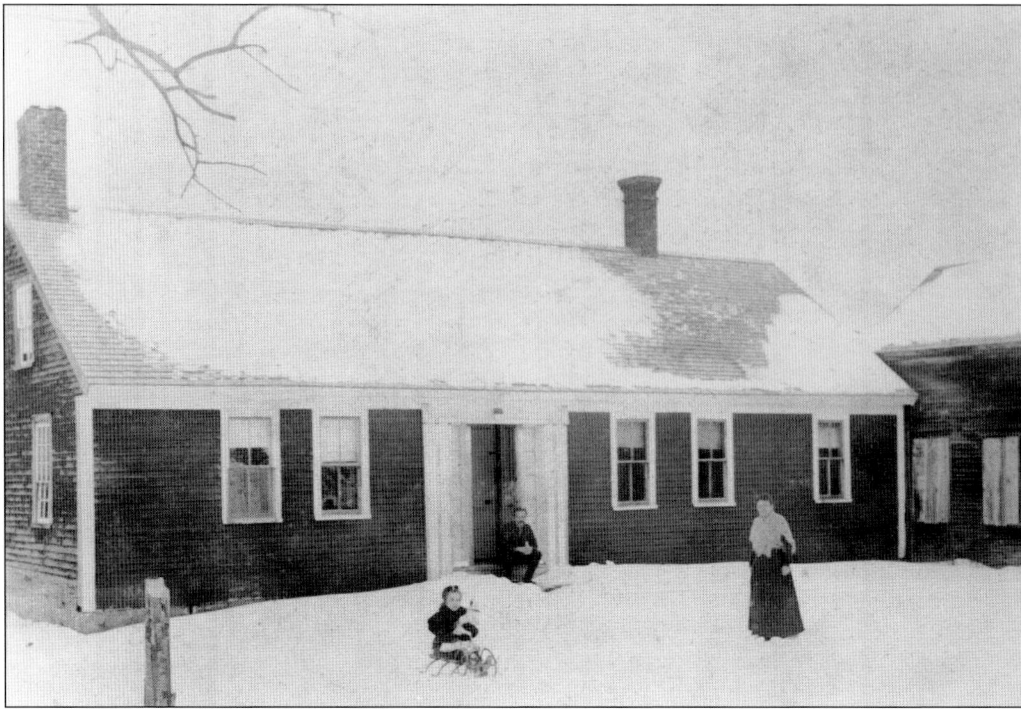

Apphia Bailey of the North Village wrote that winter clothing was made at home. Nearly everyone kept a flock of sheep. Their wool was spun and woven to make blankets, shirts, and drawers for the men. Women knit stockings by hand. Girls were taught to sew and were expected to knit a certain number of rounds every day before they could go out to play. (WHS.)

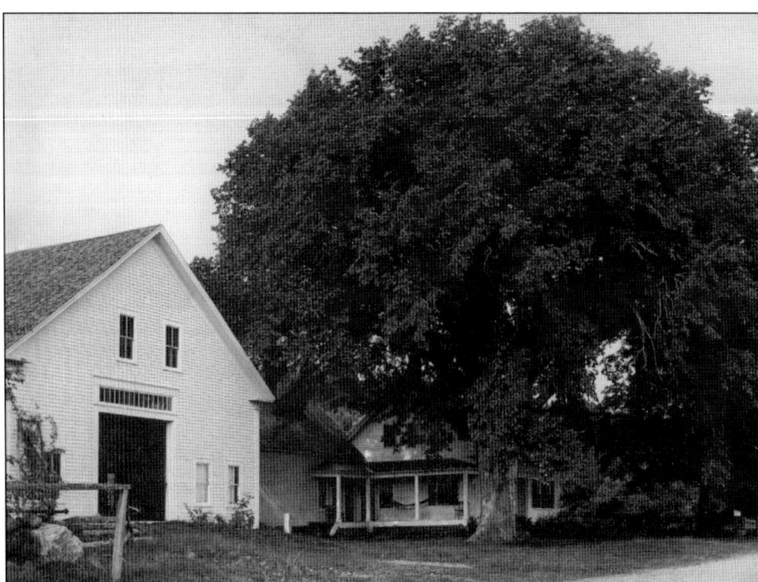

There are many stories about how the majestic Tewksbury Elm came into existence. One says a visitor stuck his whip in the ground, drove off without it, and the whip took root. Another tale says Philip Flanders built a log cabin here in 1798 and transplanted the elm to the front yard. This elm succumbed to disease in the 1970s. (WHS.)

Three

We Gather Together

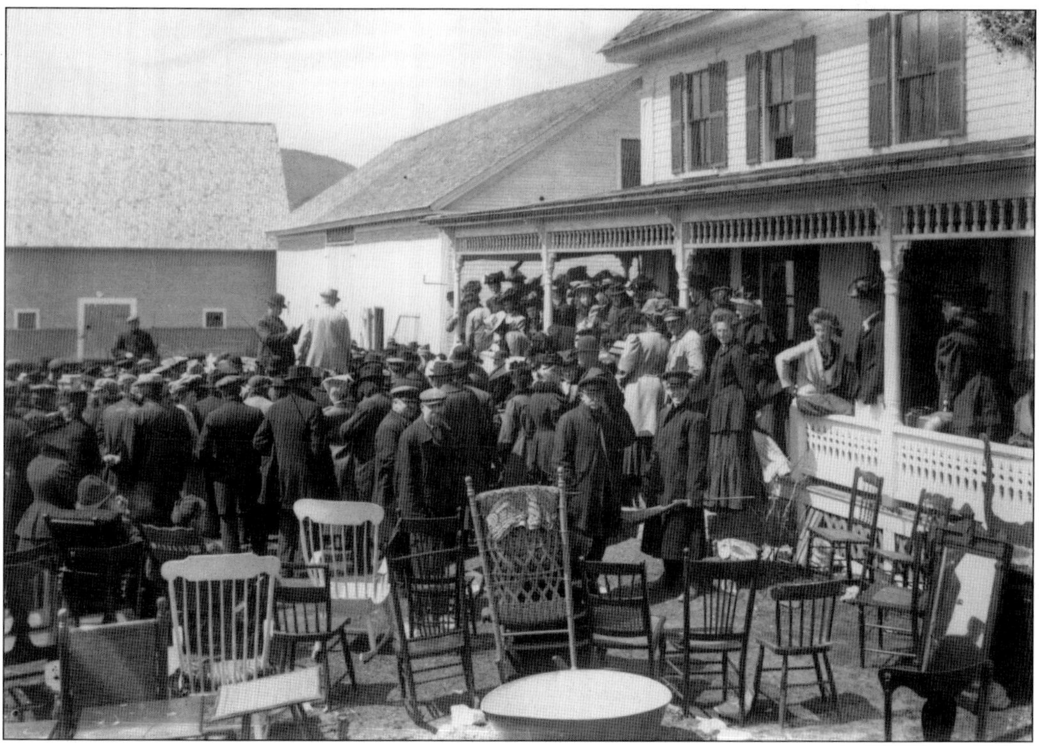

Hotel proprietor Charles Gillis conducted auctions in the early 1900s. People gathered for commerce, communion, and celebration. Fairview Farm, pictured here, was built in the 1820s by John Peaslee. His family ran the farm as a boardinghouse in the 1880s, charging $7 a week for both room and board. John later donated land to the Bradford-Newbury Fair Association to be used as a fairground. (Courtesy of Steven Hansen.)

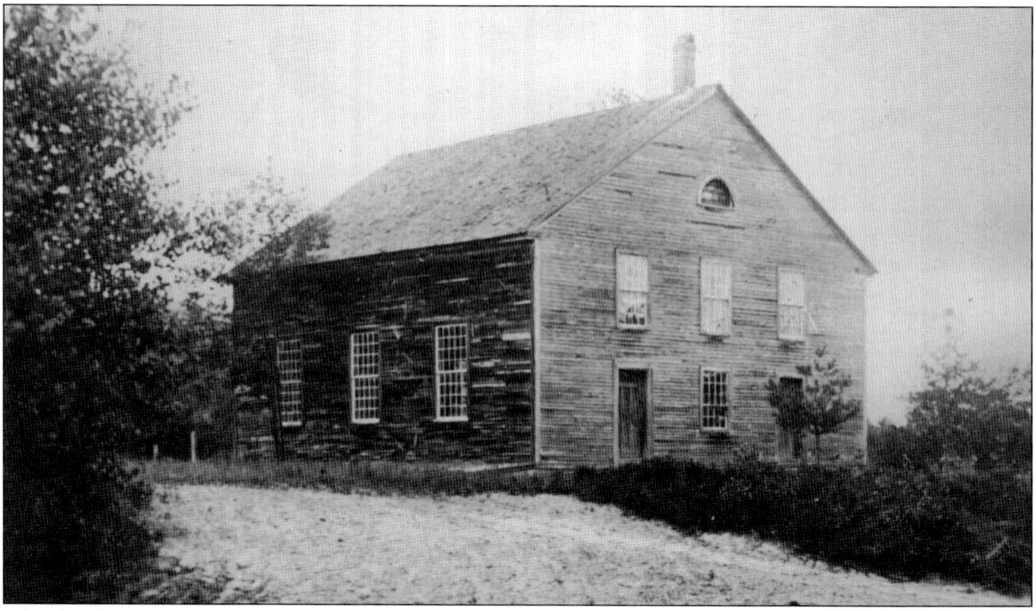

Pond Meetinghouse was erected in 1833 on a sandy knoll overlooking Lake Massasecum. The building was actively used until it burned in 1941. Built by men of various beliefs, it was unlocked so anyone could hold meetings. A marker honoring Warner philanthropist Ida Redington is located near the adjacent Pond Cemetery in gratitude for her support. (BHS.)

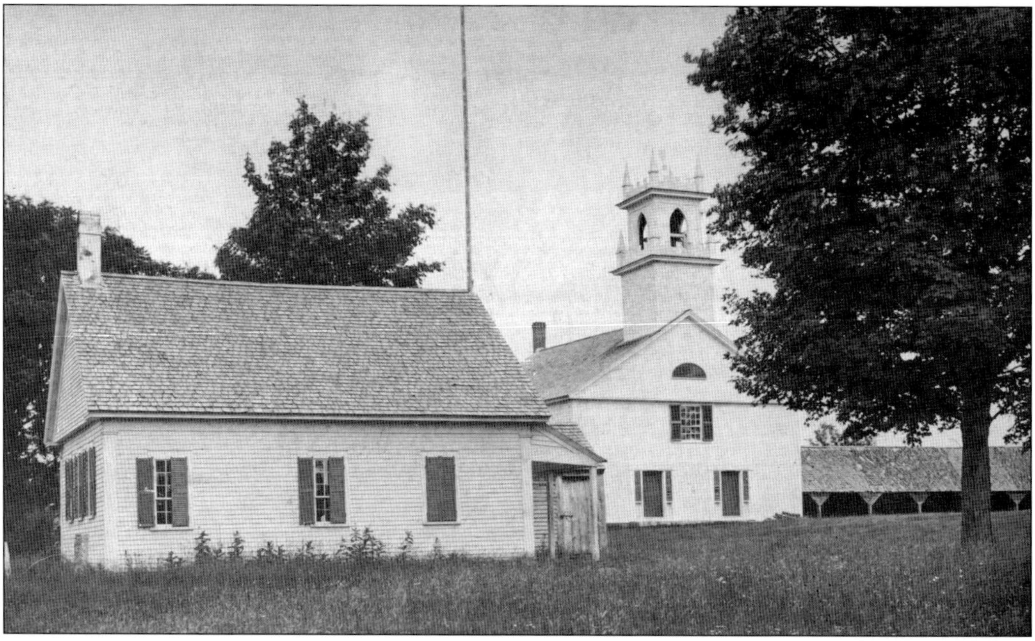

Bradford Center still boasts the original schoolhouse, meetinghouse, burying ground, town pound, and the only town green. Horsehair-cushioned pews were used by Congregationalists, Baptists, Universalists, and Methodists alike. The famous abolitionist and feminist Abby Fulsome was bodily removed from here after voicing her views. At the Centennial Celebration in 1938, a dinner of oyster stew was served to 300 people in the vestry and snow roller sheds, visible here on the right. (BHS.)

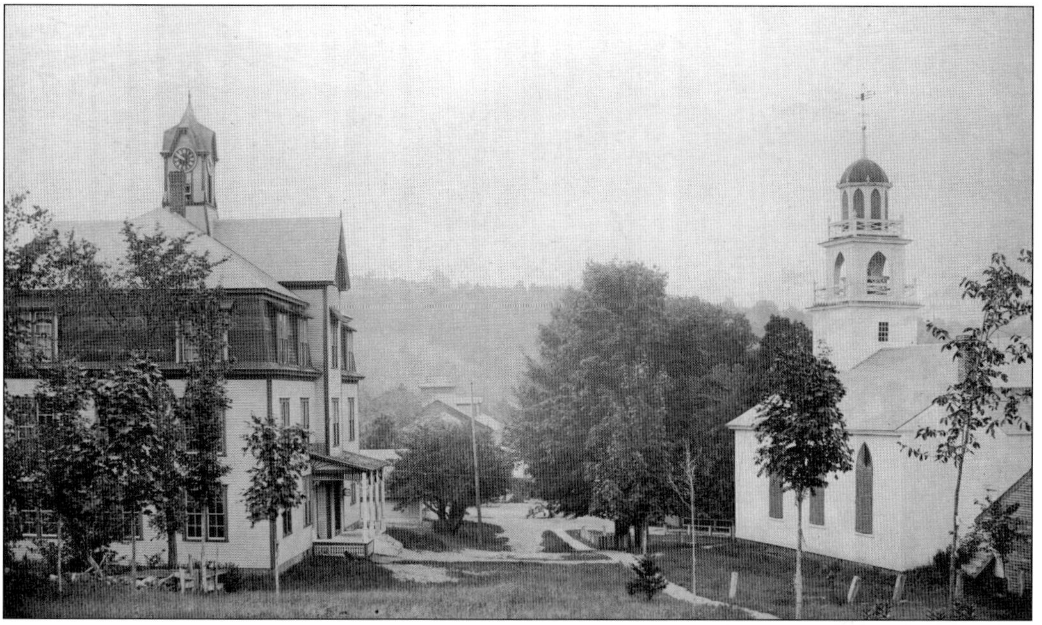

The First Baptist Church was built by 22 men for $1,500 on grounds purchased from Dr. Nathaniel Eaton in Warner. It was dedicated on September 25, 1833, in the presence of its 29 members: 12 men and 17 women. The original lap organ (or elbow melodeon) was the first instrument used in the church and is currently owned by the Warner Historical Society. The bell tower was removed in the mid-1960s. (WHS.)

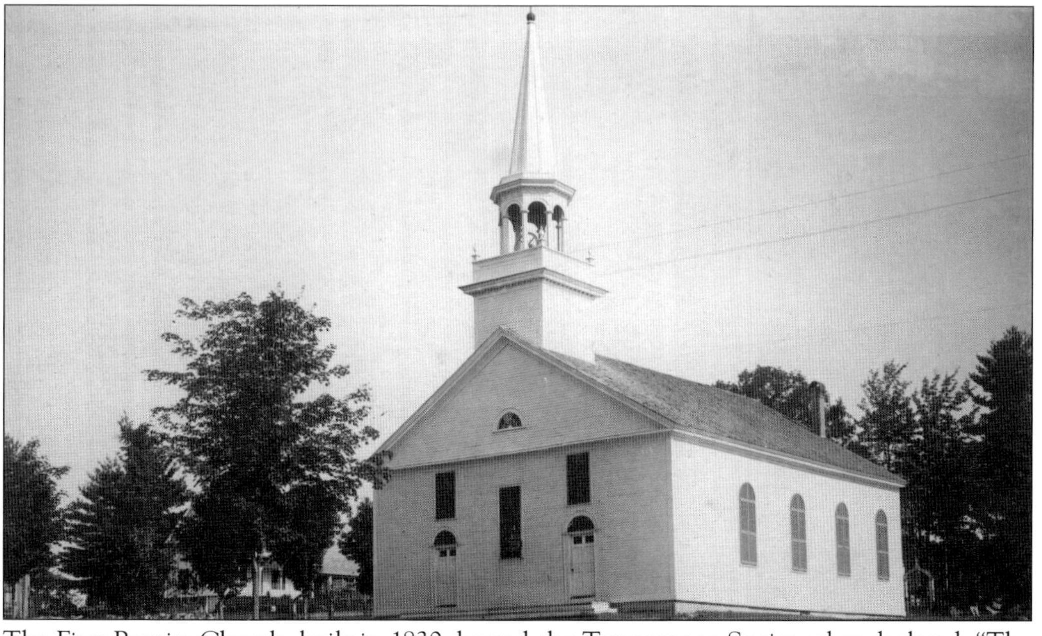

The First Baptist Church, built in 1830, hosted the Temperance Society that declared, "The church cannot be the salt of the earth or the light of the world while it holds those in good church fellowship who trade and traffic in ardent spirits or use it as a beverage." The organ was pumped by janitor Henry Bellows, whose fondness for wrapped candy added rustles to the hymns. (Courtesy of Steven Hansen.)

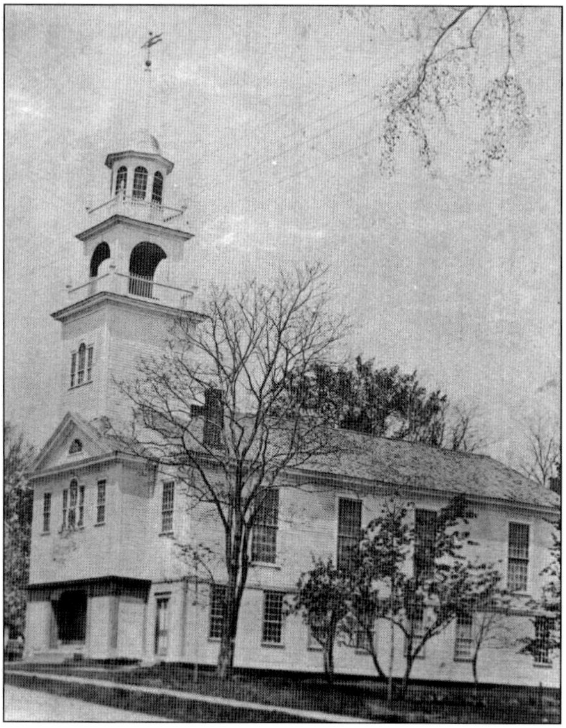

The Congregational church, known as the United Church of Warner, was originally built in 1819 and moved to this location from Old Main Street in 1845. Sunday services were not affected as church was held in the shored-up building while it was being moved. Ida Redington gifted stained-glass windows, a porte cochere over the front entrance, and a new pipe organ in the 1930s. (WHS.)

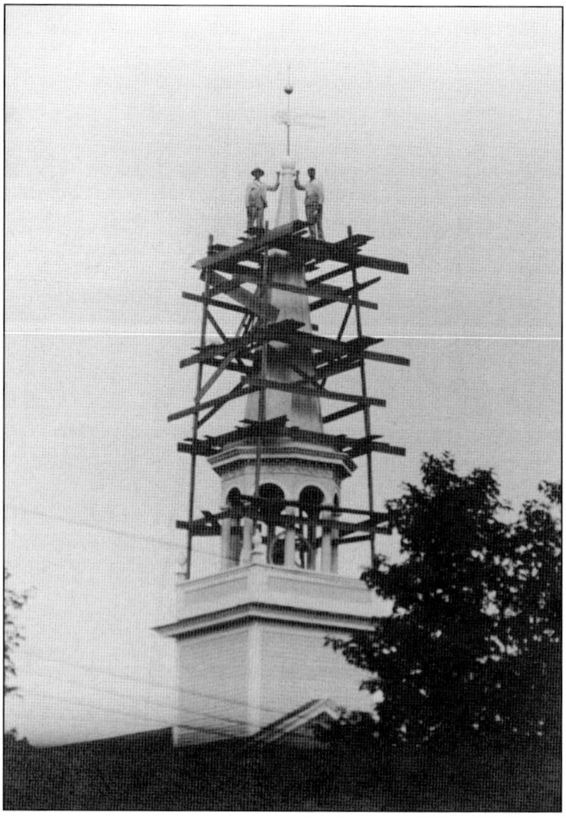

Painters Ned Smith and Albert Jewett help with one of the many renovations to the First Baptist Church in Bradford. Earlier painters advertised "varnish graining" and frescoing. The steeple bell, purchased in 1856, is still in use, and the baptismal tank is in place under a platform. Later, Reverend Bartle's sermons were recorded for radio broadcast. When loud train whistles interfered, the schedule was changed to accommodate the pious. (Courtesy of Steven Hansen.)

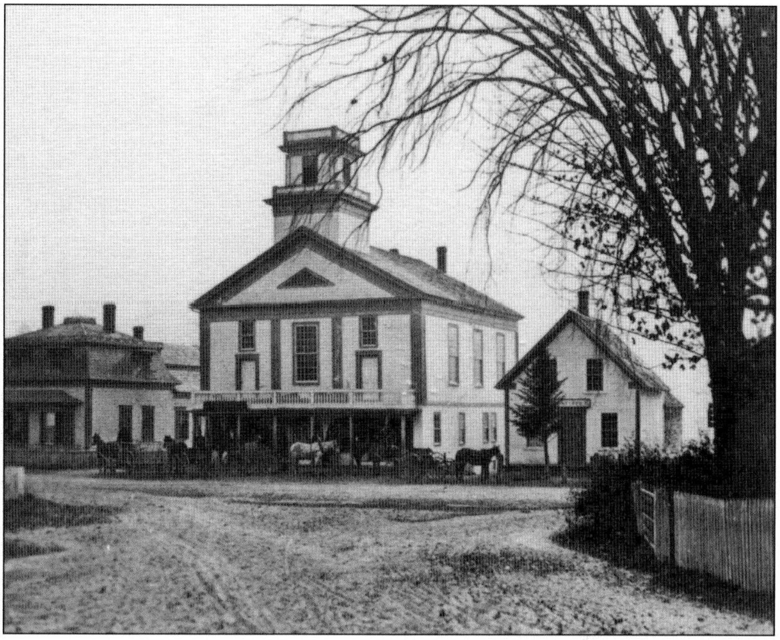

The Universalist Society Church in Warner was built in 1844 under the leadership of Daniel Bean and was located on the corner of Main and Mill Streets. Nehemiah Ordway purchased it in 1863 for $200 and moved it by oxen to this location. A first floor was added for a dry-goods store operated by Alonzo Carroll & Son, and the upper story was used for public meetings. (WHS.)

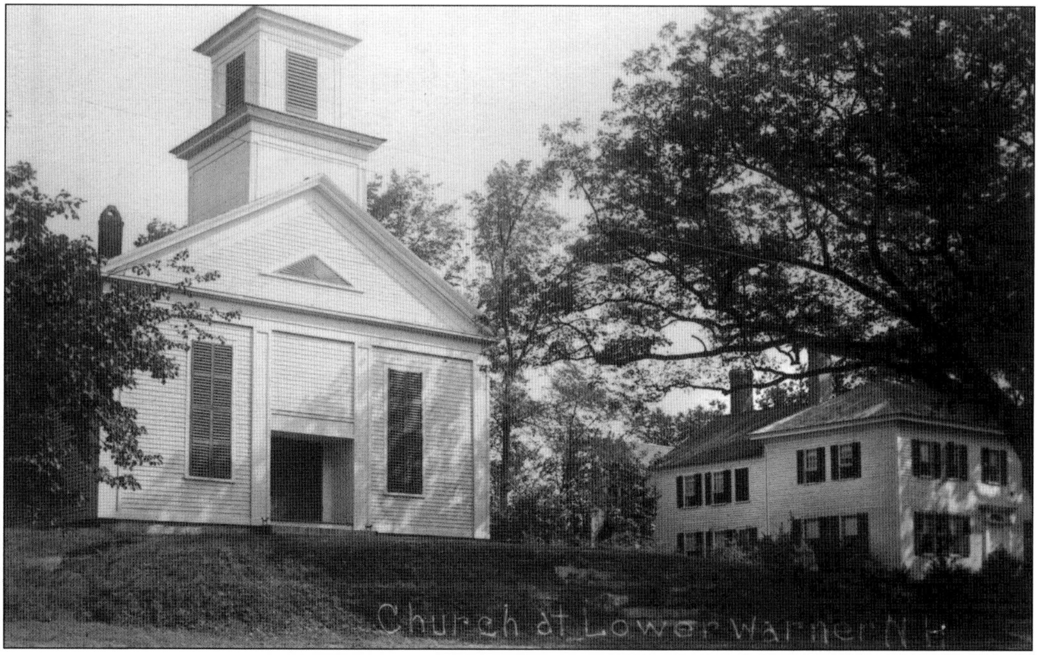

The Congregational church's move to the Main Village in 1845 caused a split in the congregation. Several members of the George family in the Lower Village perceived the movement of the church as a threat to their livelihood, so they formed the Second Orthodox Congregational Society. The meetinghouse was donated to the Warner Historical Society in 1969 by Nancy Sibley Wilkins, a descendant of the George family. (WHS–Pratt.)

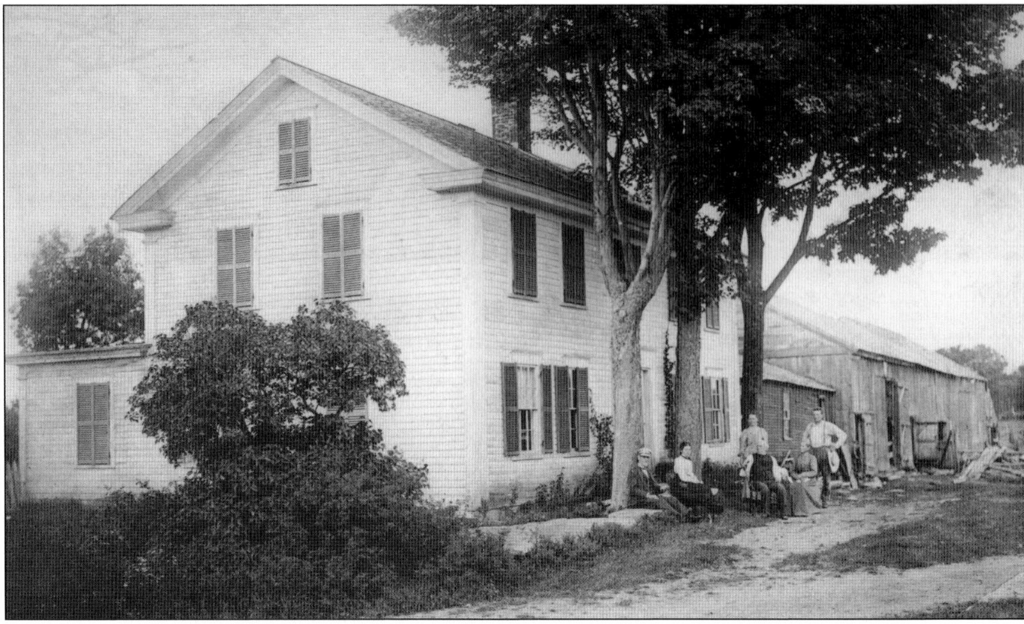

The Peter Ayer Cook home on West Road saw the beginnings of the First Baptist Church, which was organized here in 1821 under the guidance of Rev. Isaac Kimball, a visiting missionary. In a day when a congregation was commonly addressed as "Brethren," it was decided here that "Sisters" could vote in church meetings, as they made up half of the membership. (BHS.)

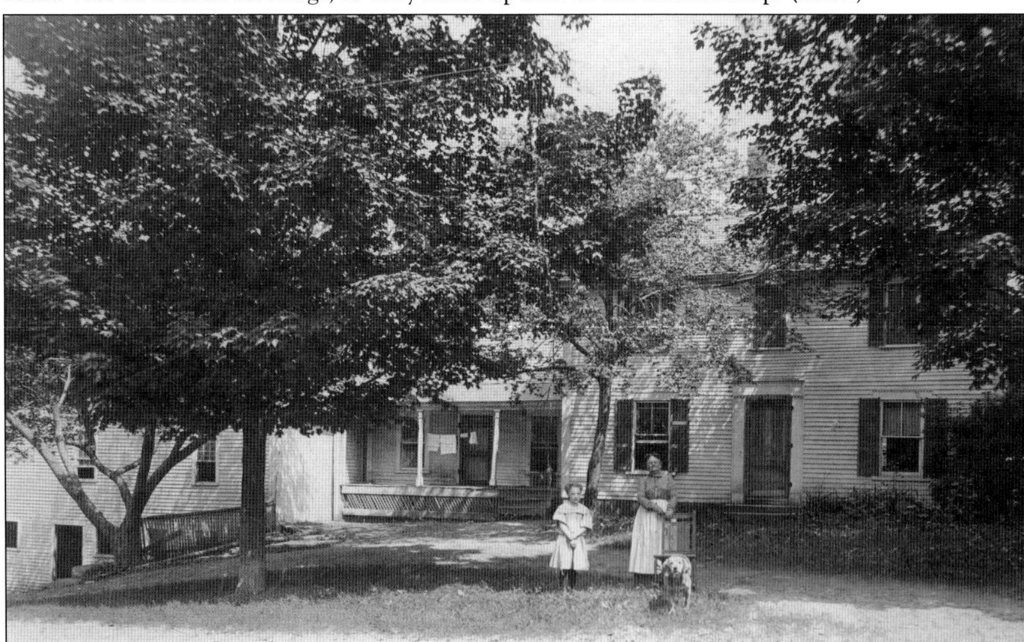

In 1849, New Hampshire became the first state to authorize public libraries. By 1811, Bradford had a subscription library. The donated collection was housed in various dwellings and stores with the goal to preserve books, promote social discourse, and "improve the intellectual welfare of the community." The first free public library was housed in Nellie Peaslee's home beginning in 1893. She was the first in a line of many fine librarians. (BHS.)

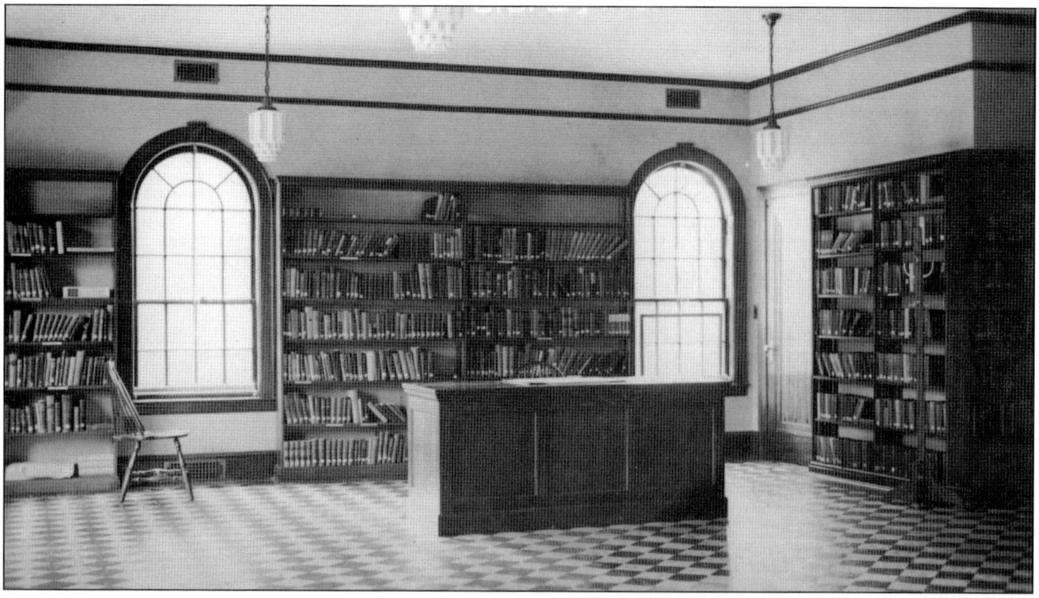

The Brown Memorial Library was built in 1932 from sizable gifts made by James Brown and John and Emma French. An impressive dedication ceremony featured speeches, music by the Simonds Free High School Orchestra, and Boy Scout assistance. The original circulation desk is still in use, and the library continues to provide free collection access and serve as a cultural center for the town. (Courtesy of Steven Hansen.)

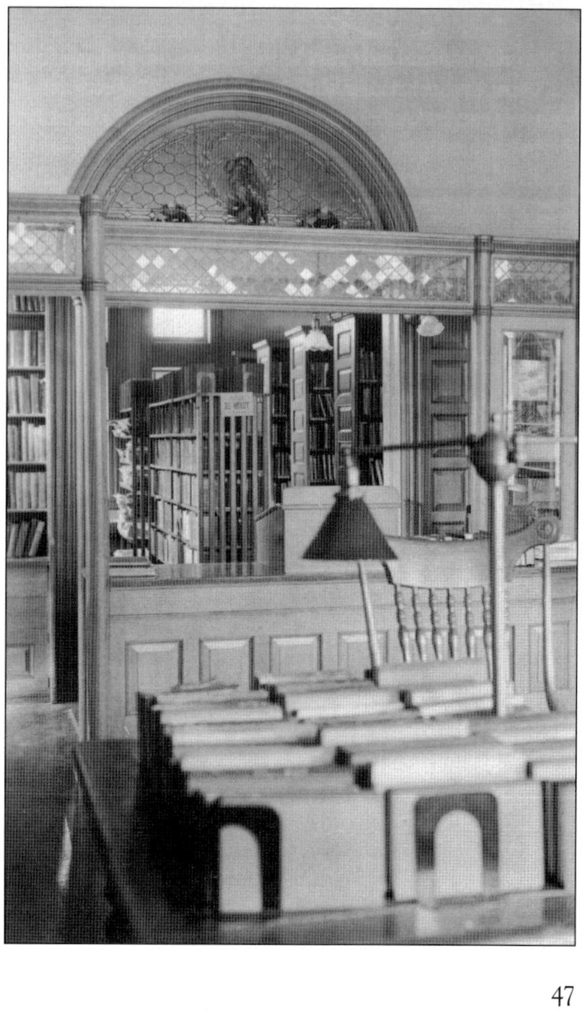

The Pillsbury Free Library was dedicated on October 2, 1891. The official opening day was held on February 6, 1892, and 12-year-old Lloyd Cogswell received the first library card. The Romanesque Richardson Library was a gift of George and Margaret Pillsbury, former Warner residents who had made their fortune in the Pillsbury Flour business. Harry Wild Jones of Minneapolis, Minnesota, was the architect. (WHS.)

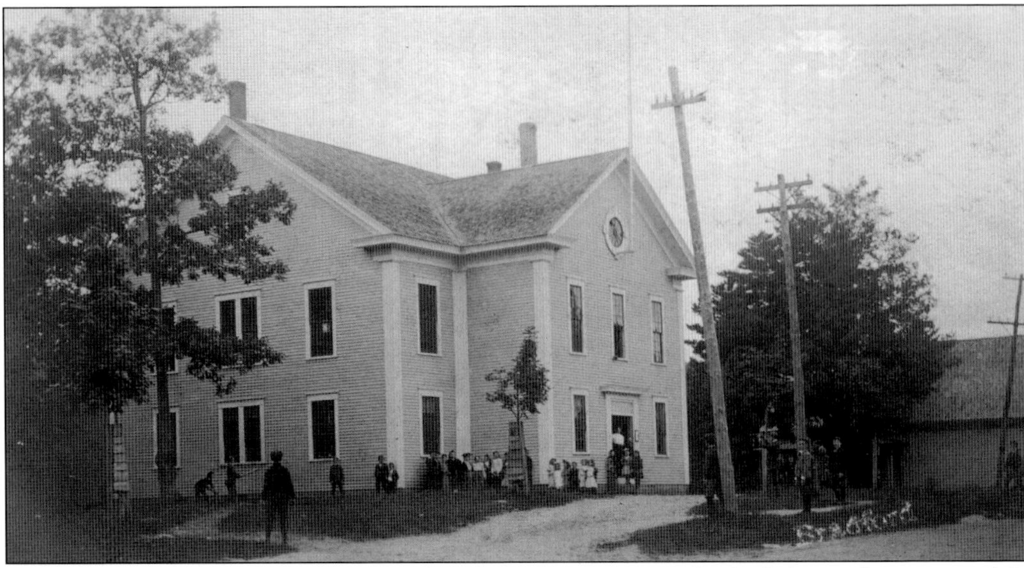

Bradford Town Hall was originally built at the center in 1796. The high box pulpit was used for divine worship as well as public gatherings. In 1863, it was dismantled and moved to the village for proximity to the railroad line. Before women's suffrage in 1920, only men attended town meetings. The floor was lined with sawdust to absorb the tobacco spit. (BHS.)

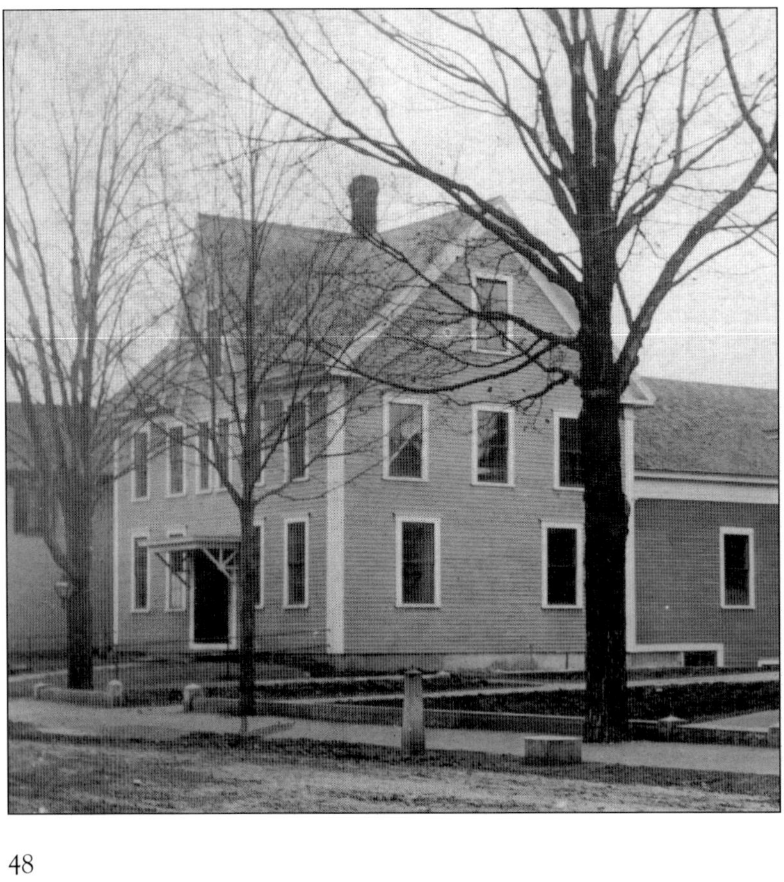

The townspeople decided to build a new town hall in 1854 because the barn-like structure in the Lower Village was unsuitable. The new hall was the site of fiery political speeches debating the merits of the Civil War and calling on men to enlist. Lyceums, musical events, and high school graduations were convened on the second floor. After being torn down in 1910, it was rebuilt as a barn on Pumpkin Hill. (WHS.)

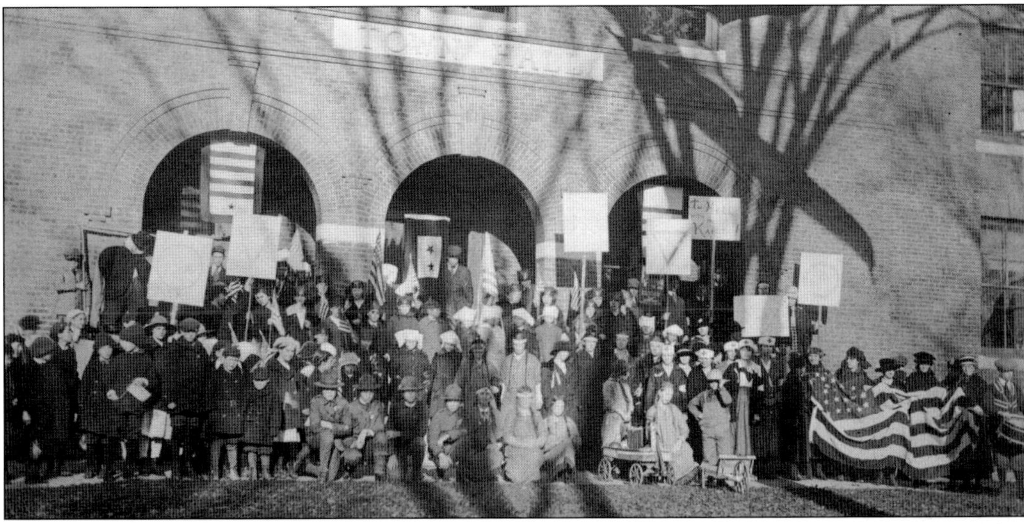

Warner celebrated on November 11, 1918, when they heard that World War I was over. Flags were flown and houses were draped in buntings. An impromptu parade was held in the afternoon with children dressed as soldiers and nurses. The Camp Fire Girls and the Boys Scouts wore their uniforms. A torch light parade was held in the evening, followed by a bonfire and music by the Bradford Band. (WHS.)

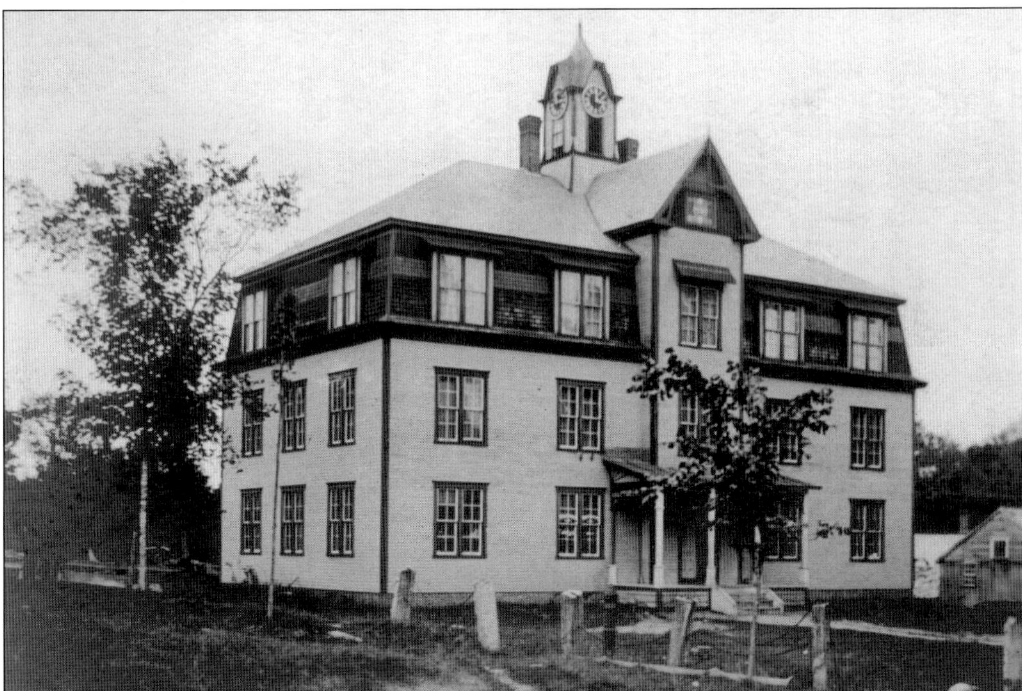

The Odd Fellows building, constructed in 1892, was topped with a mansard roof and cupola. Built by Isaac Connor's crew and painted yellow with brown trim, the three stories correspond with the three links in the order's symbol. The first floor was rented out for retail space, the second floor held the kitchen and large dining room, while the top floor was reserved for their private meetings. (WHS.)

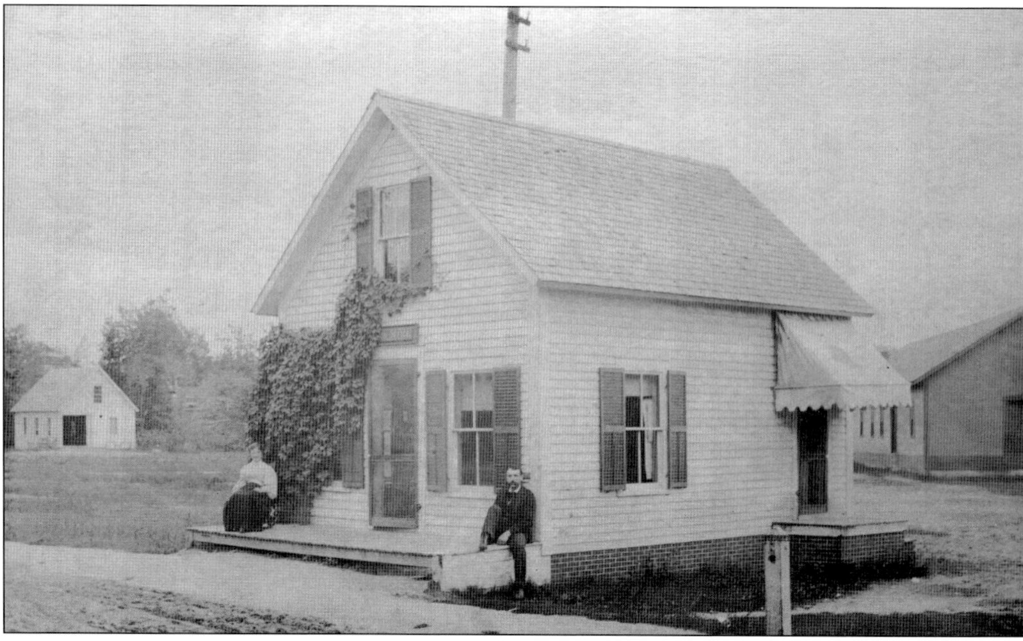

In the late 1700s, weekly post riders carried the mail up to 40 miles. This post office was built in the late 1800s by postmaster George Cressy, pictured here with his clerk and fiancée Amie Cheney. In 1900, this building hosted the King's Daughters, a charitable organization dedicated to performing neighborly deeds. Charles Newman's blacksmith shop and the railroad freight depot can be seen in the distance. (Courtesy of Steven Hansen.)

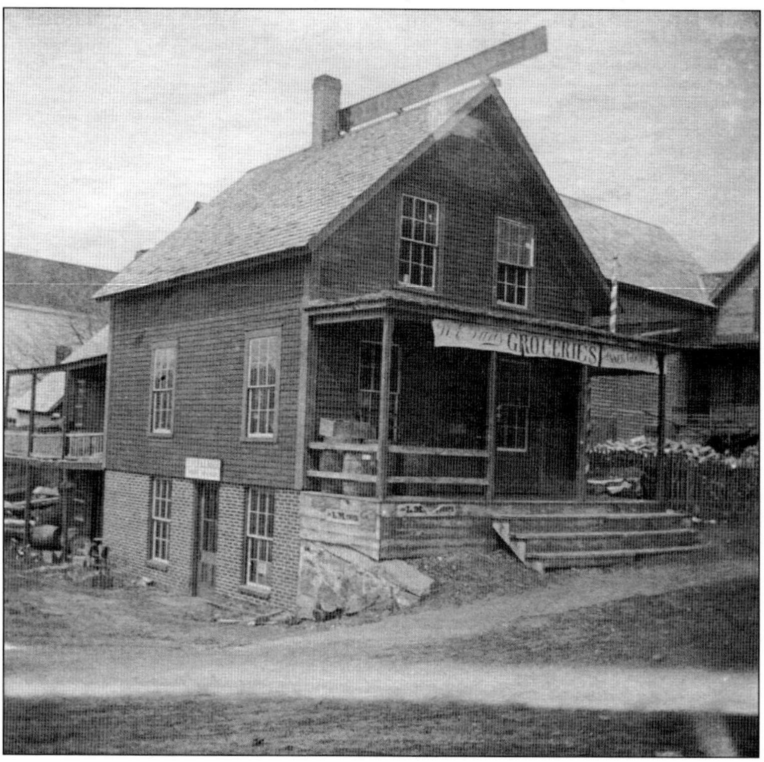

Hiram Buswell was the postmaster in Warner from 1861 to 1877 and operated his paint shop in the rear of the building. Many letters and packages were sent to the boys serving in the various regiments of the Civil War. It would be here that townspeople would gather to read the latest news from the front and rejoice or weep at the news of a loved one. (WHS.)

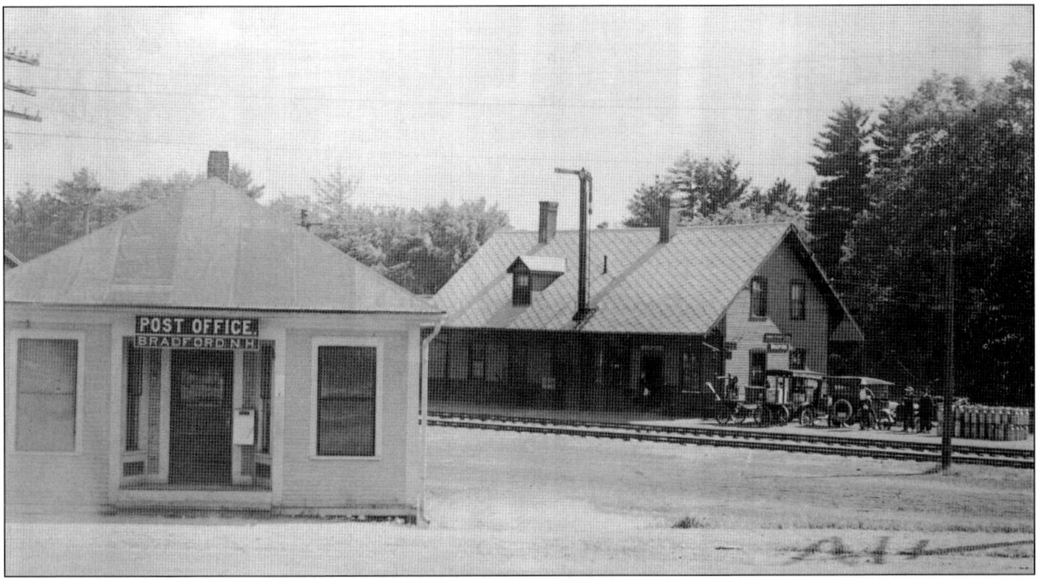

Built in 1918 by postmaster Leon Perkins, this former post office now houses the Bradford Historical Society. Bradford's first US Post Office was opened in 1812. It was housed in various hotels and stores, depending on who was the acting postmaster. There was also a special postal railroad car, with an exterior slot for quick service while the train was at the station. (Courtesy of Steven Hansen.)

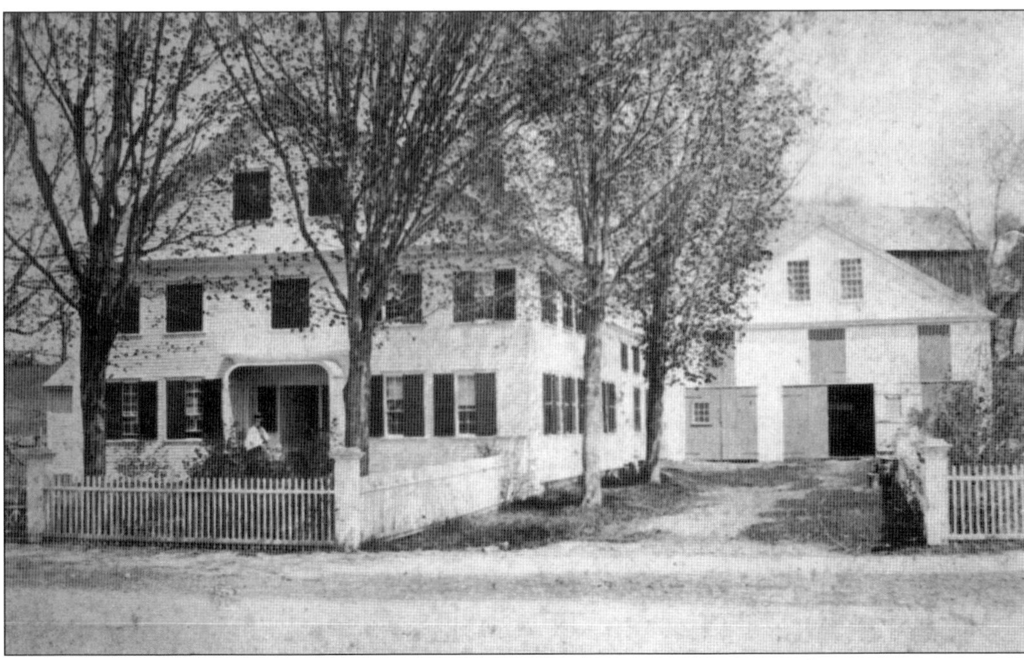

Deacon Ezra Barrett purchased a half-acre lot with a small building for $260 in 1817. Barrett operated a scythe and snath shop, employing several men between 1830 and his death in 1843. The business afforded him the ability to build this Federal-style home for his family. John P.H. Chandler Jr. donated the building to the Warner Historical Society in 2000 to use as a museum. (WHS.)

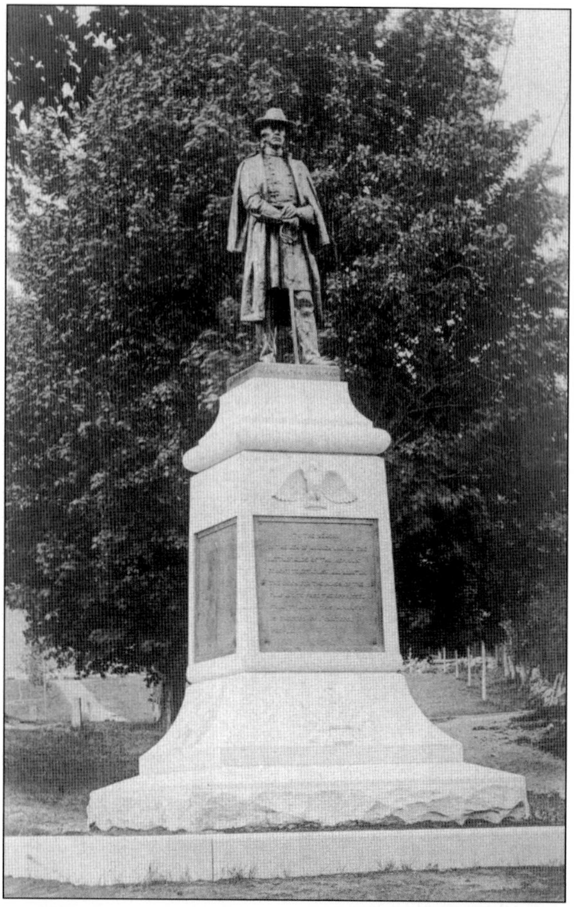

Despite the heat of the day, 1,500 people attended the dedication of the Soldier's Monument on July 2, 1903. Two women, Harriet Bartlett and Sarah Edmunds, gave bequests of $1,000 each for a soldier's monument. The town supplied a site and appropriated additional monies to complete the memorial. The Harriman family offered to provide a statue of Col. Walter Harriman to grace the top of the monument. (WHS.)

Angie and former Massachusetts governor John Brackett are standing with young Julian and Ralph Dodge at the 1913 dedication of this monument. The base was made from the original stone doorstep of the Raymond House, through which Revolutionary War hero, General Lafayette passed during his visit in 1825. The monument originally stood in the center of Lafayette Triangle but was moved slightly to accommodate traffic. (Courtesy of Brackett Scheffy.)

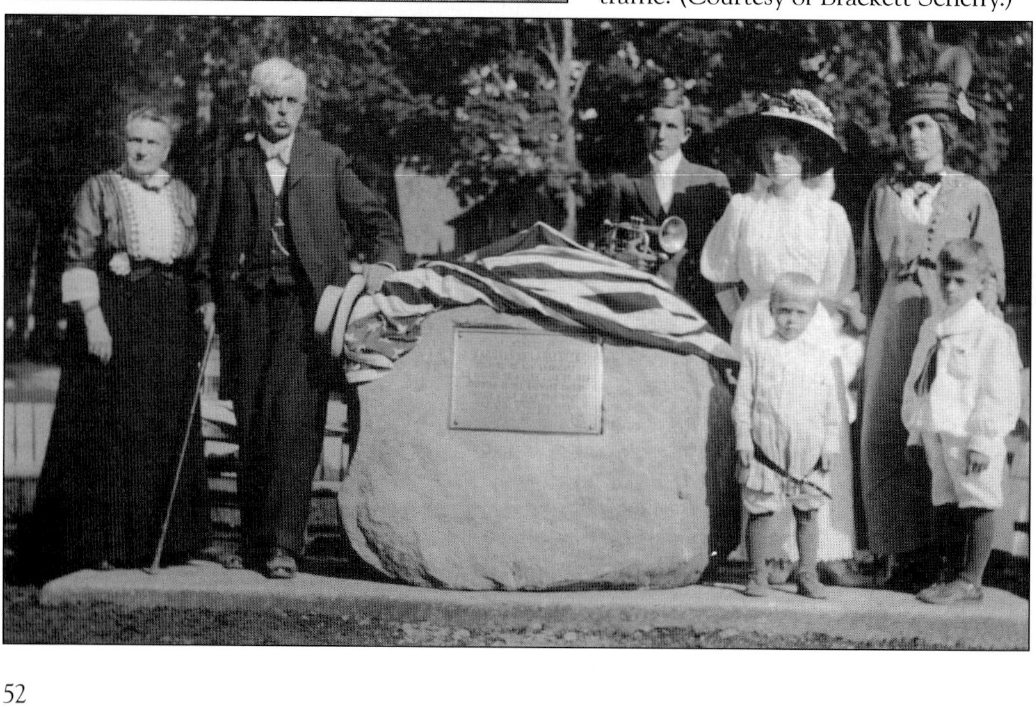

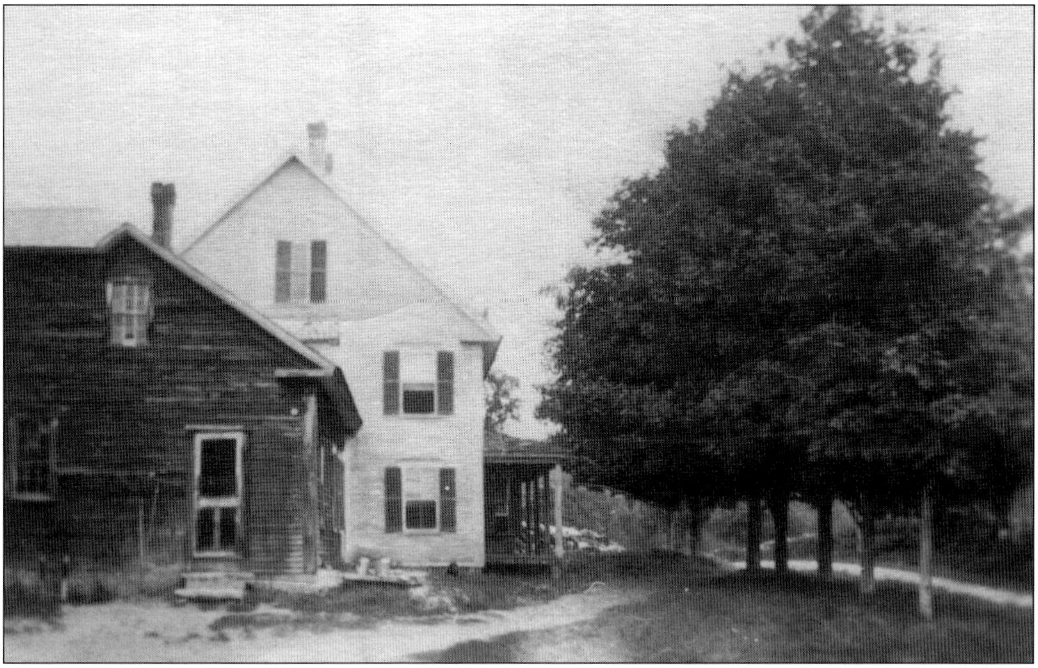

This farm on Rowe Mountain Road was the town's poor farm in the mid-1800s. Down-and-outers were offered succor under the management of an agent. Transients were warned out of town while resident paupers were provided with food, shelter, clothing, tobacco, health care, and burial. Elsewhere in town, tramps followed the railroad tracks and looked for marks on ties to indicate where they could get a handout at the Tramp House. (BHS.)

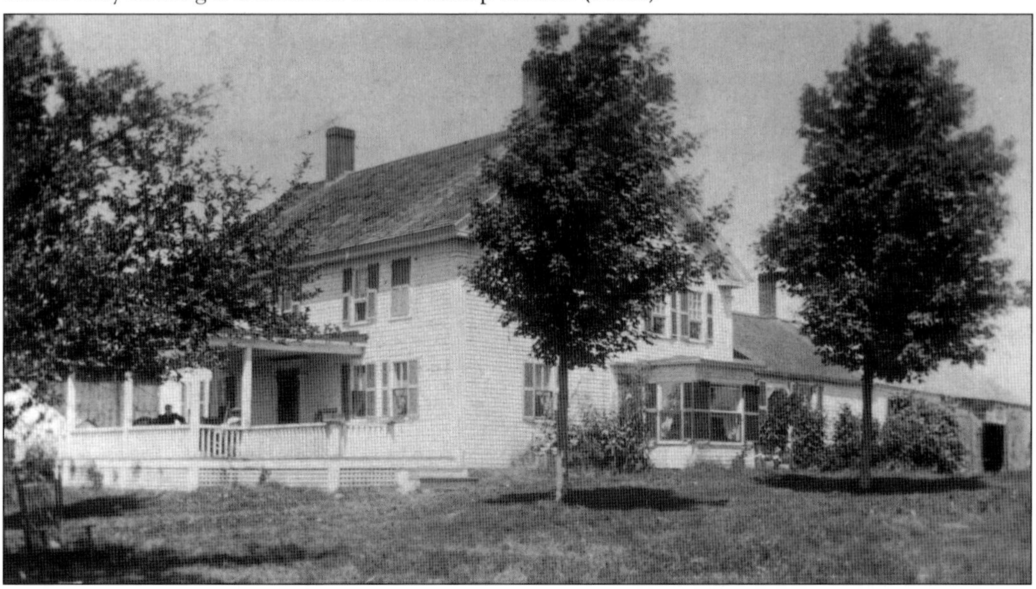

Support for the town's poor was struck off to Samuel Hill for $279.50 in 1829. The town purchased the property in 1832 to operate the town poor farm. A burial plot contains the remains of African Americans Prince Hastings and William Bradish. Bradish was a veteran of the War of 1812. Thomas Foster, a Civil War veteran of the 9th Regiment, is also buried here. The town closed the farm in 1899. (WHS.)

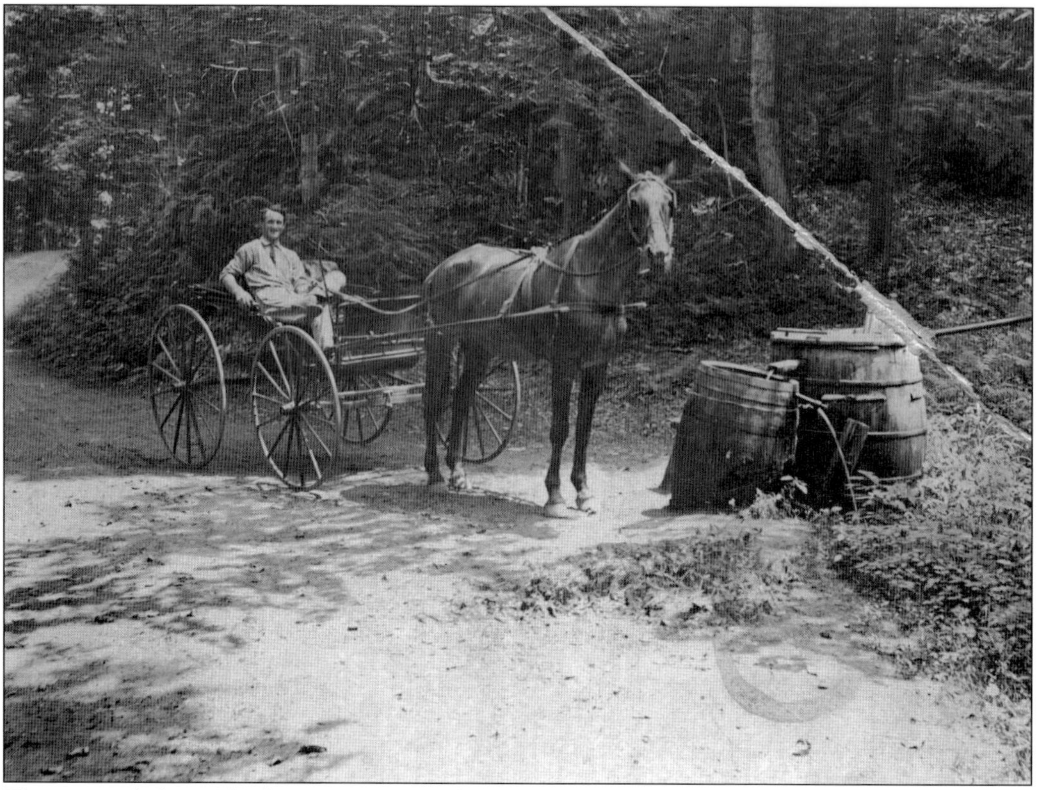

The state ruled in 1858 that every town, "shall abate a sum not exceeding $3 from the tax of any inhabitant, who shall construct, and during the year keep in repair, a watering trough, well supplied with water, sufficiently elevated and easily accessible for horses attached to carriages." Warner had over 20 troughs, and this one was located on the road to Mount Kearsarge. (WHS.)

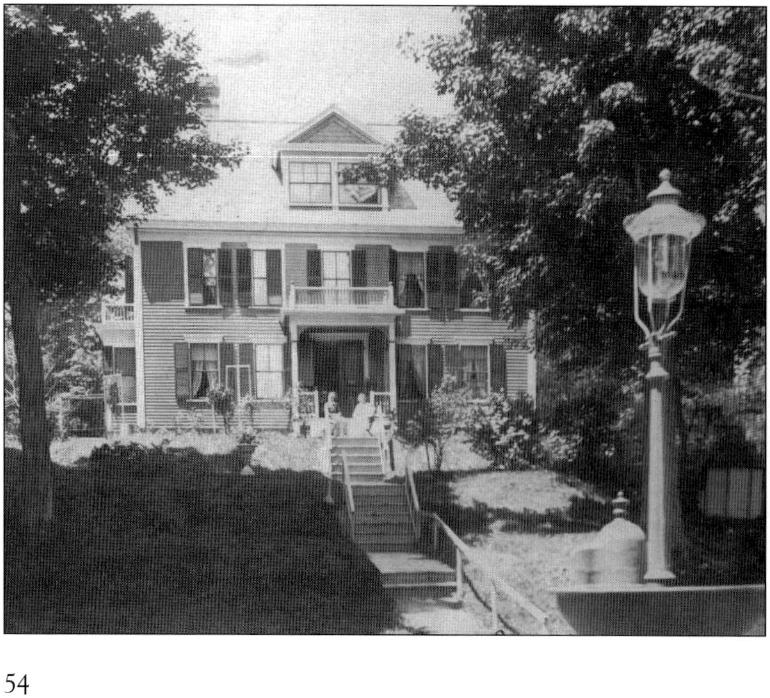

A public water supply was necessary for humans and animals alike. This watering trough served travelers at the west end of Main Street. Later, it was adorned with a traffic lantern and dubbed "the Silent Policeman." It was removed in 1929 when it proved to be a hazard for speeding motorists. Built by Silas Wilkins, a stately home stands in the background, serving as lookout for the Mills community. (BHS.)

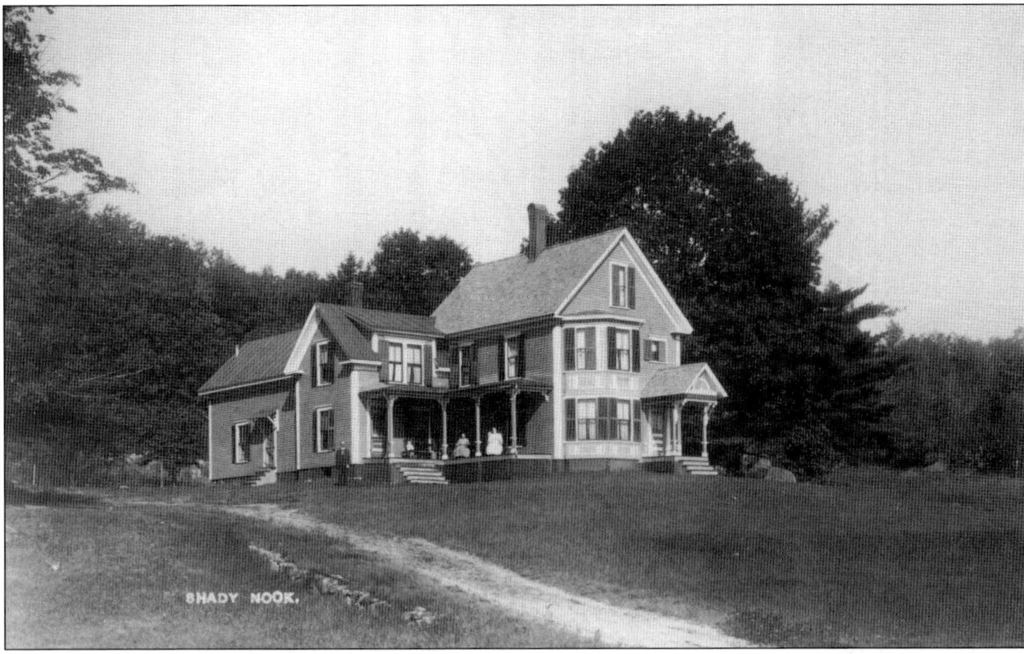

Rev. George Trow and his wife, Etta, lived in this home on Old Sutton Road. During his retirement, the reverend served the Baptist congregation as clerk, deacon, Sunday school teacher, and interim pastor. He was also town clerk and, with his wife as witness, he conducted wedding ceremonies in this house. (Courtesy of Steven Hansen.)

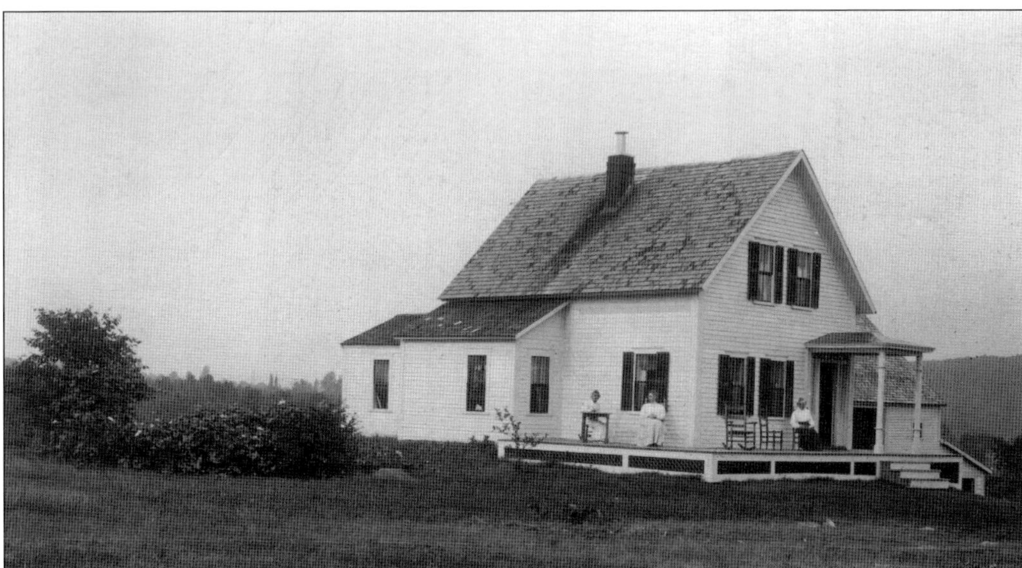

The so-called Badlam place was built on the site of the original home of Nathaniel Presbury. He acted as both constable and tax collector for Bradford Center as was the custom of the day. The first town meeting was held here in 1786. This house was nicknamed the Outlook because one could espy arrivals from a great distance. (BHS.)

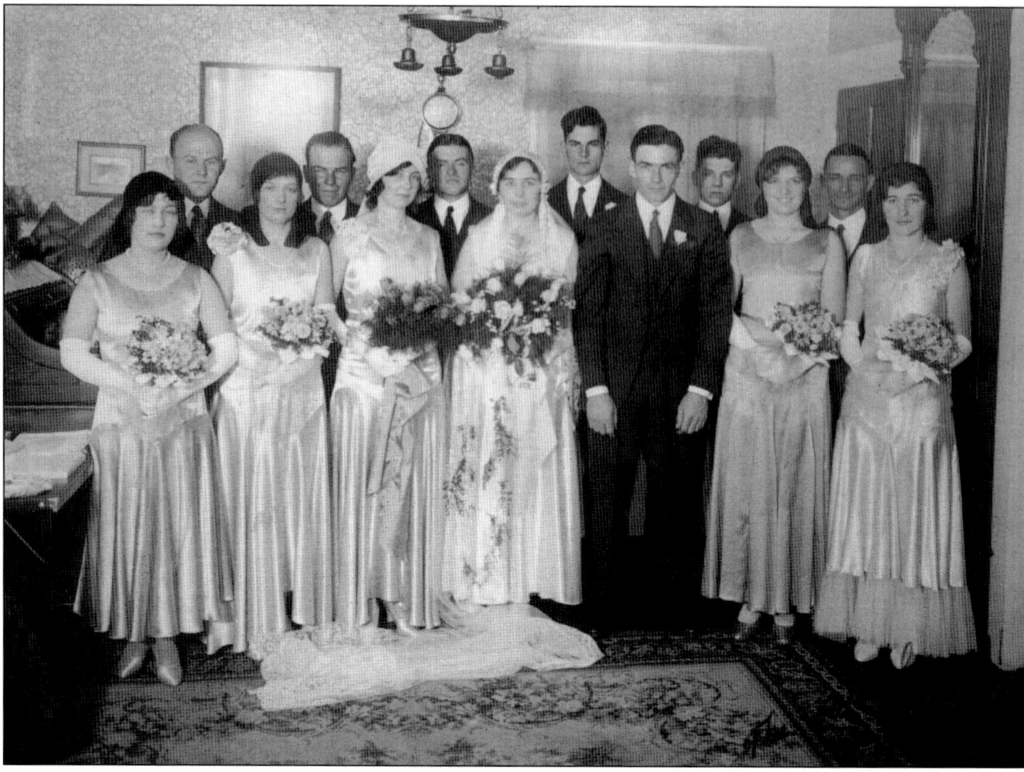

Through the years, families gathered in their homes to celebrate the birth of an infant, the death of a loved one, or the marriage of their children. Upon one's death, it was customary to attend to the body at home and prepare it for viewing in the "best" room. On this happy occasion, Gerald Wheeler wed Myrtie Annis in 1930 at her parents' home. (WHS.)

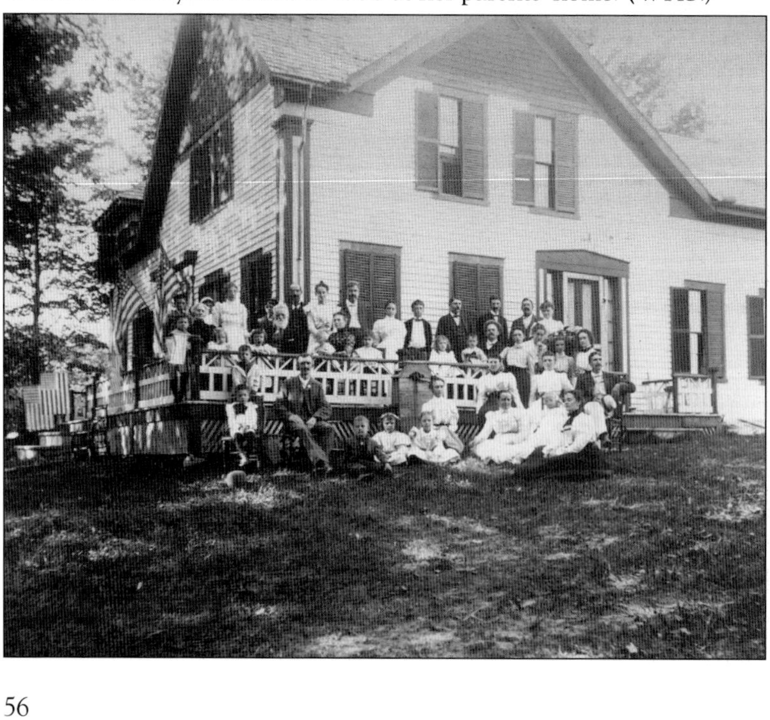

Held in 1899 at Maple Grange Farm, the Pattee-Davis family reunion, was hosted by Stephen Pattee. An educator, he remarked, "I had the muscle and the boys and girls the brains, and they were not softened by examining as we had not time for it. This cramming system in our schools for the purpose of showing off to 'ye committee men' is all wrong, and is working a great evil to the future generations." (WHS.)

The Center School (1793–1937) was the first of 12 schools in Bradford. Students decorated nearby graves with lilacs on Memorial Day and took nature walks behind the meetinghouse, hunting for the yellow lady's slipper and chucking apples at the steeple bell when the teacher's back was turned. A centennial address acknowledged, "In language of thankfulness and love, we owe our preparation for work to the schools of Bradford." (BHS.)

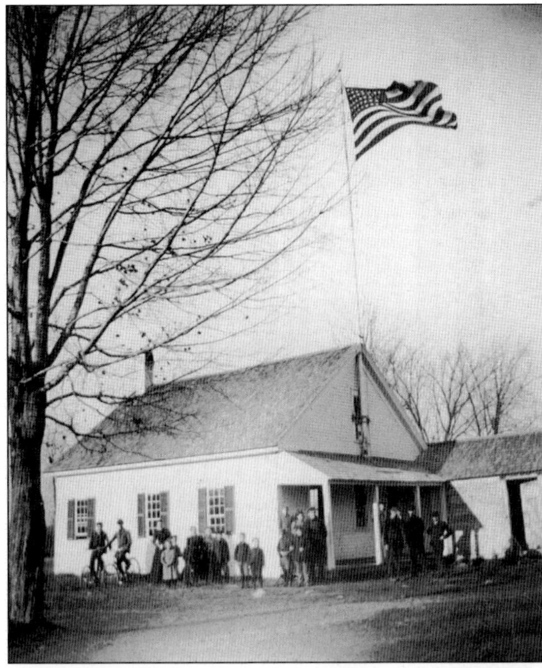

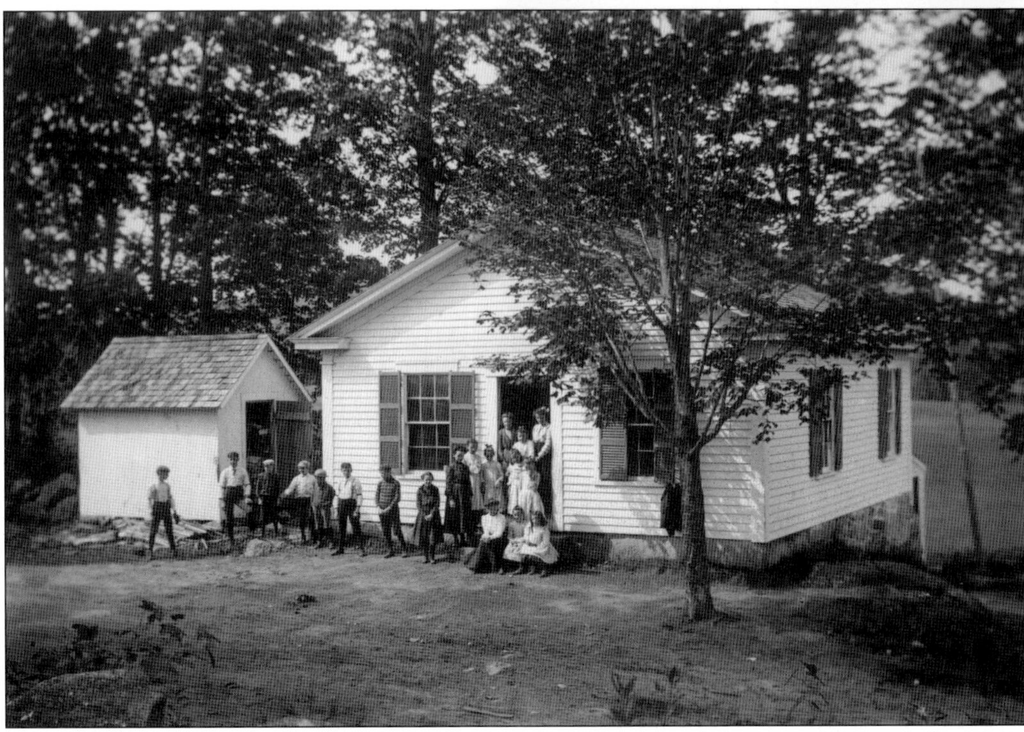

Ada Ring of Bradford was an excellent teacher in Waterloo. She wrote, "The scholars feel a natural desire to excel by reason of efforts of parents and citizens to give them a pleasant school house, and their interest in planting shade trees around the building, making it a most delightful spot, and by their strong endeavors, repay a hundred fold to those who have looked so kindly and wisely for their welfare." (WHS.)

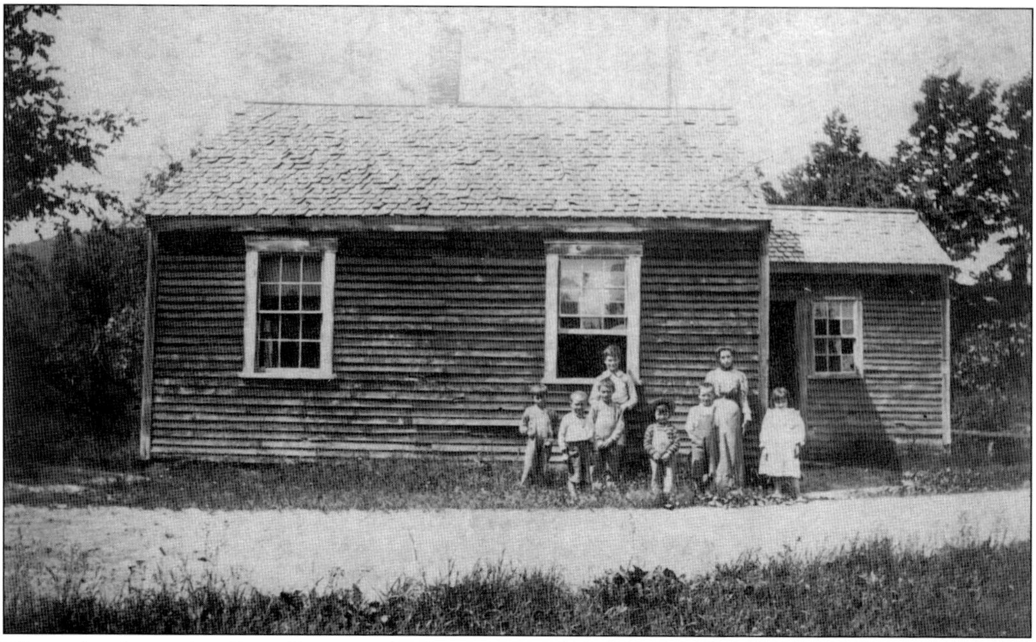

This school stood at Box Corner, which was named for the mailboxes that sat at the juncture of many roads. Corporal punishment was condoned in schools. The 1897 town report stated, "We expect teachers to bring our children up to a higher standard of behavior at school than we can possibly do at home." In another part of town, Olive Presby taught school in her father's barn. (BHS.)

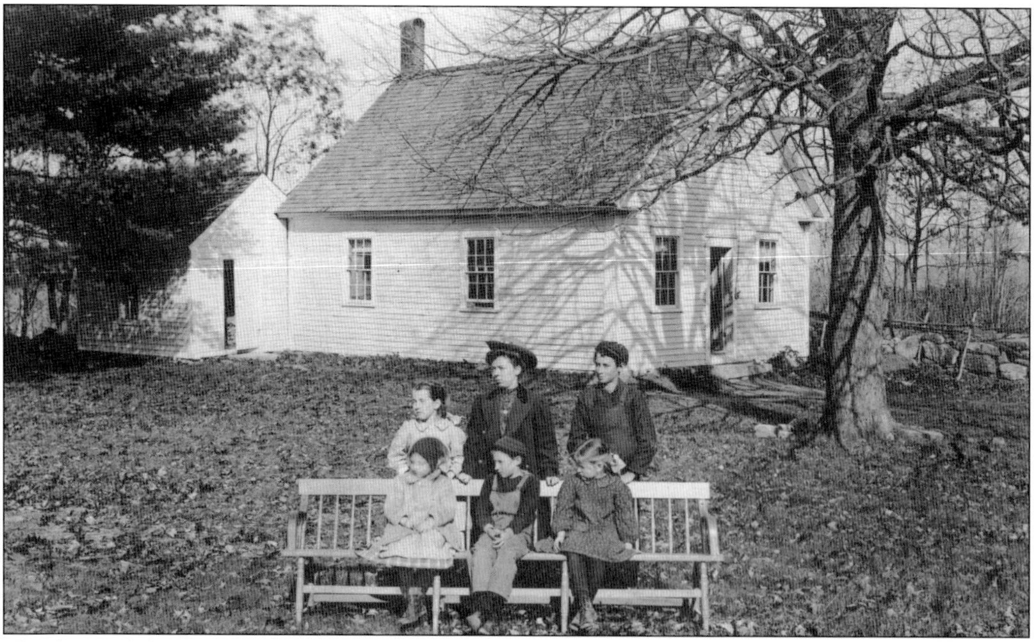

The focus of these six pupils at the Collins District School has been drawn away from the camera. Children attended school ages three to nineteen. A student was responsible for laying a fire in the morning before the pupils arrived. Water was drawn from a well and children sipped from a common dipper. The bathroom was an outhouse. (WHS.)

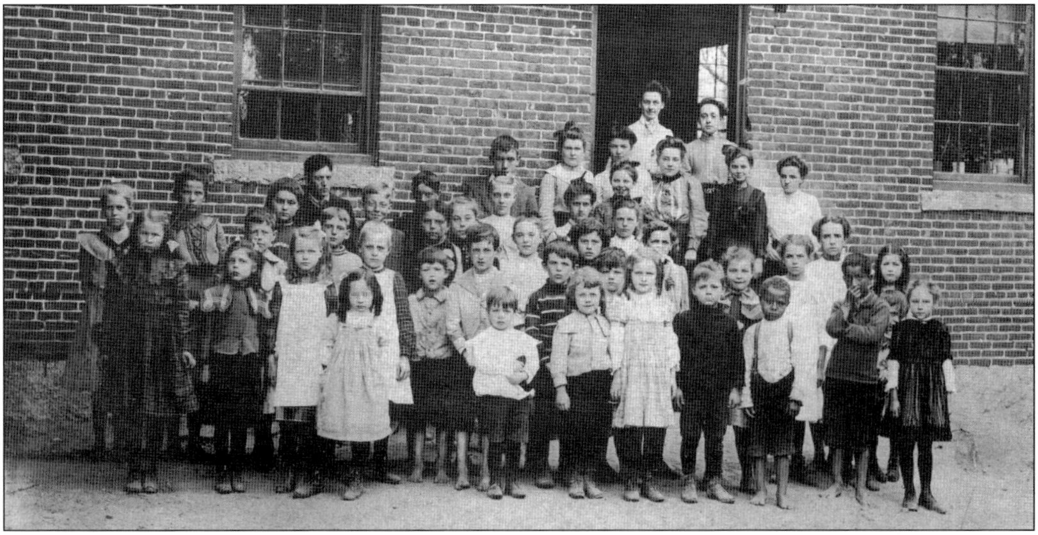

The School Street School consisted of two rooms, one for primary classes and the other for grammar classes. Stephen Pattee taught 80 children here by himself. There are two teachers and 43 pupils in this c. 1898 photograph. The two African American children on the right are probably Fred and William Sanville. (WHS.)

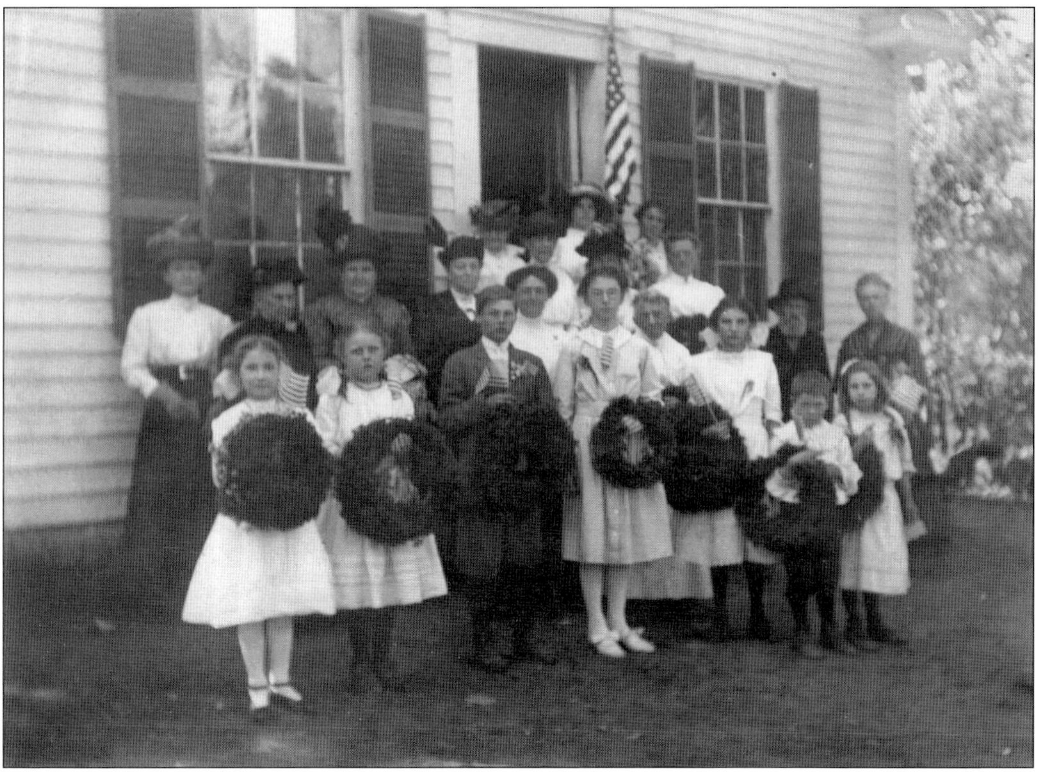

The pupils, teacher, and parents from the Waterloo School District No. 19 assemble with their homemade wreaths and flags to decorate the Old Waterloo Cemetery for Memorial Day in 1913. Before proceeding to the cemetery, there was probably a program of recitations, songs, and the reading of the Gettysburg Address. This was one of 24 schools located in Warner. (WHS.)

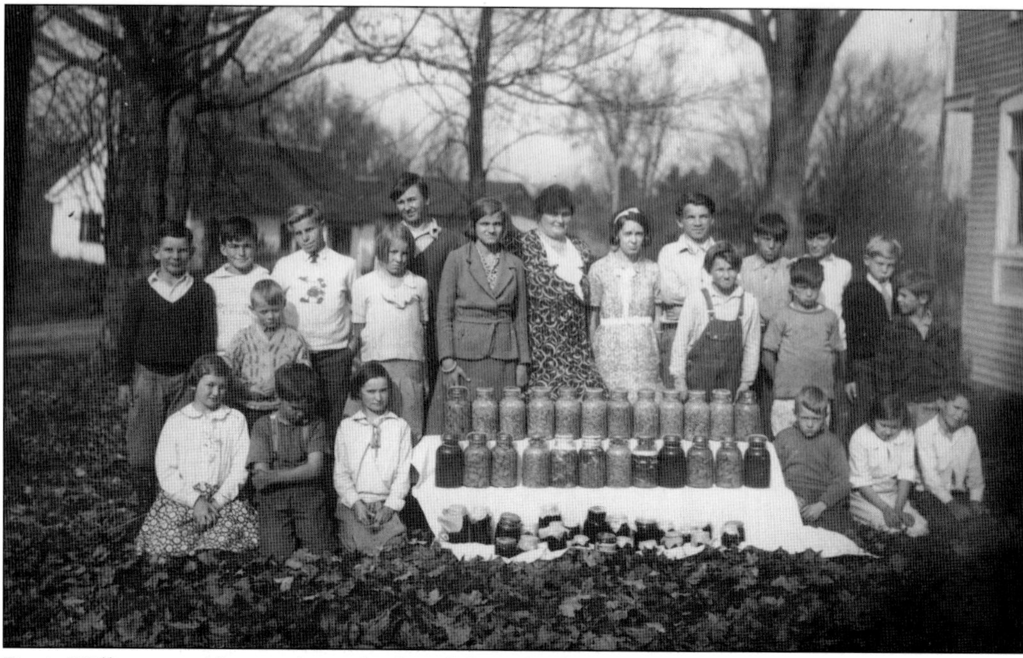

Doris Williams and her students displayed their food stores at the center during the Depression. She had a stern hand, but was beloved for her generosity. Walter Heselton Jr. claimed "my teeth came out early and I always thought she shook them loose." She could hold up a student in each hand. Heselton later owned and resided in this schoolhouse, which he donated back to the town for restoration. (BHS.)

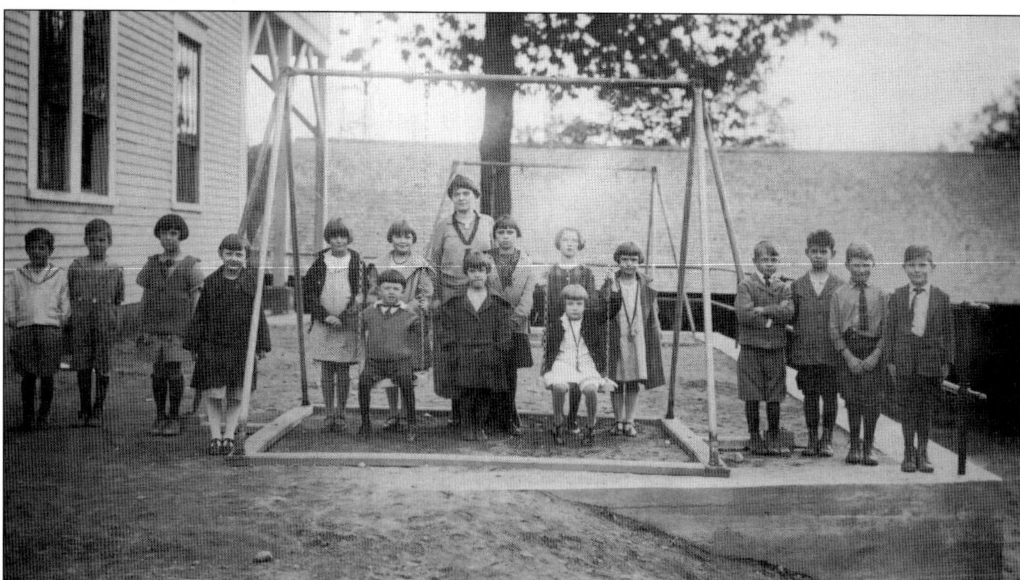

The rivalry between the Mills and Corner Villages resulted in lively tug-of-war games at recess when they shared the same school, first in a small brick structure, then at the town hall. Village schoolteacher Martha Cilley kept order with the phrase "Put your hands in position and listen to the clock tick." In many schoolhouses, students made cups from folded paper and drank water from a crock. (BHS.)

Baseball was a popular summer pastime in many communities. This game was played on the lawn of the Simonds Free High School. In June 1893, the paper reported that the town observed a game on Memorial Day between Waterloo and the Warner Second Nine. Waterloo was defeated by a score of 31-30. (WHS.)

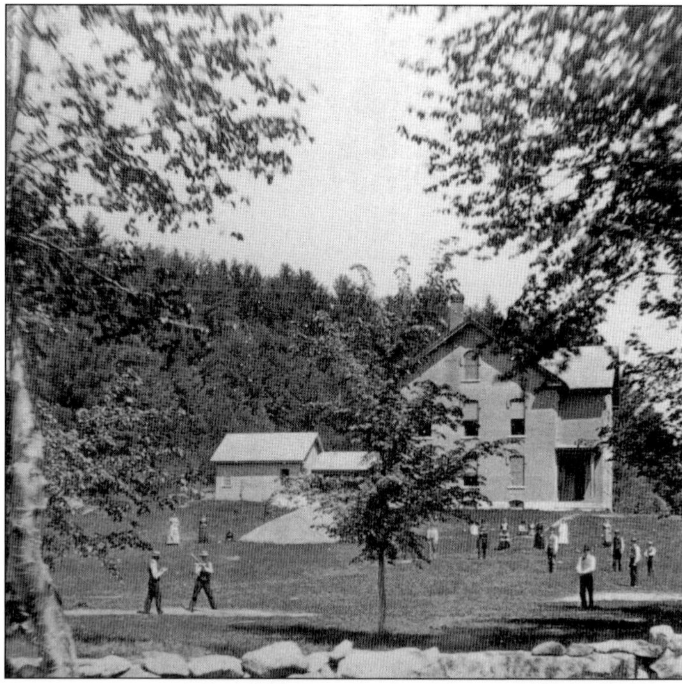

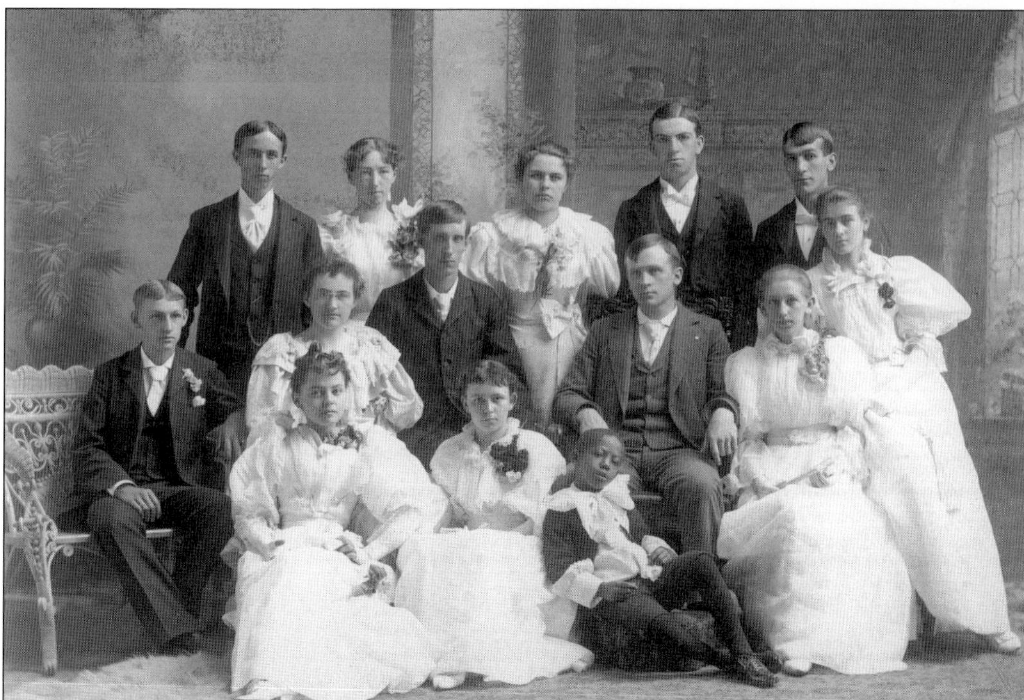

The graduating class of 1896 from Simonds Free High School is shown with Principal Jesse Barton. They chose Tony Jones, who lived in student Marion Davis's home, as their young page. His mother was the cook in the Davis household. Upon graduating, five classmates went to college, four became local teachers, and one clerked in the Upton & Upton dry goods store on Main Street. (WHS.)

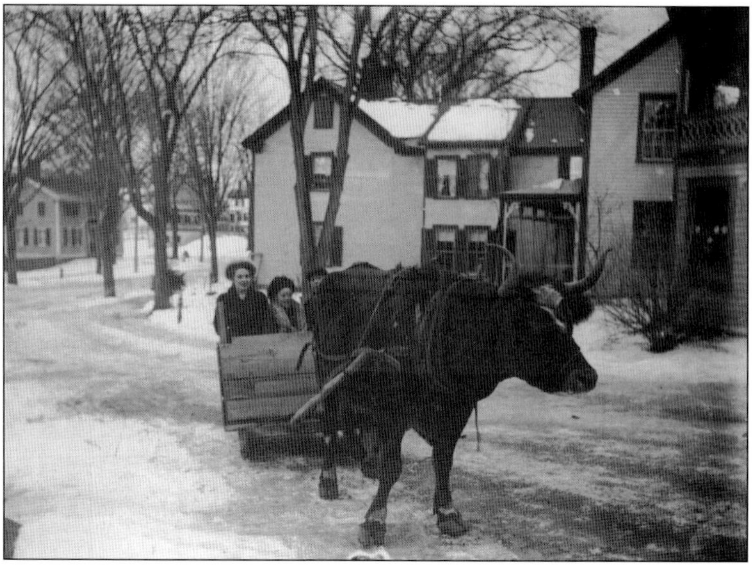

Edwin and Vivian Andrews lived in the Kearsarge Gore and came to school in a wooden sled with thick buffalo robes and a lit lantern to warm their feet. A single ox furnished the power to transport them five miles to school. It meant leaving in the dark, and during the winter months, arriving home to do their chores and homework after a long, slow, uphill ride. (WHS–Hardy.)

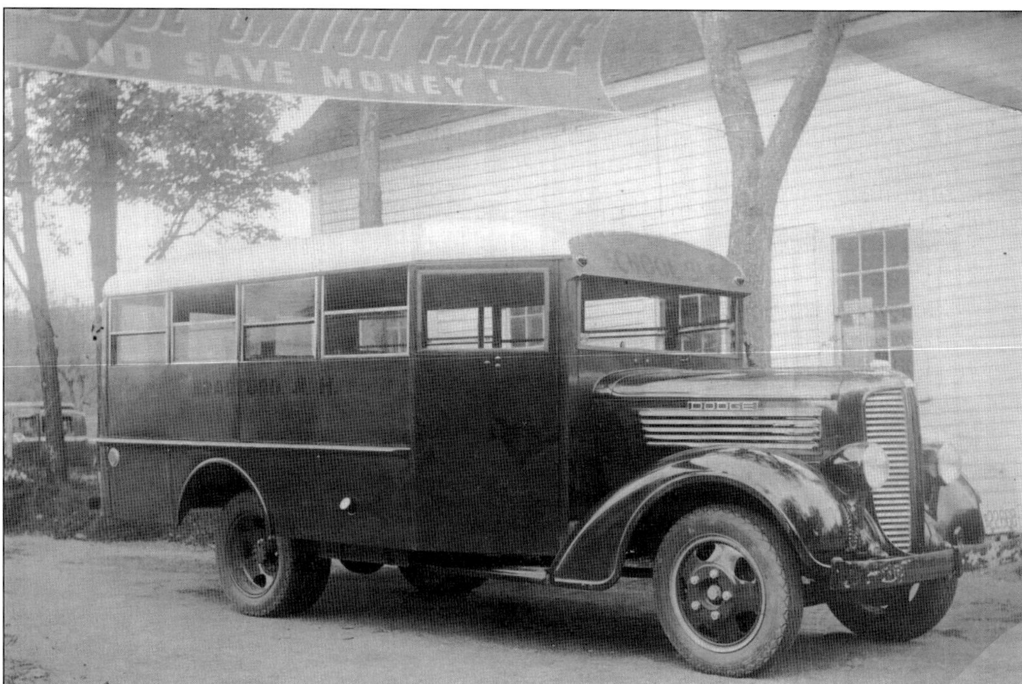

Bradford's first official school bus drove students from the outskirts to the Central School when it opened in 1937 to serve the consolidated town schools. Originally, funds that were raised for schools were payable in corn or grain. Distant students rode to school or boarded in town. It was voted in 1789 to divide Bradford into districts for schooling, just as highways were split for work. (Courtesy of Steven Hansen.)

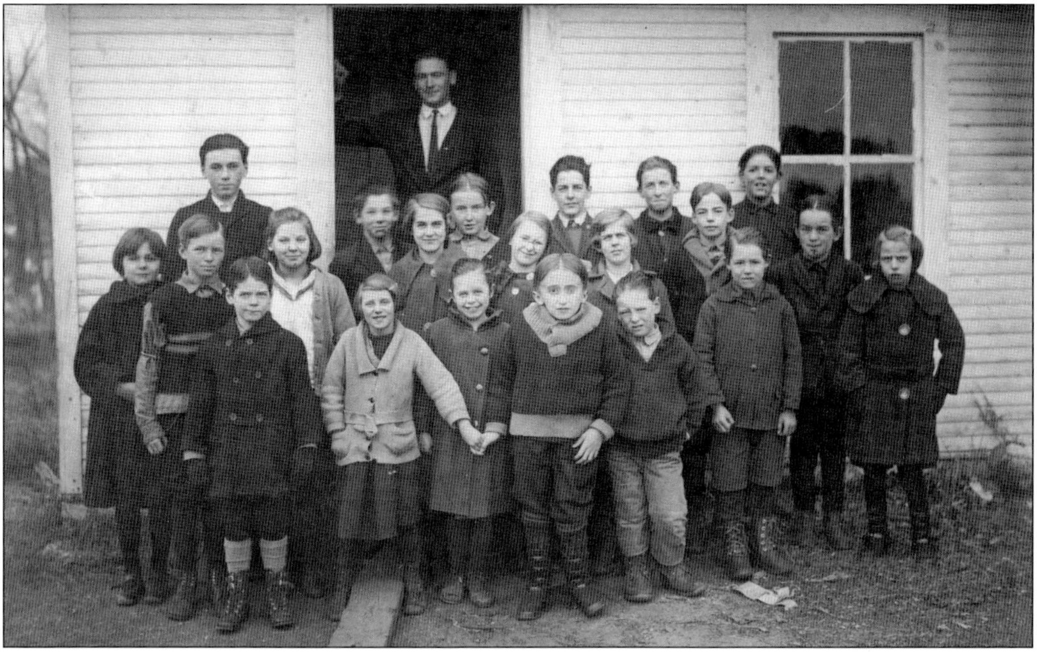

Teacher Ralph Darling poses with his students in 1924. Men were paid more than women teachers and were often hired to help with discipline during the winter months when older boys would attend. Otherwise, boys were needed for farm work. Terms varied from year to year. Older girls usually attended full-time, while younger children went when weather permitted. (BHS.)

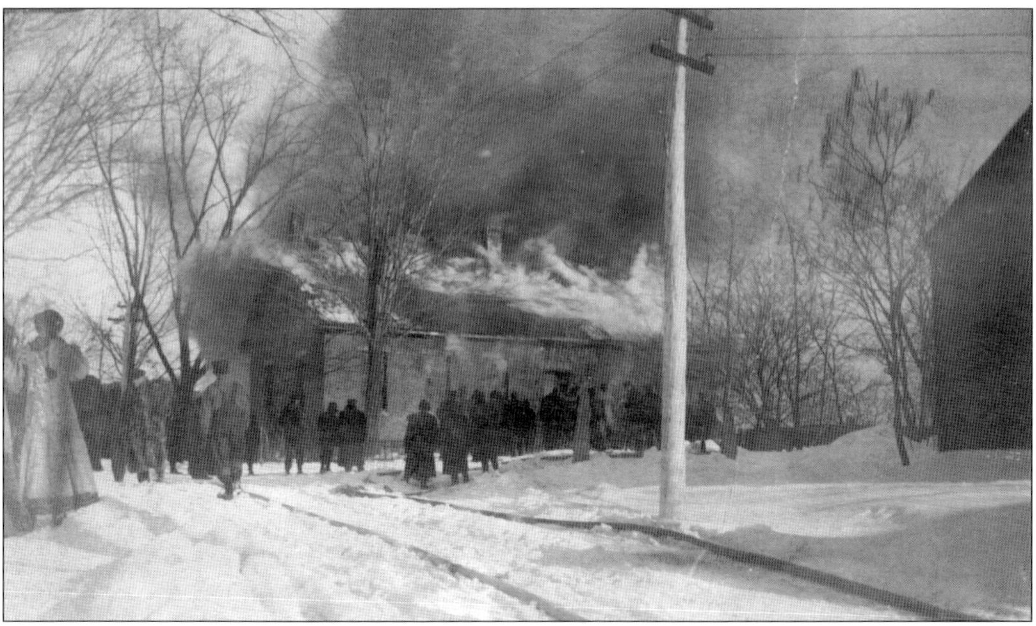

Paul Cloues missed school on February 10, 1909, due to a cold, but the clamor of "fire!" popped him out of bed. Upon arriving, the firemen were busy chopping a hole in the floor. Cloues wandered out back and "saw a place above the heater, blazing merrily." Reporting to the firemen, he was told to mind his own business. The town used the opportunity to build a new grammar school and town hall. (WHS–Pratt.)

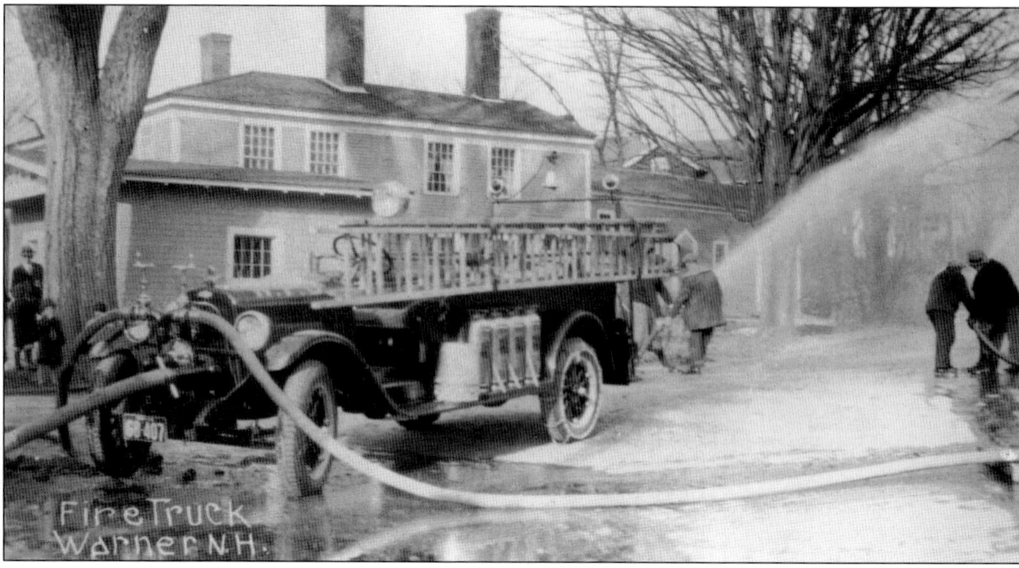

The Warner fire truck was tried out for the first time at the square on Christmas morning in December 1928. The demonstration was reported to be successful in every way. This 1928 Chevrolet chassis was purchased for $640, and a fire truck body was built by local craftsmen. Now, they could respond to fire calls outside the precinct limits. (WHS–Pratt.)

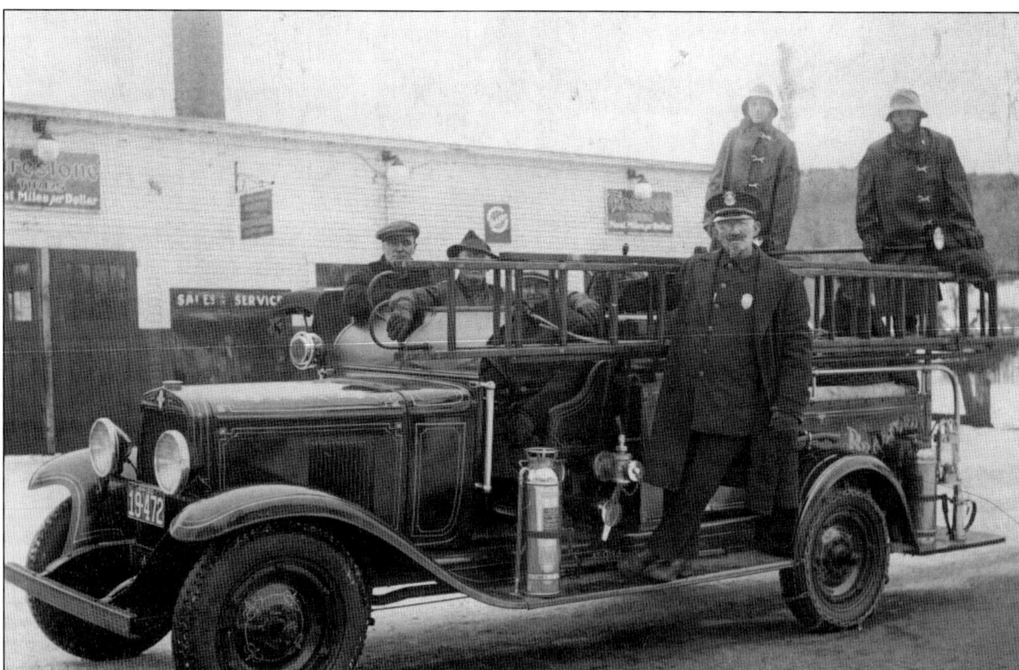

Bradford's first fire truck, featured here at the Winter Carnival in 1930 shows Chief Stevens on the running board. The first recorded brush fire took place in 1829 near Day Pond. Firemen stayed on duty for three weeks, extinguishing subsequent fires that burned in the sections of the corduroy road en route to Henniker. The largest conflagration was in 1918, when Bradford lost three main business blocks and the King's Daughters' Hall. (Courtesy of Steven Hansen.)

Four

TRANSPORTATION

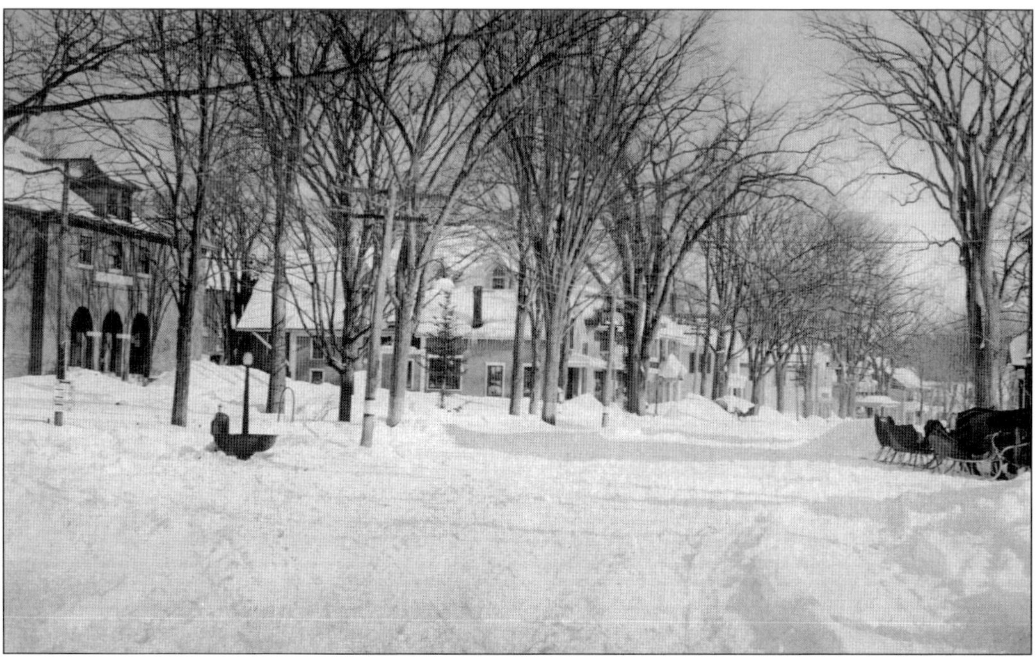

In January 1912, the *Kearsarge Independent* reported the first real snowstorm of the winter dropped eight inches of snow, and the brisk wind following the storm created large snowdrifts. Frozen water and drainpipes were reported. The street had been rolled for the convenience of sleighs pulled up in front of Martin's store. The water fountain was originally placed in this location. (WHS.)

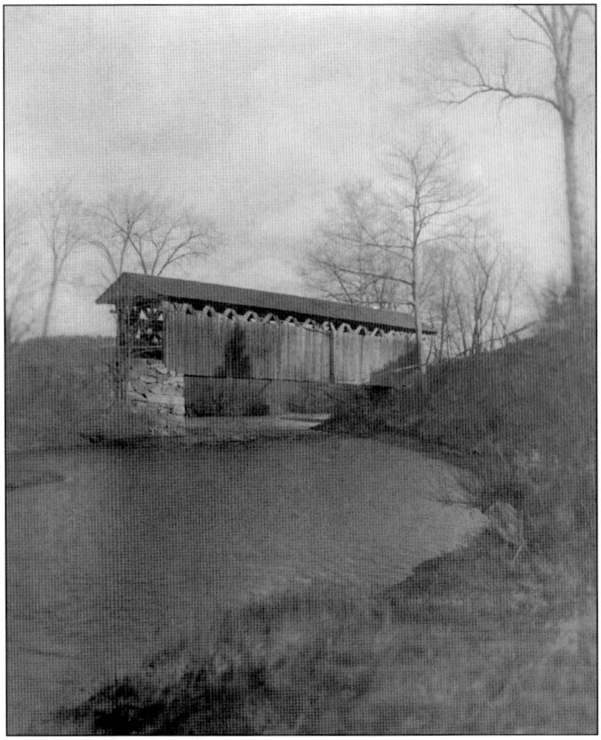

This covered bridge spanned the Warner River at the intersection of Jones Road and Henniker Road (Route 114). It was replaced right after World War II by a temporary, pier-less structure, known as a Bailey Bridge, constructed quickly with nuts and bolts. In 1948, a concrete bridge was built and designated as a memorial to Col. Mason Weare Tappan, a notable citizen of Bradford. (BHS.)

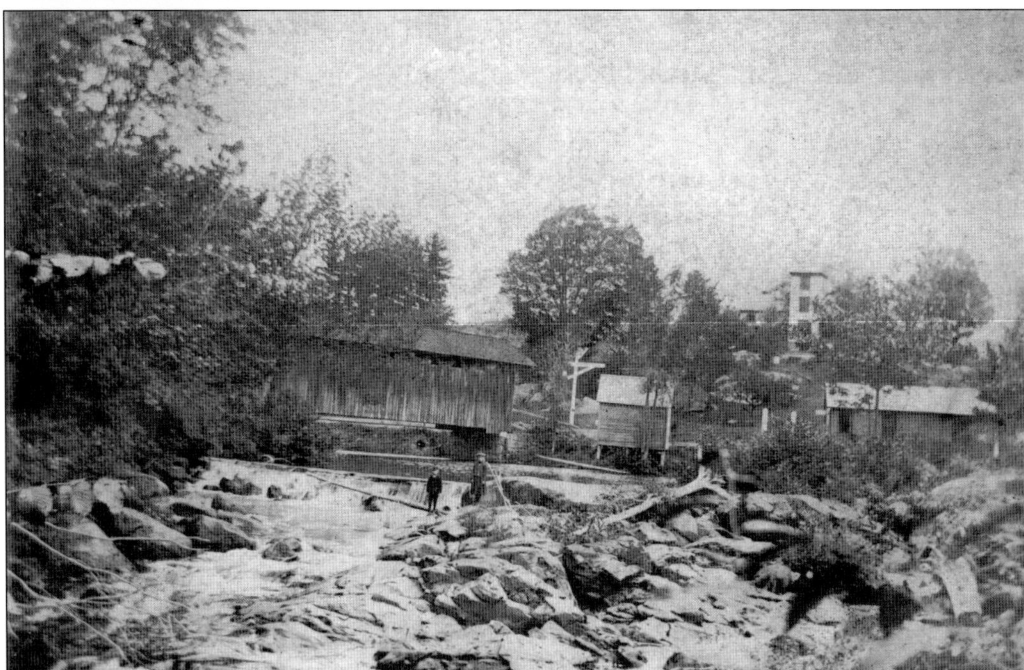

The low water during the summer at the Waterloo covered bridge allowed children to leap from rock to rock and afforded good fishing holes. Waterloo railroad station (right) serviced eight passenger trains and two freight trains a day. The station had a siding for 12 railroad cars. By May 1941, service had been discontinued. (WHS.)

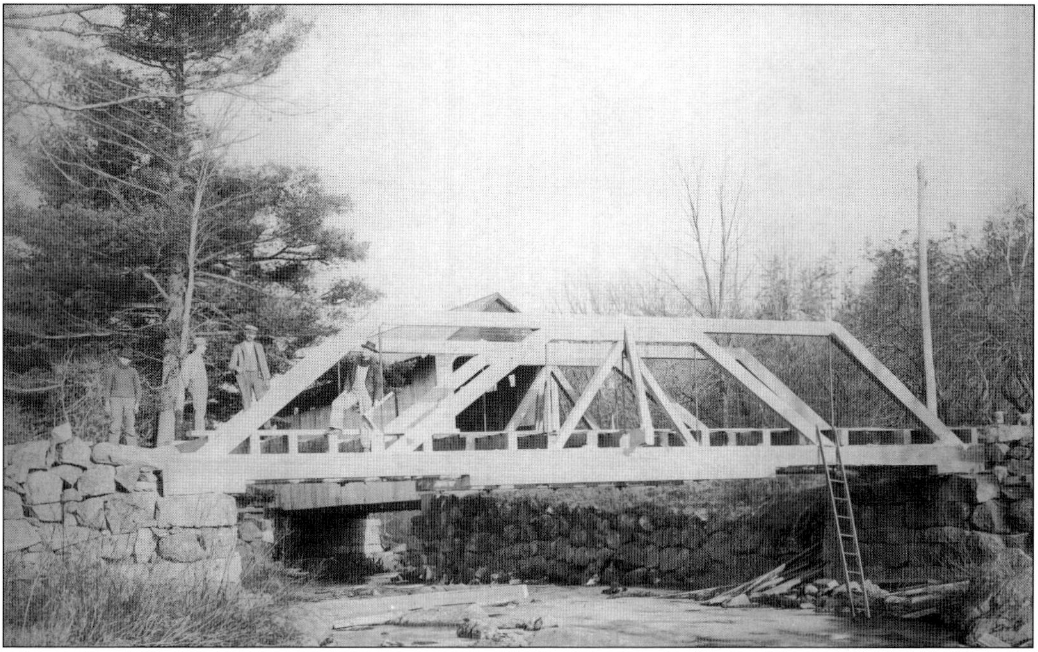

The bridge connecting Roby's Corner to South Sutton is being built by these men. The man on the decking is holding a square. Notice that the foot of the ladder is in the river. This bridge, which became covered, was torn down in 1920. The covered bridge in the background was used by the railroad. (WHS–Hardy.)

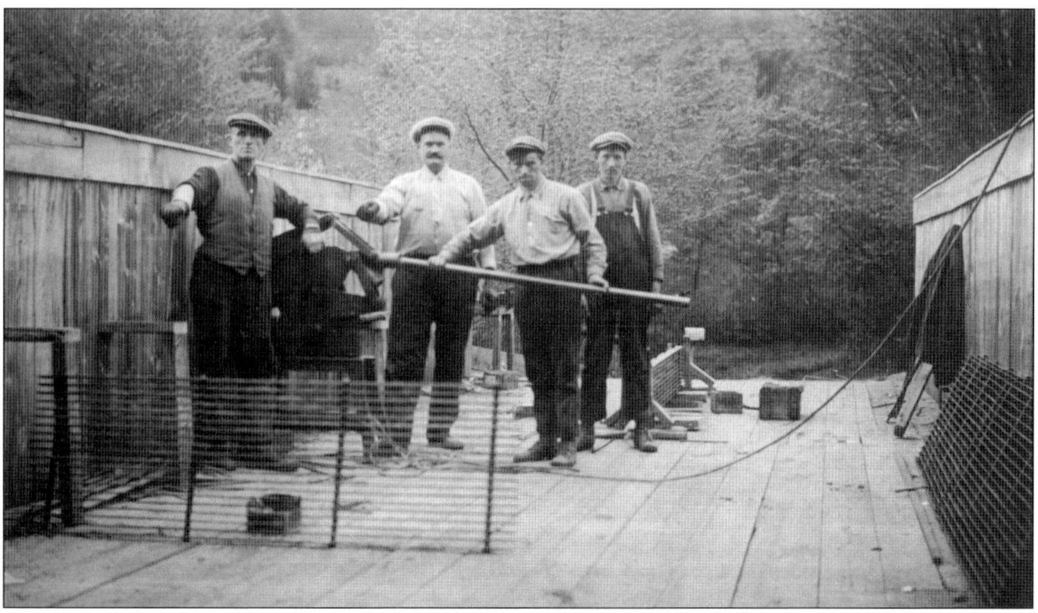

These men are working on the bridge on Breezy Hill Road by Lake Massasecum in the 1920s. Workers installed grates (often bed springs) below the bridge to prevent beavers from damming the river. This bridge was considered a covered bridge because the trusses were covered, even though it did not have a roof. Earlier in the 1820s, men were paid the same wage as the driver of a team of oxen for a day of labor. (Courtesy of Steven Hansen.)

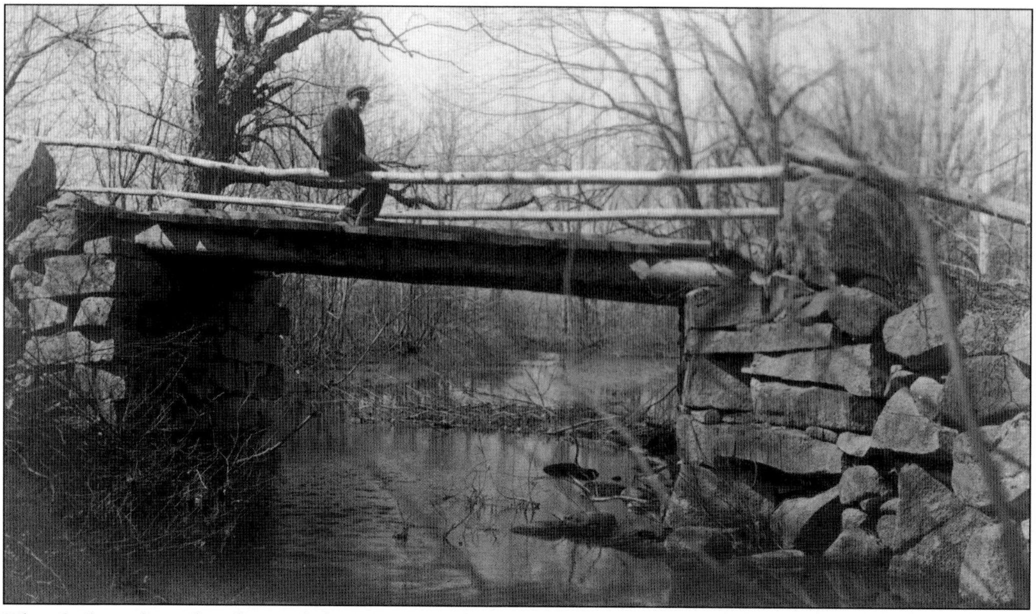

This lad studies the flow of the West Branch, a tributary of the Warner River. He may have been the town eccentric, gentle Jimmie Johnson, who visited the local schools to show children the wonders of nature. The Warner River is fed by a reservoir and several brooks. It provided an important power source for early local mills and continues to inspire recreation and reflection today. (BHS.)

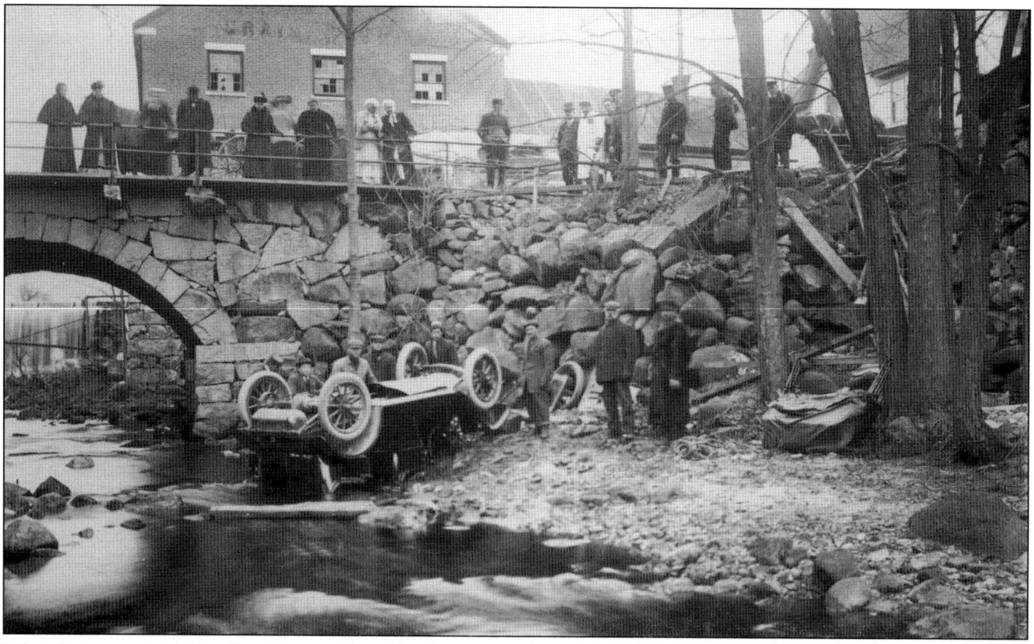

The first automobile fatality in Bradford occurred in 1911 by this arched stone bridge on Main Street. Bradford's first roads were laid out as early as 1787. Main Street was eventually macadamized in the early 1900s when this bridge was widened and covered by a concrete superstructure. The Lucius Woods brick gristmill and Todd Pond dam can be seen in the background. (Courtesy of Steven Hansen.)

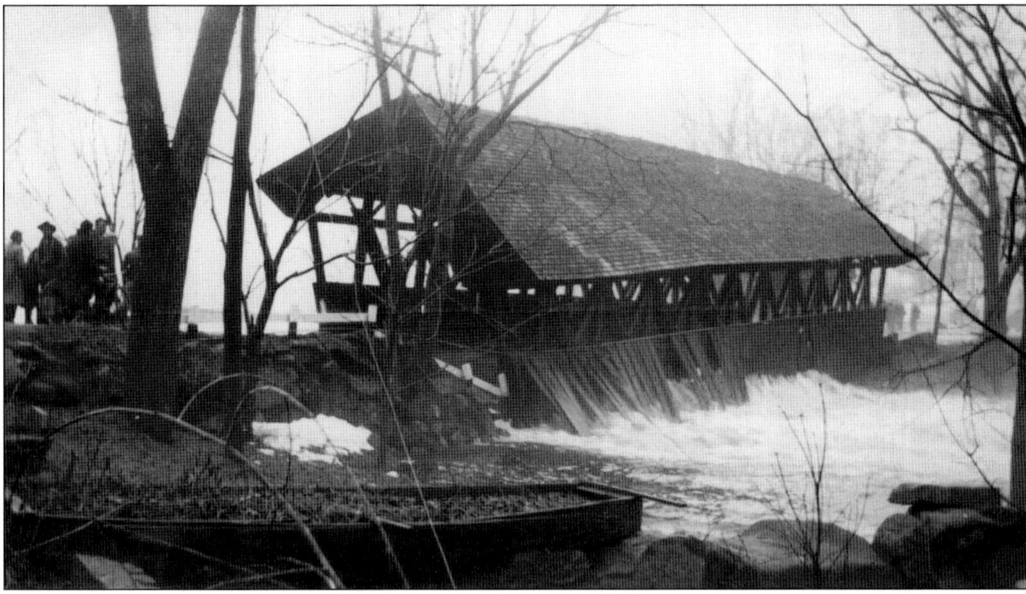

In May 1936, the *Kearsarge Independent* reported that the Warner River was probably the highest in its history, with ice floes causing lots of damage to property and railroad tracks. The bed was undermined in numerous places with rails underwater and the track off its course. The rail line did not reopen until September 8, 1936. The Davisville Covered Bridge was swept off its abutments minutes after this photograph was taken. (WHS.)

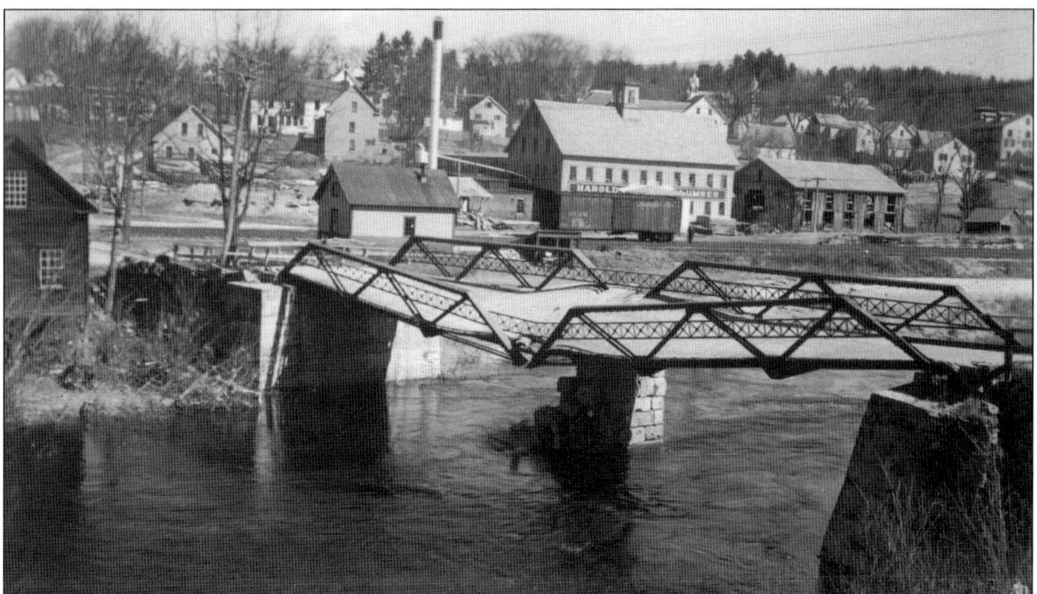

The middle pier of the Ela Bridge was badly damaged in the 1936 flood. People living along the Warner River were warned that the Todd Pond dam at the upper end of Bradford village might let go. Roads were badly washed out and the new cement bridge in Lower Warner sustained damage. Townspeople were glued to their radios to hear the news of the outside world. (WHS–Pratt.)

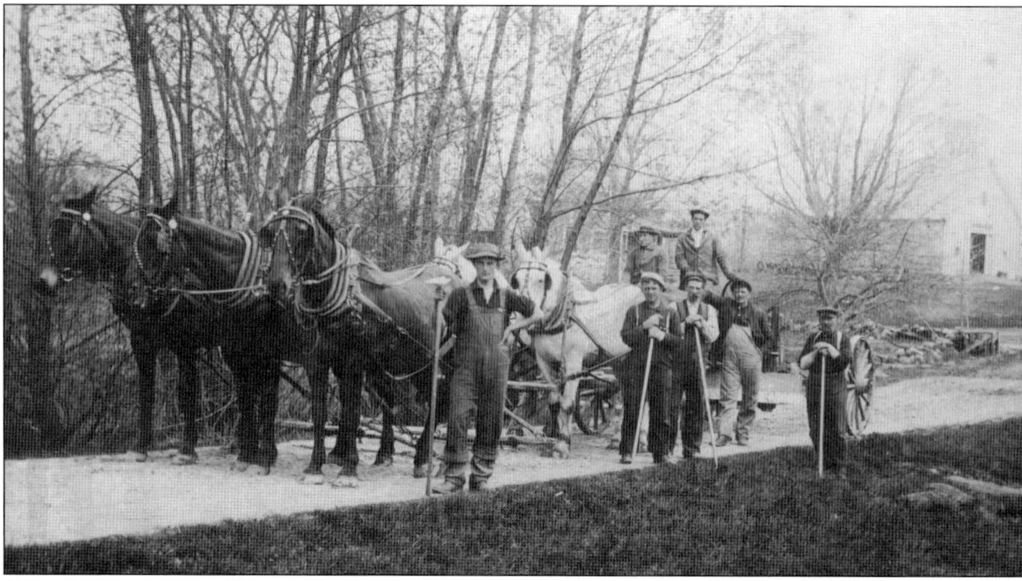

Horsepower was used to grade the early dirt roads. The Old Post Road (Route 114) was just a forest trail, the trees marked with the letter "H." Settler William Presbury brought his family on snowshoes over this route in 1771, and he hauled corn to be ground on his back to Henniker. In 1904, the town was still purchasing a yoke of oxen to maintain the roads in this traditional fashion. (BHS.)

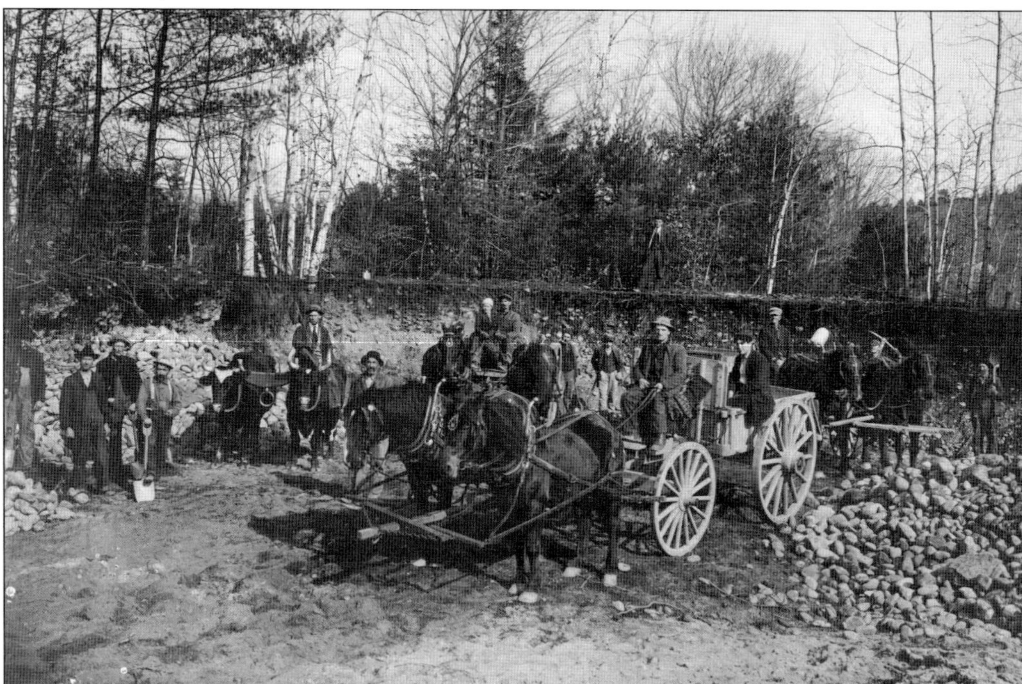

Frank I. Hill was the "go-to" guy when it came to building roads. He was awarded a contract for building 1,800 feet of road for $1,375 to commence in October 1905. His crew is filling carts with rocks on this bony piece of ground and hauling them away. Building roads was done by hand and was slow, tedious work. (WHS.)

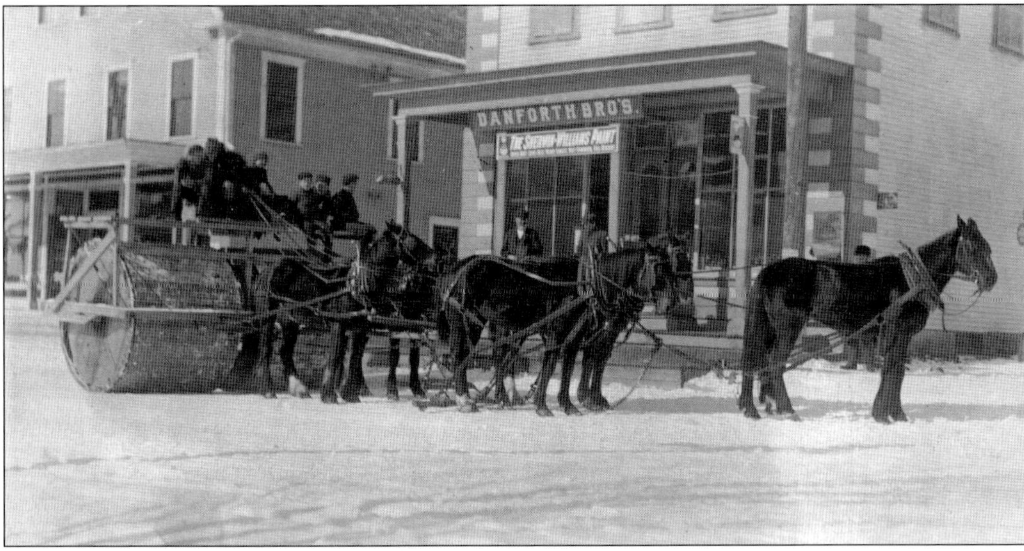

Up until the 1930s, snow rollers were used to pack, rather than plow, the roads. The rollers were filled with stones to add weight and were slatted so melted snow could escape. Until 1960, there was a law on the books that required towns to "snow" the bridges to allow for the passage of sleighs. (BHS.)

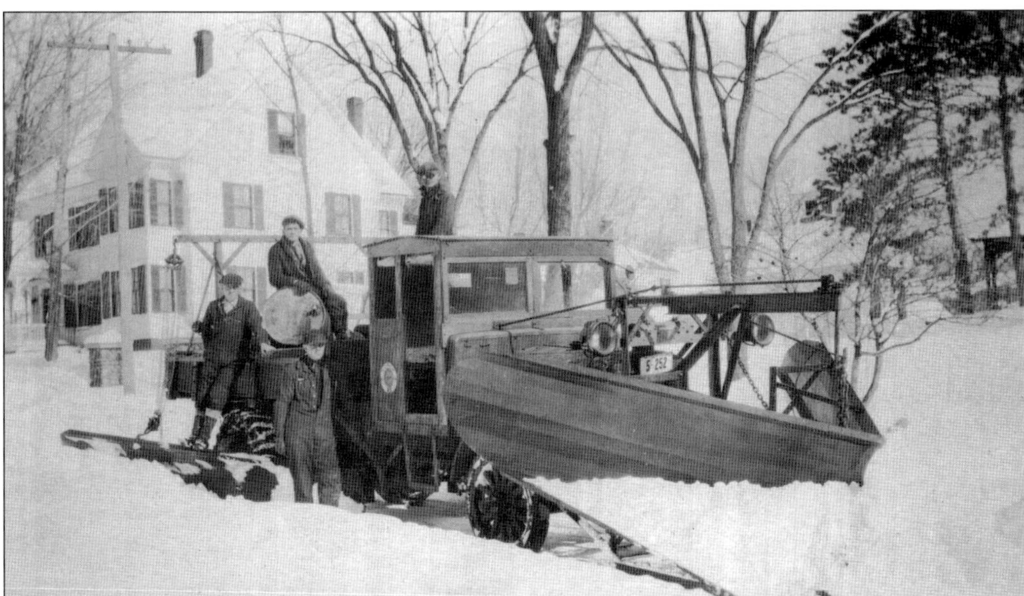

In November 1926, the *Kearsarge Independent* stated, "a building for storing the snow plow, furnished by the state for keeping the main road open during the winter, had been constructed under the direction of the selectmen on the hill at the upper end of the plain." Jim Henley was the driver, and Harold Dow manually operated the wing. Everett Jewell and Orton Hill just happened to get in the picture. (WHS–Pratt.)

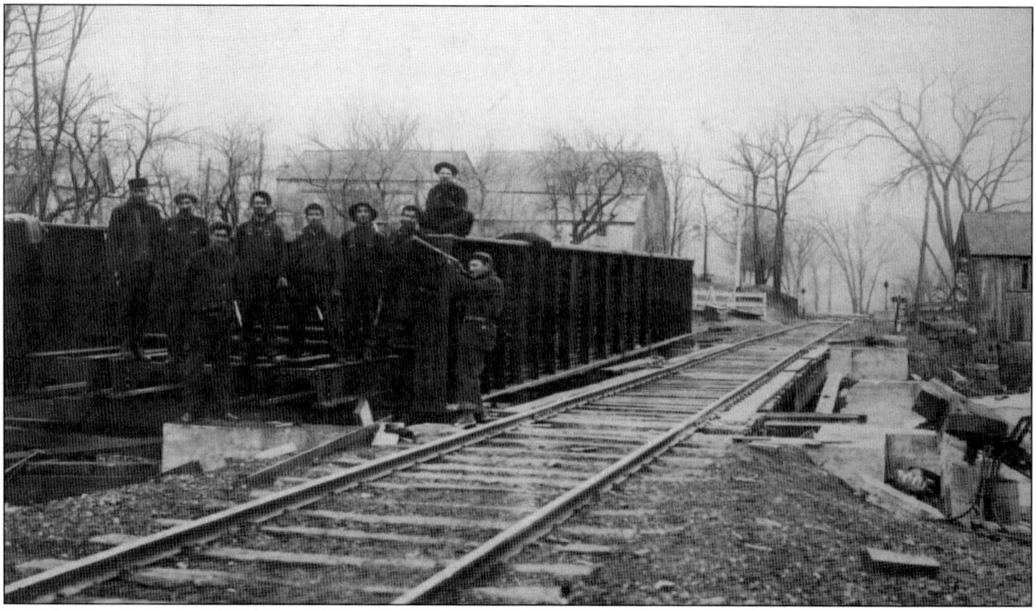

In July 1911, the sparks from a locomotive set fire to the covered railroad bridge at Roby's Corners. There was a delay in train service until a temporary bridge was installed and then replaced by this steel structure. Teams conveyed passengers to the Birch Hill crossing to board another train. It was not unusual for sparks from a train to set grass, bridges, mills, and homes on fire. (WHS.)

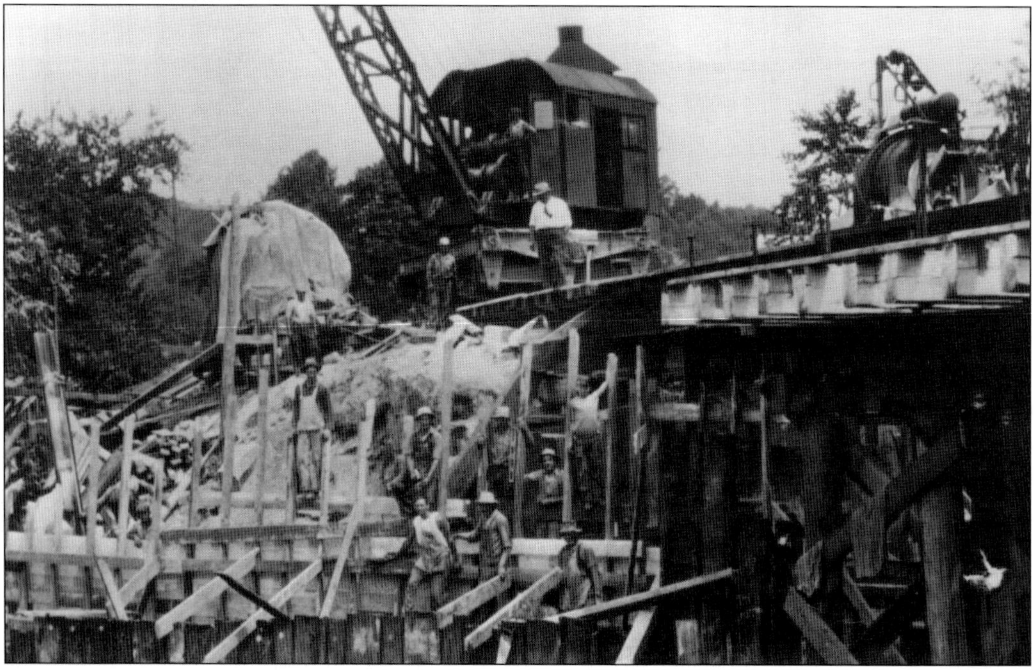

The Bartlett Excelsior Mill and the railroad trestle were destroyed by fire in September 1905. Help was summoned from Concord, and a fire steamer with 25 men raced to Warner. By the time the equipment was unloaded in Roby and transported a mile to the fire, it was too late. Trains ran close to the site and transferred passengers and baggage around the high banks until a temporary structure was built. (WHS.)

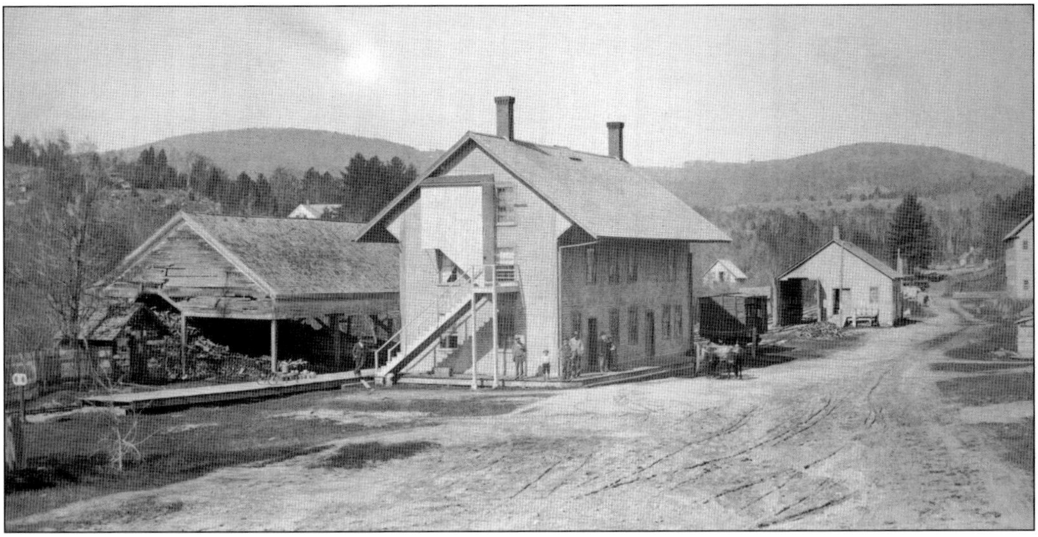

On September 21, 1849, the first train from Concord to Warner arrived with great fanfare and 1,300 passengers. Two locomotives were required as the train was so heavy. A tragic accident occurred on the way, resulting in injuries to several people and the death of 20-year-old Moses Gould. After the accident was dealt with, the train continued on to the festivities of speeches, music, and refreshments at the Warner Depot. (WHS.)

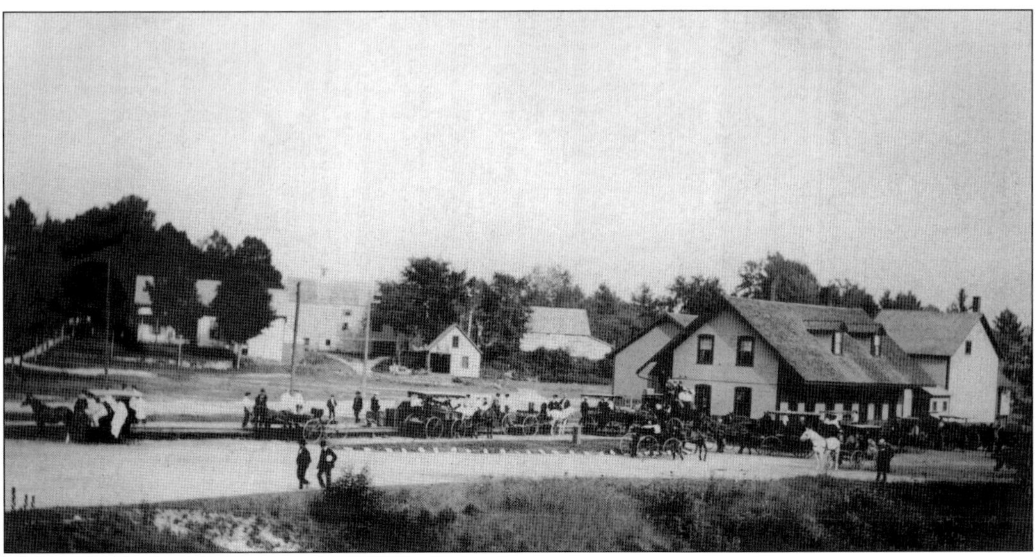

Bradford progressed from a frontier to a thriving destination in its first century. This freight depot later became the Merrimack Farm Store. For two generations, high school students rode the train to Warner for $4.09 per month. There were plush, green seats, but the windows were always filmed with coal dust, so riders had to make peep holes to see out of them. (BHS.)

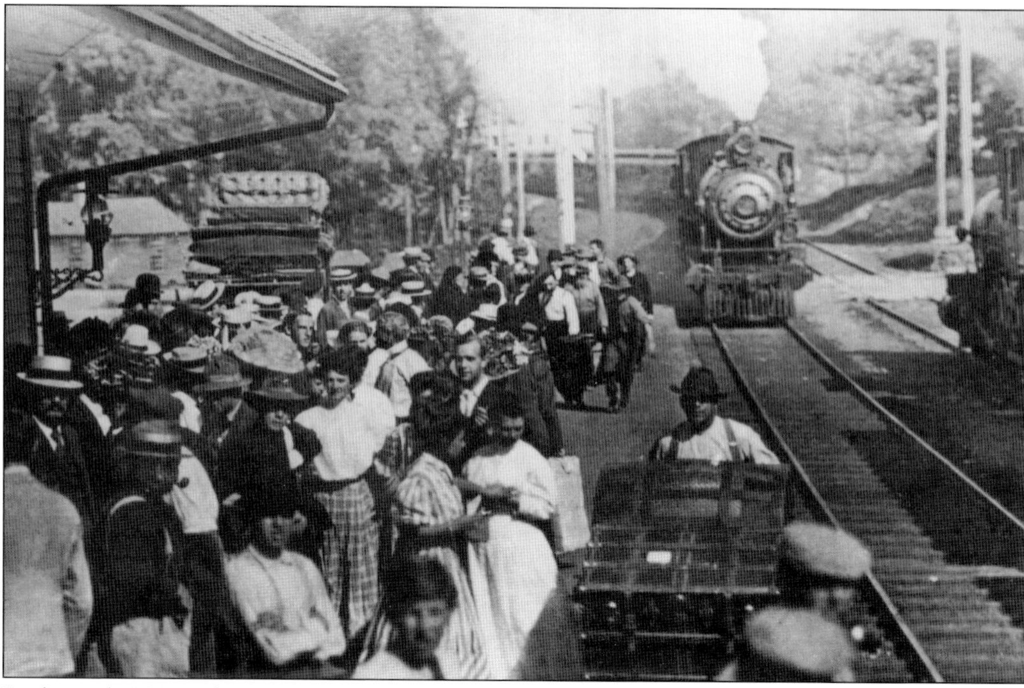

In the early 1900s, the train is arriving from Claremont Junction. Boys were often hired to follow the trains to check the lines and wooden bridges for incendiary sparks. The advent of the railroad opened the town to manufacturing, and an active merchant class developed. For 20 years, Bradford was the end of the line. (BHS.)

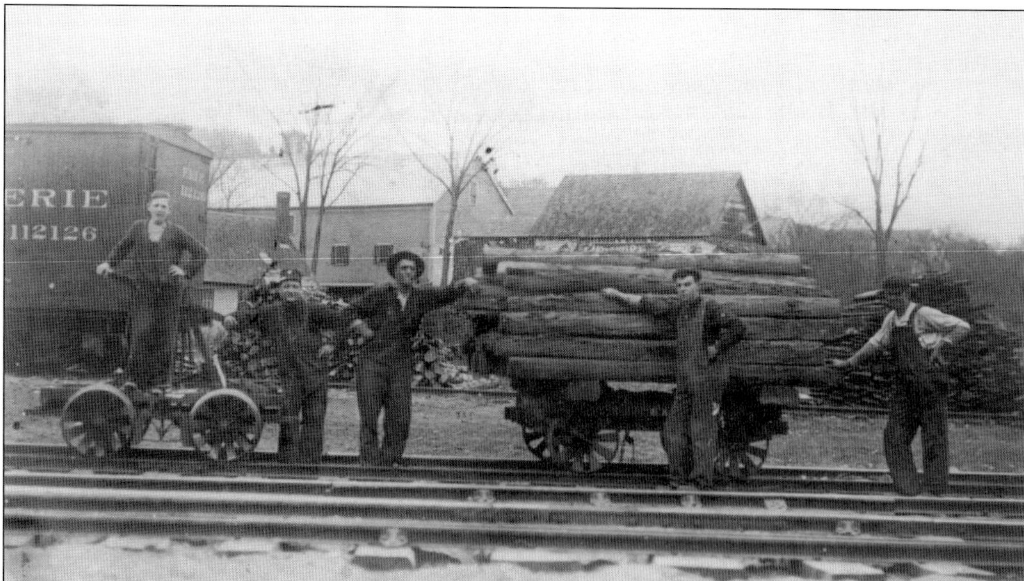

These yard workers, known as section hands, were responsible for repairing and maintaining a 10-mile stretch of track. Boarding cars (that held sleeping bunks) and a cooking galley were available to workers during major repairs. Handcarts were pumped up and down the track. New Hampshire was nicknamed "the Railroad State" for its short-line service and the profound difference this type of transportation wrought in financial stability and progress. (Courtesy of Steven Hansen.)

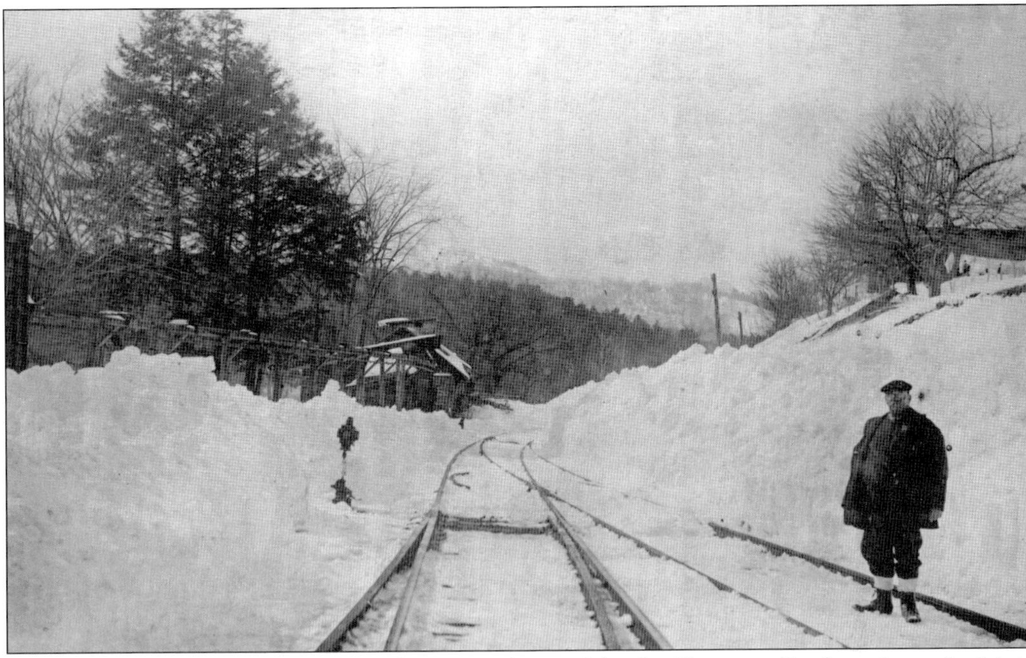

An April 1932 storm left 32 inches of snow on the track by the Ela sawmill siding above the Main Depot. The lighting device to the left of the tracks would indicate when the train was approaching a siding or depot. The engineer would also be alerted when to drop off or pick up cars located at the various sidings throughout town. (WHS.)

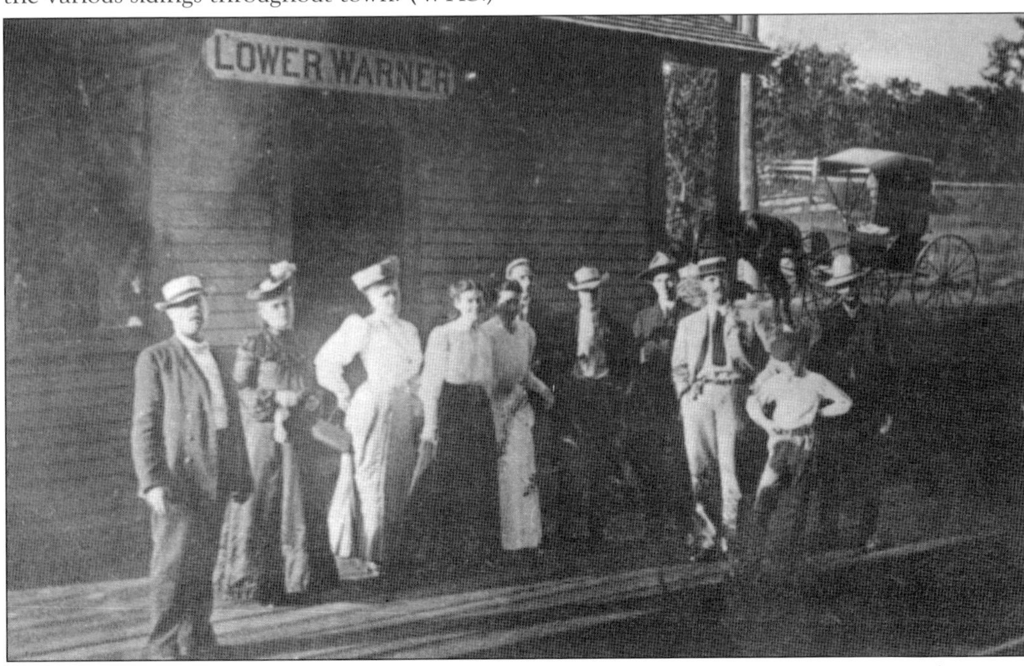

Ed Dudley earned his nickname "Everyday Dudley" because he would reliably wait at the Lower Warner station as each train pulled in. There, he would offer assistance to any passengers who needed a ride home. Schoolchildren used to hitch a string to an apple and lower it to the engineer when the train stopped under the bridge at the Lower Warner station. (WHS.)

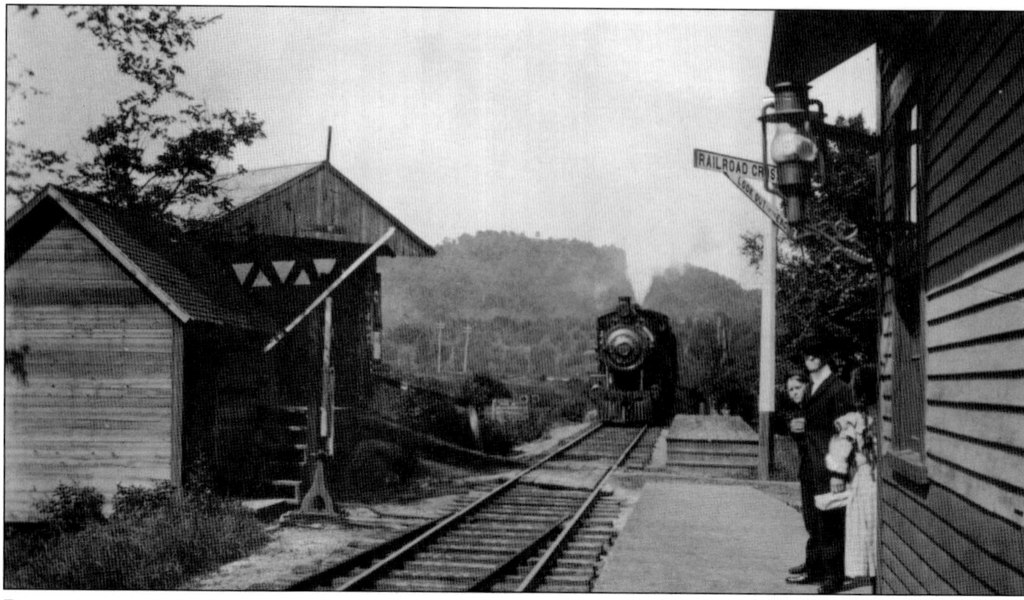

Passengers are waiting to board the "down" train to Concord from the Waterloo station. The contraption by the bridge caught the mailbag if the train was not stopping. Stations served as social hubs of the community, offering a post office or small store. Roger Gage, the stationmaster, sold chocolates and packs of Lon Bean's Seegars, three for 5¢. Complaining customers were told that candy and tobacco improved with age. (WHS.)

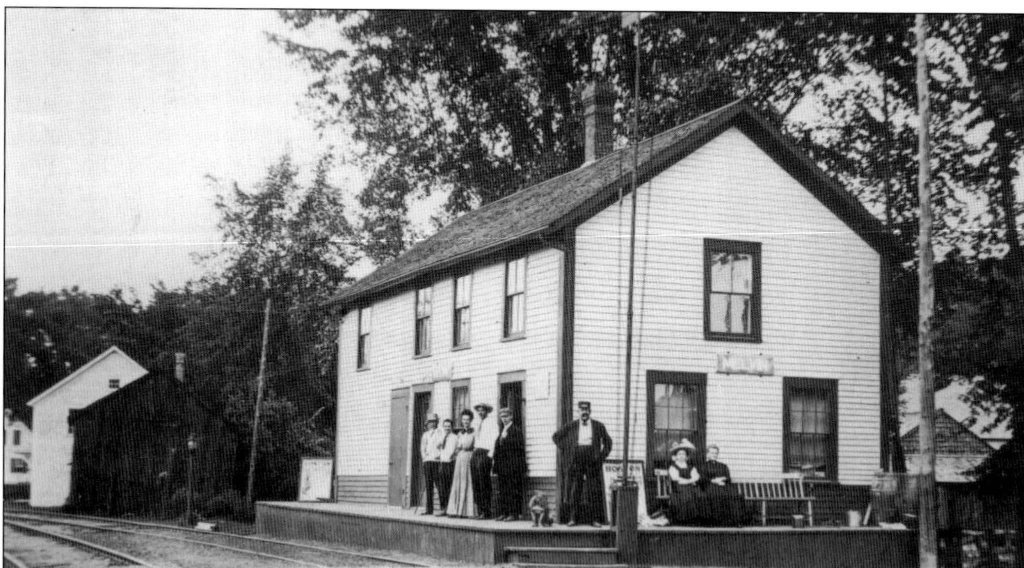

Melvin Mills was the last stop in Warner before the train reached the depot in Bradford. It was a quaint village with mills, the Calico schoolhouse, and several boardinghouses. Walter Melvin was the stationmaster. In 1921, the freight and passenger ticket business was discontinued and it became a flag station, which meant the train only stopped when signaled. The post office was located in this village from 1894 until 1955. (WHS.)

The Bagley station was a passenger station and a freight house for deliveries from the local farms. In the mornings, one could hear the wagons bringing the clinking cans of milk. Samuel Dow erected his farmhouse and barns in 1876. For 20 years, his son-in-law Fred Savory operated a general store until it was destroyed by fire in 1919. (WHS.)

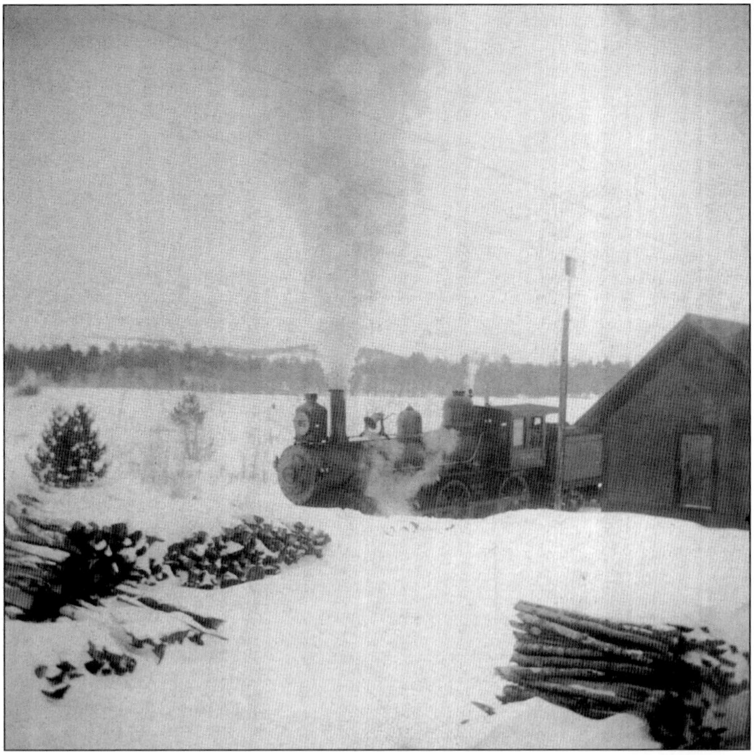

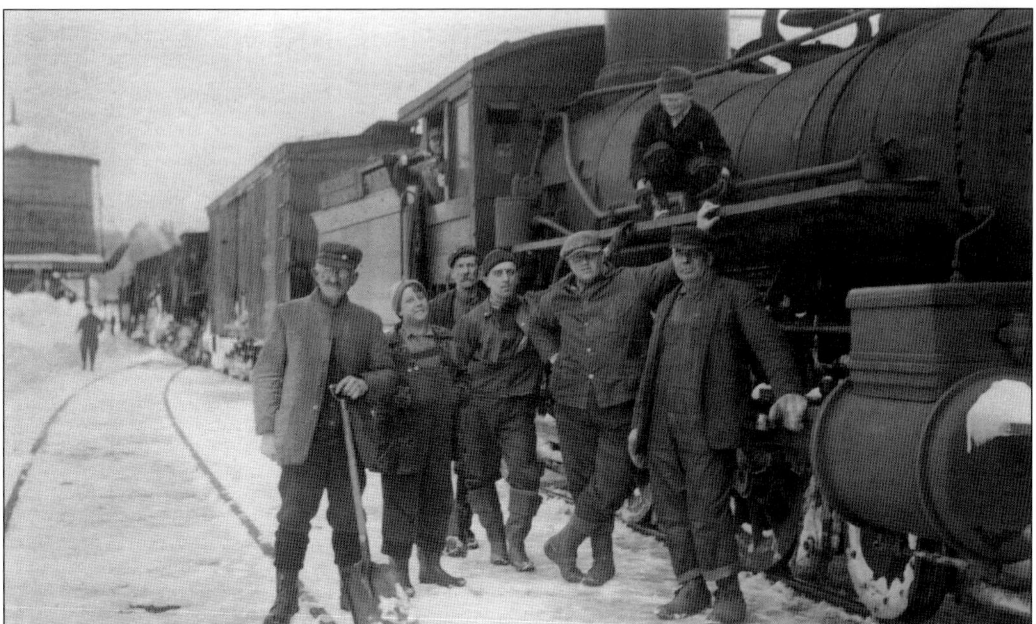

Many blizzards have raged through the Newbury Cut. In February 1873, three locomotives were hooked behind a wooden plow to brave the 10-foot drifts of snow in a vain attempt described by Conductor Perry as the "rashest folly." Passengers sought lodging in town and the train eventually had to back down. The railroad closed in the 1950s but was briefly reopened in the 1960s as a tourist attraction called Steamtown. (BHS.)

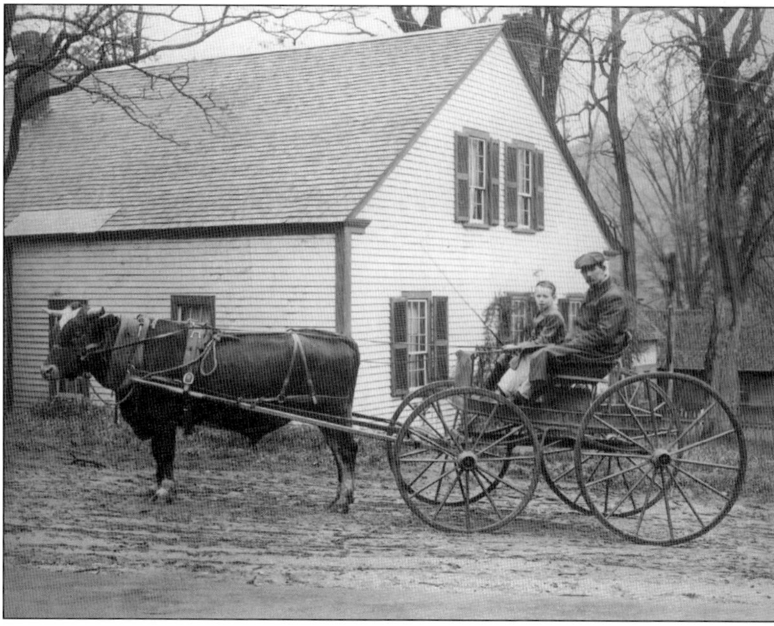

Bert Mason and young Horace Martin pose in front of the Hardy Studio with a single ox harnessed to their light gig. It was no easy feat to teach an ox to pull a carriage, and they were certainly slower than horses. There were several livery stables in town where townspeople or passengers from the train could rent a gig. (WH–Hardy.)

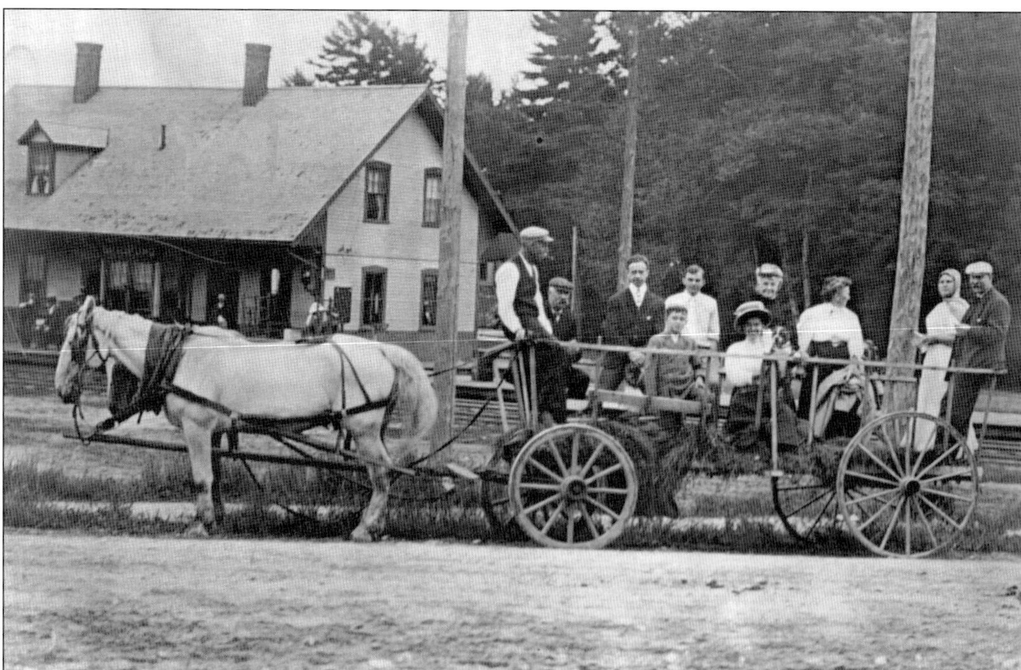

Until the railroad came, horse-drawn wagons, sleighs, and stagecoaches were the only transport besides "Shank's mare" (horseback). Horse teams hauled food and goods to market. Family buggies would often be hired for short trips. Here, a hayrack, usually employed for farm work, is loaded with folks on a summer outing. This reflects the gradual shift from function to recreation and from survival to pastime. (BHS.)

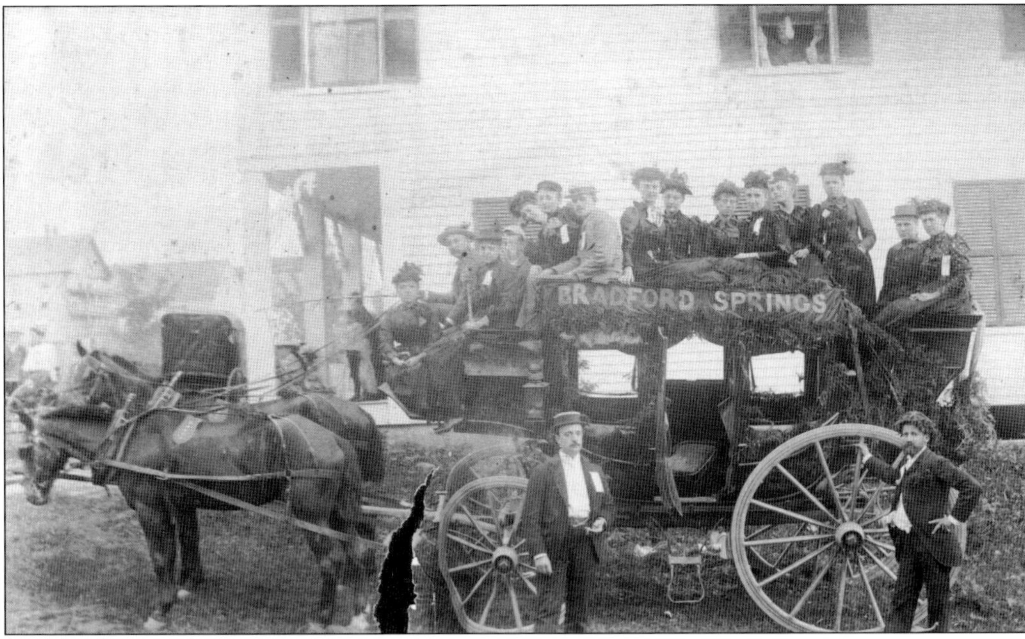

This photograph, titled "Outing to Franklin," depicts an excursion from the popular Bradford Springs Hotel. A trip from Bradford to Franklin would take all day, but it was an opportunity to visit a booming metropolis. The resort catered to a new leisure class that expected to be refreshed not only by the sulfur springs but also by diversions such as this. (Courtesy of Steven Hansen.)

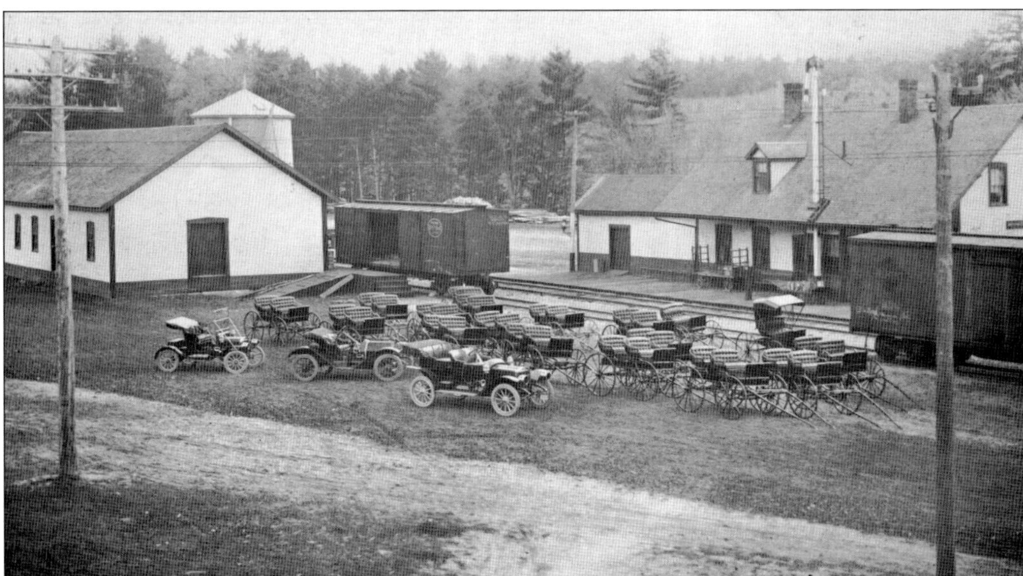

A consignment of carriages has arrived at Bradford Depot for Messer's Carriage Repository. The presence of one automobile among the carriages speaks to the gradual transition to the horseless carriage. The water tower in this photograph was fed by a spring on Ring Hill and its overflow filled the fish-rearing pool. A nearby tank was used for fire safety and clandestine dips on summer nights. (BHS.)

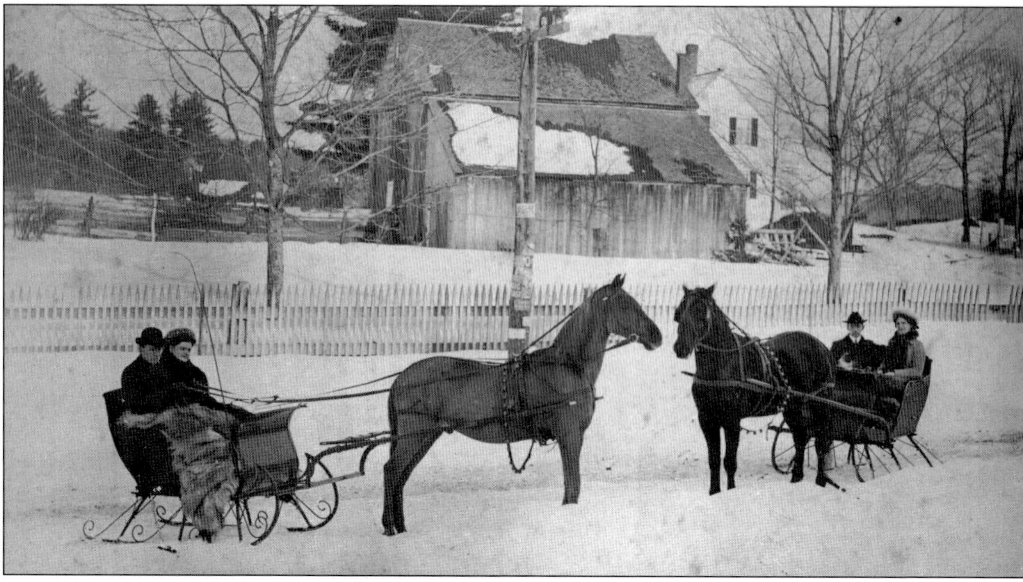

Two couples take their sleighs out for a ride. They are seen near the present site of the public library. Isolation took its toll on the outskirts of town, especially during the winter. People looked forward to town meetings as a time to reconnect with others. The first Bradford town meeting was held on February 11, 1788, but neither women nor the two African Americans in town were allowed to vote. (Courtesy of Steven Hansen.)

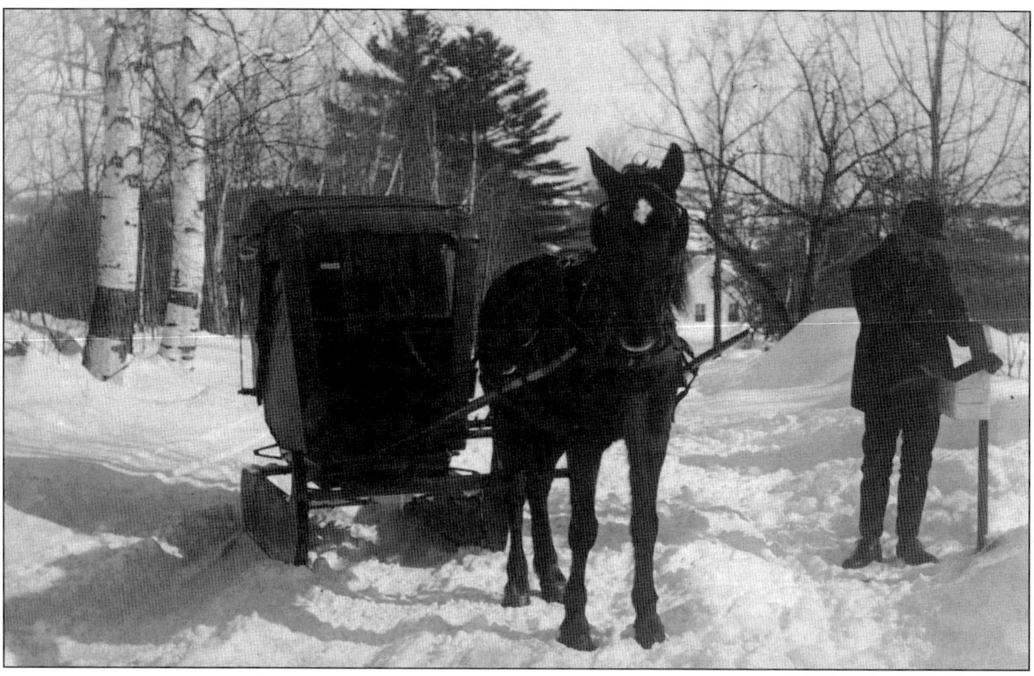

Rural free mail delivery began in July 1901. For 30 years, George Flanders was a carrier for Route 1, maintaining his travel by horse and buggy and by covered sled in winter. The route was 21 miles with 159 households extending through Schoodac, Burbank's Mills (Webster), Smith's Corners (Salisbury), and Pumpkin Hill. Sometimes, he would use a boat to deliver mail in the spring at Smith's Corners. (WHS.)

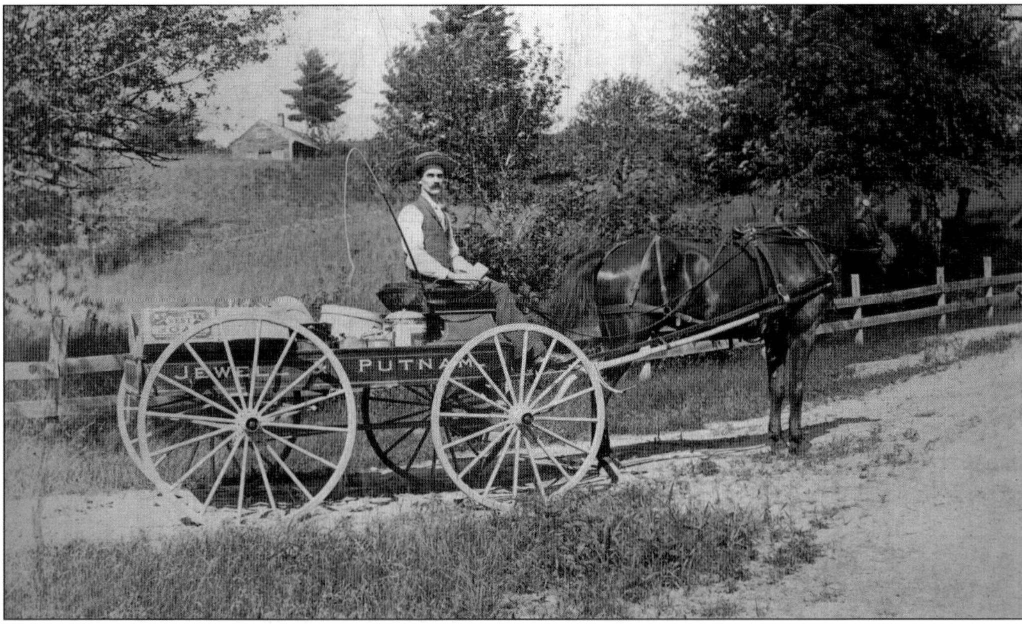

Oscar Jewell and Edward Putnam operated a grocery store at two different locations on Main Street. Stores had regular delivery days. The farmwife placed her order and had it delivered to her dooryard. If a customer ordered in the store, the clerk would scurry to fill individual items as he or she recited them. People were not allowed to wait on themselves. (WHS.)

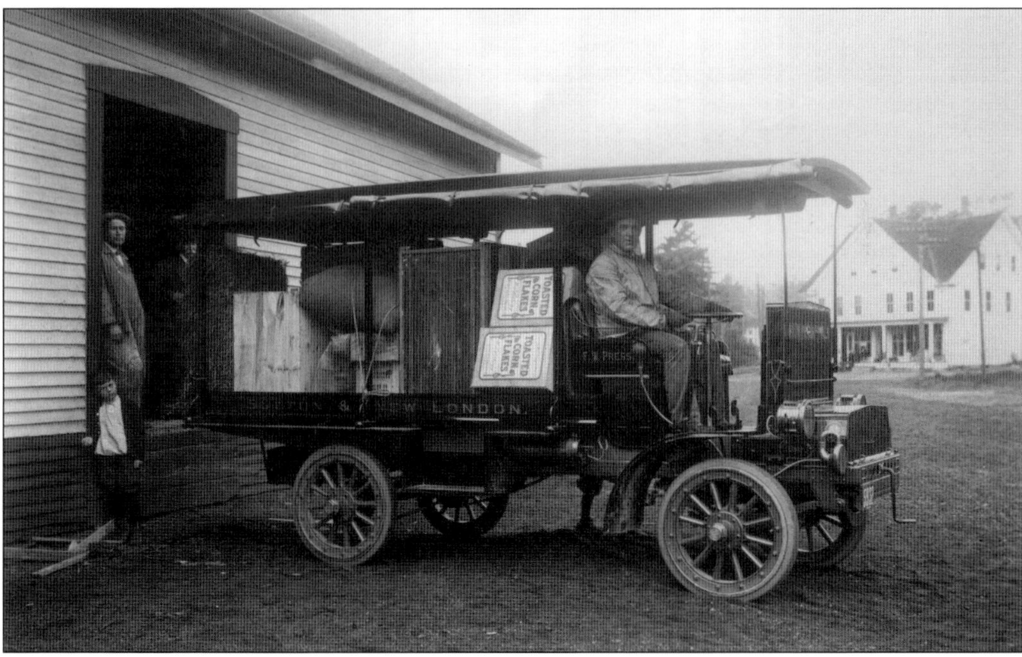

The Bradford–Sutton–New London Stage was operated by Amos Whipple starting in the mid-1880s. It was horse-drawn and would travel on runners in winter. In this photograph, Frank Pressey drives a full load in the motorized version of the stage, which also served as a passenger bus service in the early 1920s. Before automobiles arrived, livery services, often connected to hotels, provided transportation. (BHS.)

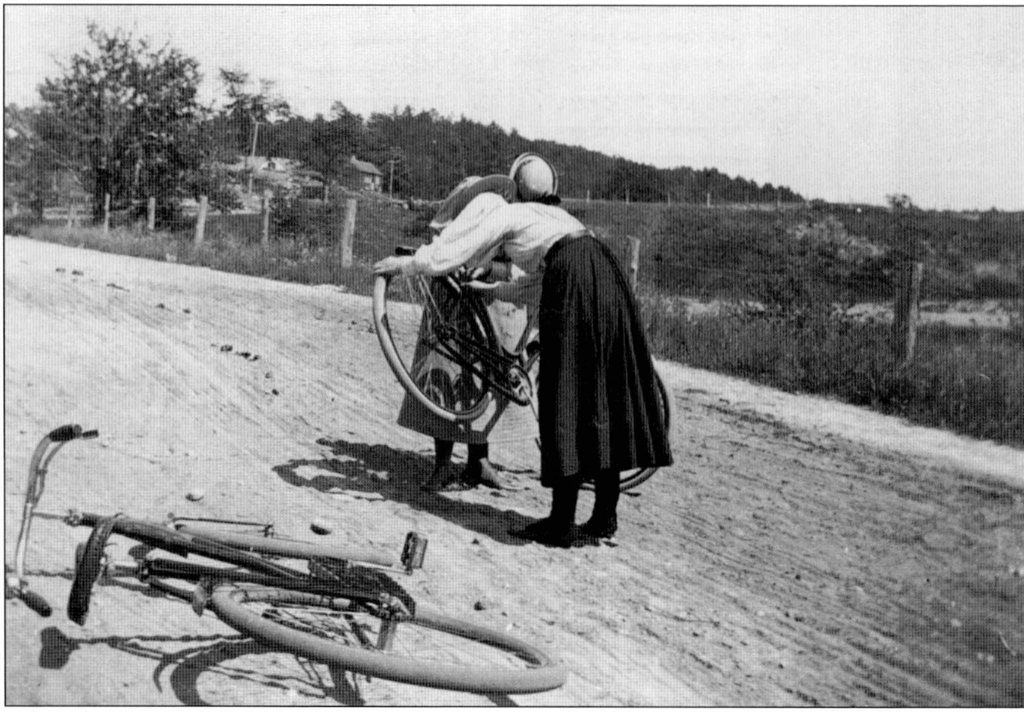

Susan Sawyer's photograph album contained this image of two young women repairing the chain on one of their bicycles in the Lower Village. The paper reported in July 1895, "Girls, where are your bloomers? Long skirts are dangerous, and awkward on the wheel. Keep up with the times." Owning a bicycle gave young women a sense of freedom to visit friends without relying on the use of their parents' horse and buggy. (WHS.)

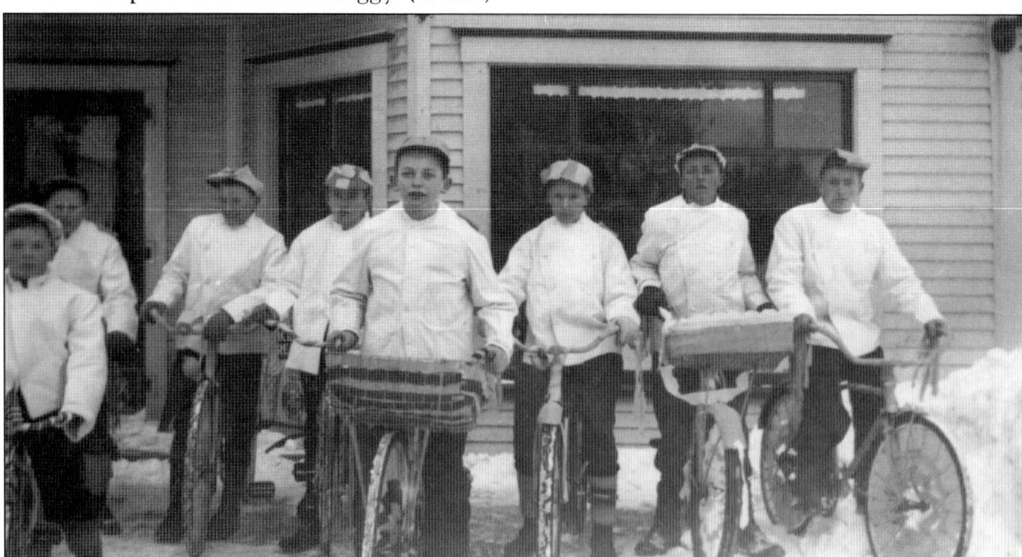

"Slice It Thin" Peaslee ran a meat market in town in the 1940s. These delivery boys, dressed in butcher jackets, are part of a festive Winter Carnival parade. Some of these boys used their bicycles to deliver newspapers for 3¢ a copy. Others remember riding their bicycles, even in winter, down from the outskirts of town to catch the train to Warner for high school. (BHS.)

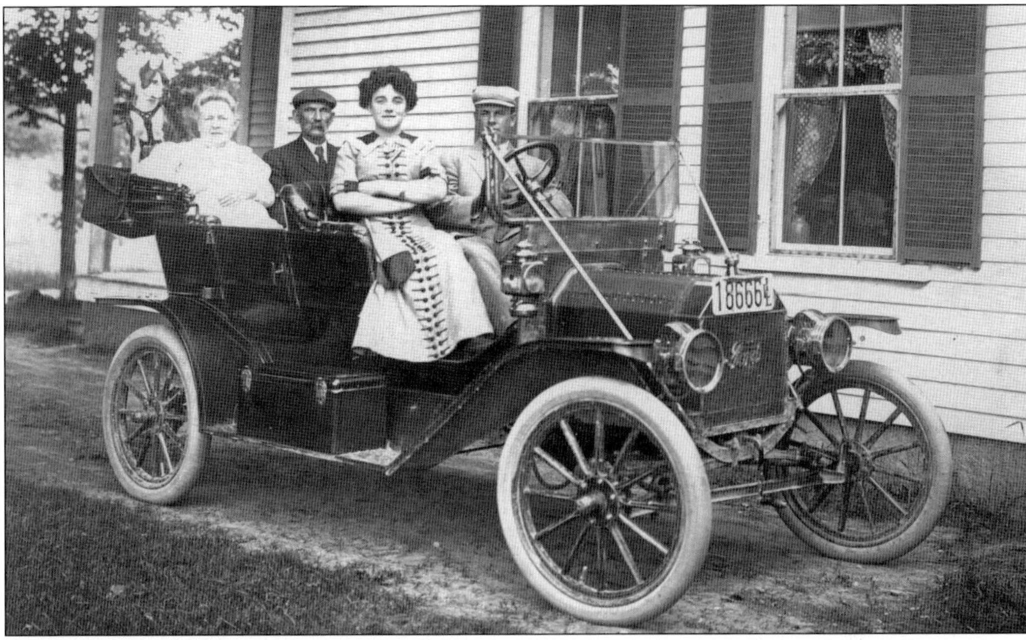

This Ford Model T touring car could go a whopping 30 miles per hour in 1910. The "rag" top could be pulled up for inclement weather. Tin Lizzies held a traveling case on one running board and tanks on the other. The acetylene gas headlights were used only occasionally. On a moonlit night, one could drive home by the light of kerosene side lanterns. (BHS.)

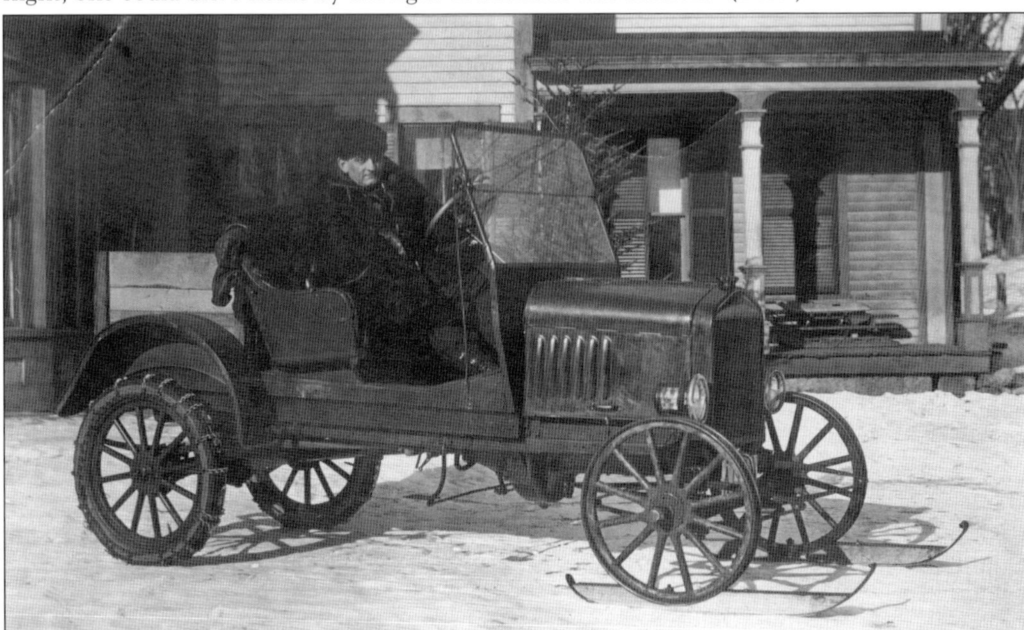

George Chase was an agent for the "snowmobile," an attachment for Ford cars. The advertisement stated it "offers 60 times the bearing surface, 40 times the traction service of ordinary autos. That is why it will go over snowdrifts at an average speed of 18 miles an hour. Sell your horse and buy a snowmobile." This advertisement convinced Dr. Lloyd Cogswell to purchase the device to make house calls during the winter. (WHS.)

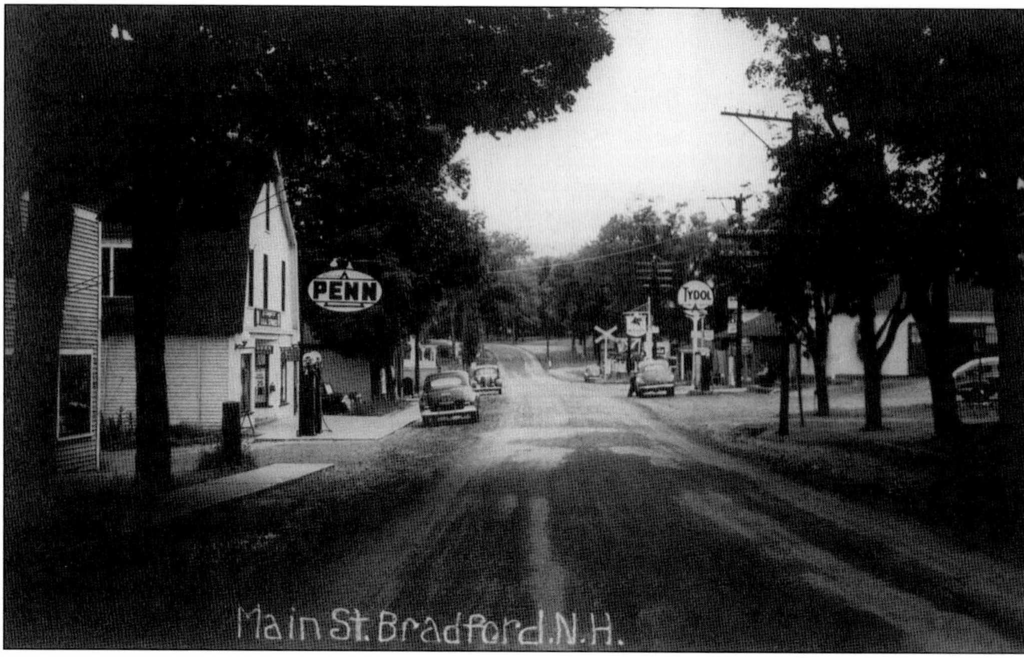

Most New England towns had lovely, tree-lined Main Streets. Stately maples and elms provided not only beauty but also shade for open carriages. The elms succumbed to disease and the maples were cut to widen the streets for automobile traffic and utility lines. Several gas stations can be seen here. In 1908, Carl Danforth installed the first gas pump in town, using fuel brought by a horse-drawn tank wagon from Hillsborough Bridge. (BHS–Pratt.)

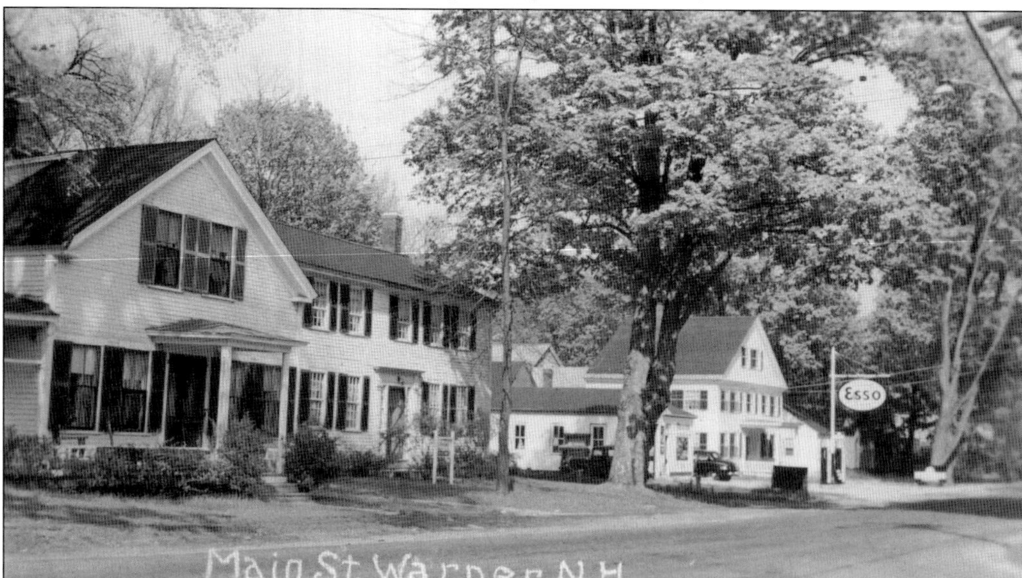

With the advent of the automobile, garages sprang up along main streets and on the outskirts to service them. The blacksmith shops slowly went out of business. In 1920, George Chase operated the first Ford Agency and the following year, switched to selling Chevrolets. The men at his garage taught many young people how to drive. The Esso station on Main Street was established by George Harris in the 1940s. (WHS–Pratt.)

Five

TRADE AND BOARD

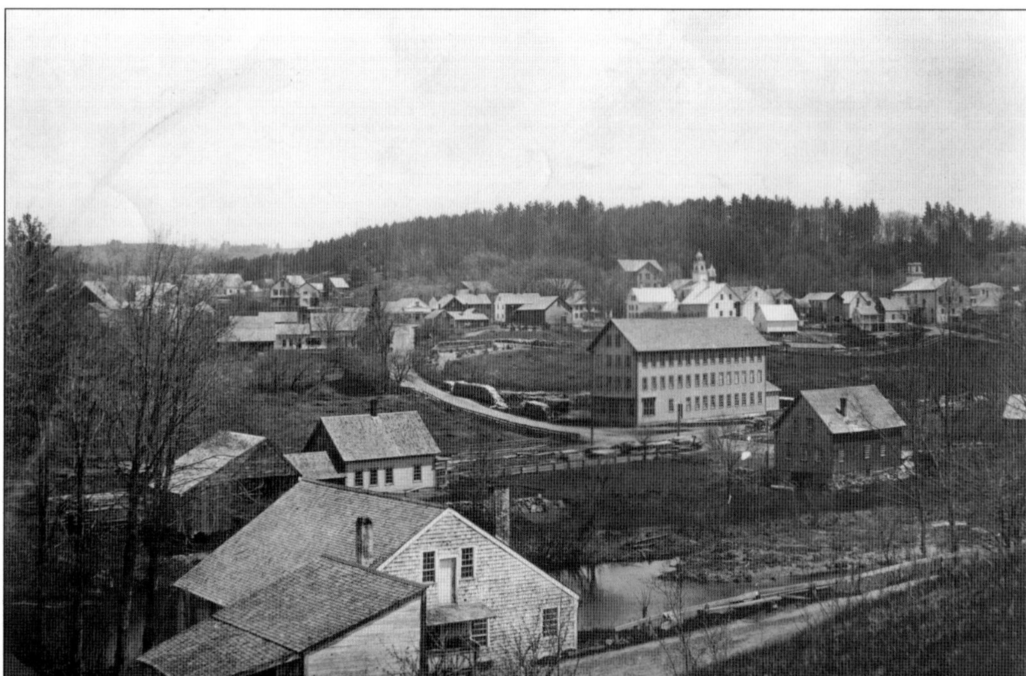

This c. 1890 photograph shows the Ela gristmill (left), Frank Turner's blacksmith shop (right), and Warner Village businesses that sprang up along the Warner River. The three-story frame building was the Merrimack Glove Factory. The steeples in the background are the Baptist church and the Universalist church, which was moved and converted into Alonzo and Edward Carroll's dry goods store. (WHS.)

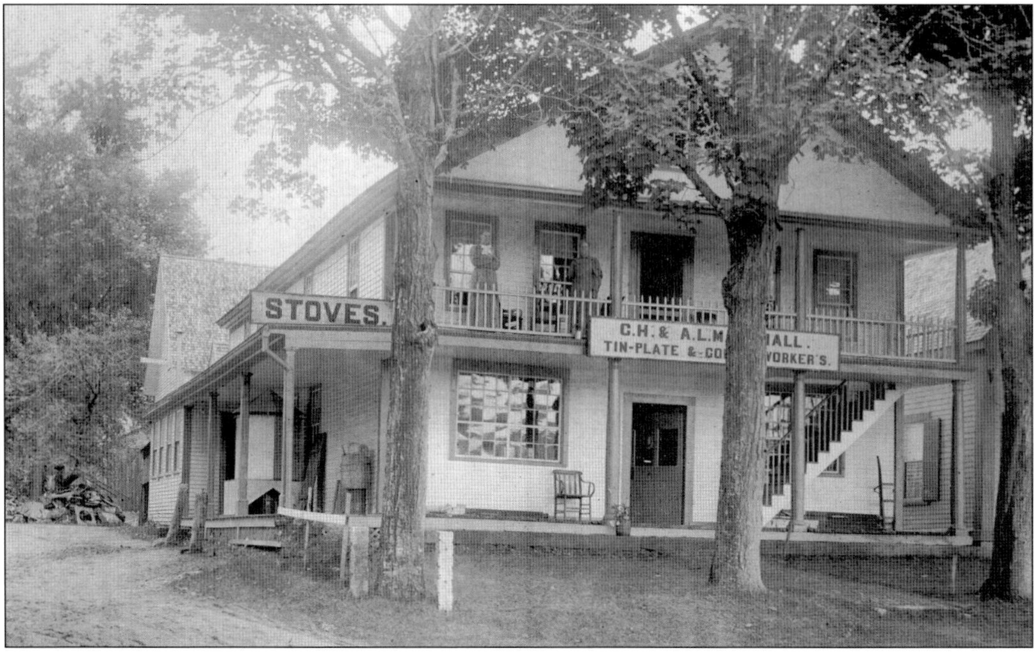

Charles Marshall's tin shop can still be seen at Lafayette Square (previously known as John Brown's Corner). There were tenement apartments upstairs. Later, it was remodeled to become the dress shop of Annie Smith, and then "Petticoat Lane" with Maude Kellar as proprietor. Bradford's first funeral home, Harry Holmes and Sons Funeral Parlor, was also located at John Brown's Corner. (BHS.)

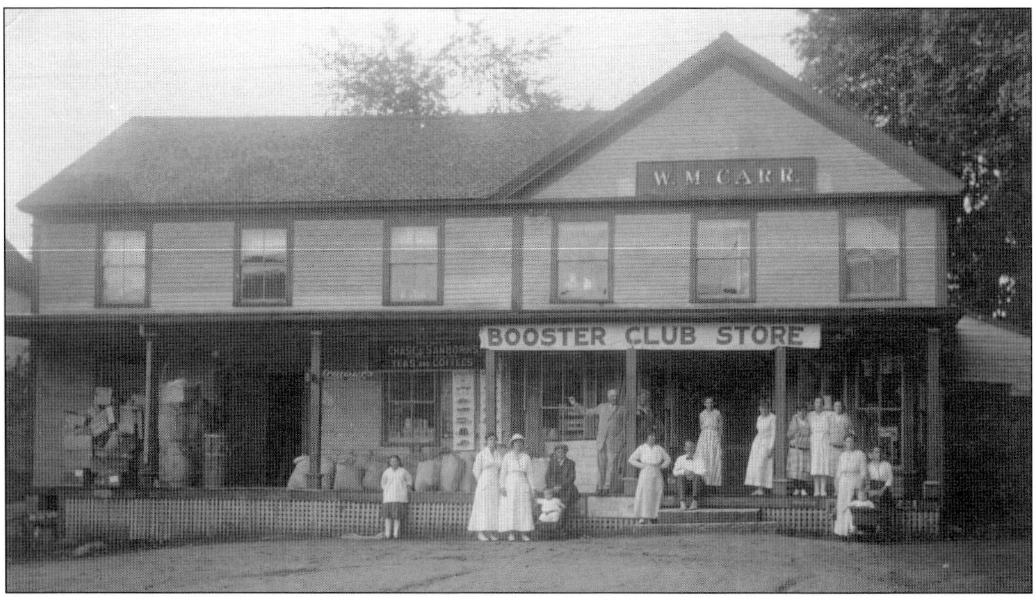

Built in 1828 by John Wadleigh, this store was run for a century by the Carr family. They sold food, hardware, sewing machines, furniture, an "elegant line of dress goods," and the favorite: penny candy. In the early 1900s, the "stamp plan" offered coupons that could be redeemed for goods. Vera Cofrin Dodge recalled, "We tried hard to save coupons . . . and we finally had enough to buy a piano." (Courtesy of Steven Hansen.)

Harrison Robertson opened a dry goods store in the 1830s and served as the postmaster. The front room of his house next door was the Warner Bank. Walter Harriman and John Pillsbury (founder of the Pillsbury Flour Company) rented the store in the 1850s. Rent was $64 for five years, including lease of the store, woodshed, lime house, and one half of the open shed. (WHS.)

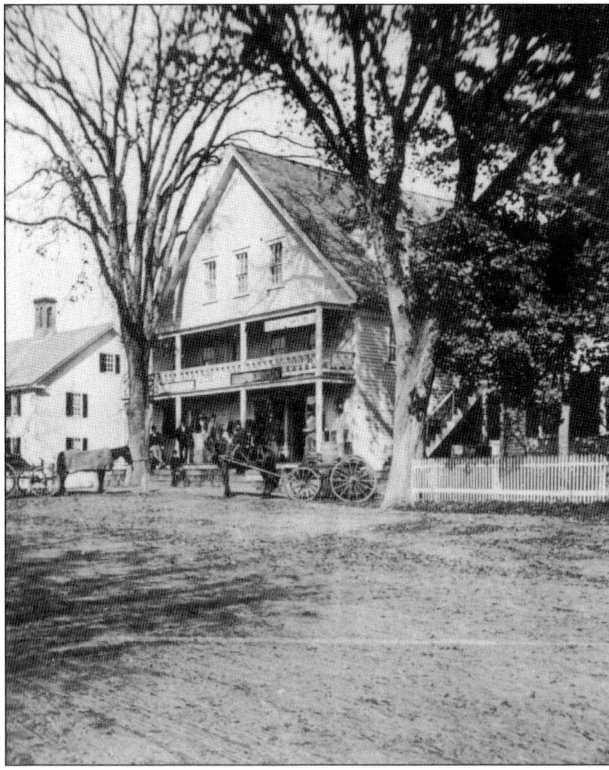

The former Union Block was operated by Horace Martin, who purchased it from his brother Herbert in 1927. Martin became a member of the Independent Grocers Alliance. A fire in April 1936 destroyed the building and the possessions of its upstairs occupants. Luckily, everyone escaped without harm. The building was soon replaced with a one-story brick structure and was operated by Martin. (WHS–Pratt.)

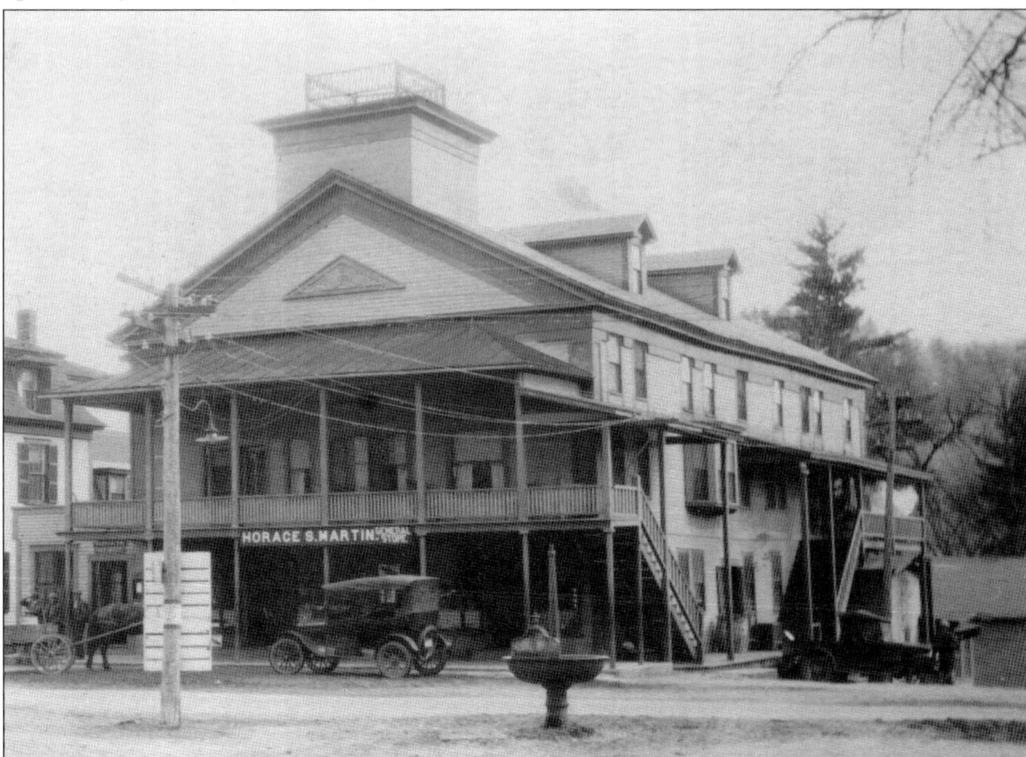

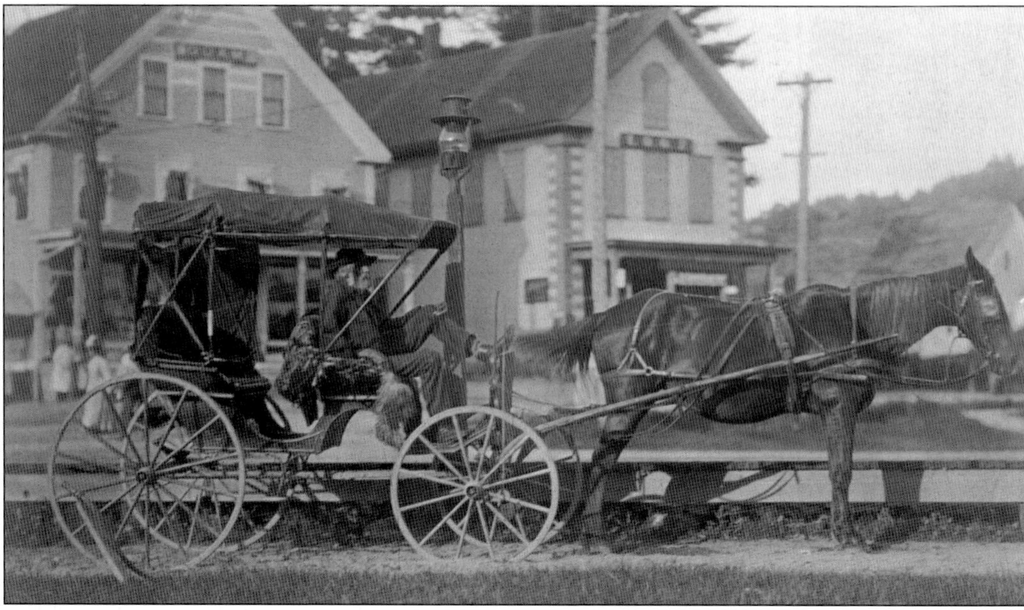

Liveryman Hiram Gillingham awaits paying passengers at the railroad station in 1908. Behind him are the Marshall and Danforth Blocks, which burned a decade later. The buildings held the telephone company and post office, stores, a barbershop, and a pool hall. They also hosted meetings of the United American Mechanics, Daughters of Liberty, Evening Star Rebekahs, and the International Order of Odd Fellows. (Courtesy of Steven Hansen.)

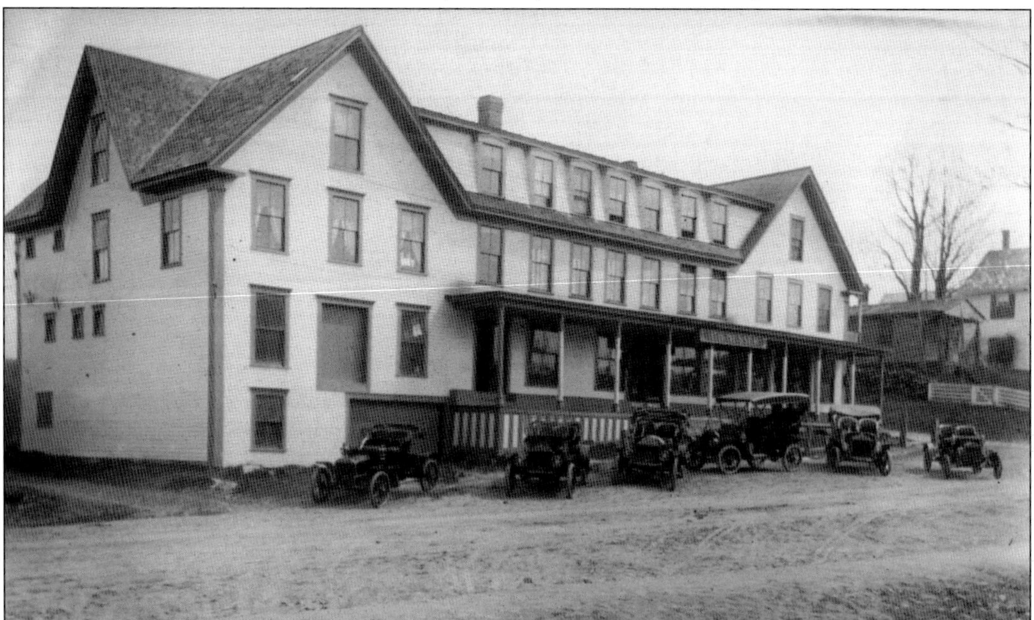

The Messer Block, built in 1898, housed many different businesses over the years. Bagley Bakery offered "wedding cakes and ice cream made to order." Charles Hadley sold grain, lime, and cement. Frank Messer sold "ready made clothing," dry goods, groceries, and Star Steel Roofing. Hurd Clothing and Shoe Company sold Ball Band and Straight Line Rubbers. The Sanitary Mattress Company occupied the space in the 1930s. (BHS.)

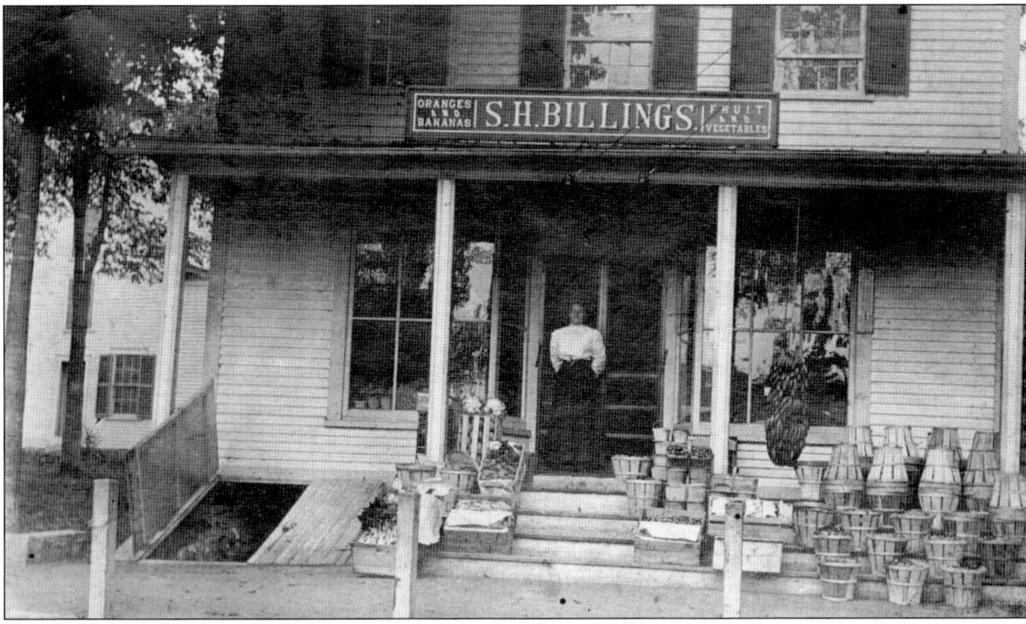

Samuel Billings operated this fruit stand under a lease arrangement at the Harvey Block from 1909 to 1912. His wife, Annie, stands on the porch underneath a sign advertising oranges, bananas, fruits, and vegetables, which are on display in the baskets and boxes on the steps. This building had been a dry goods store, tin shop, and would soon become Warner's first garage. (WHS.)

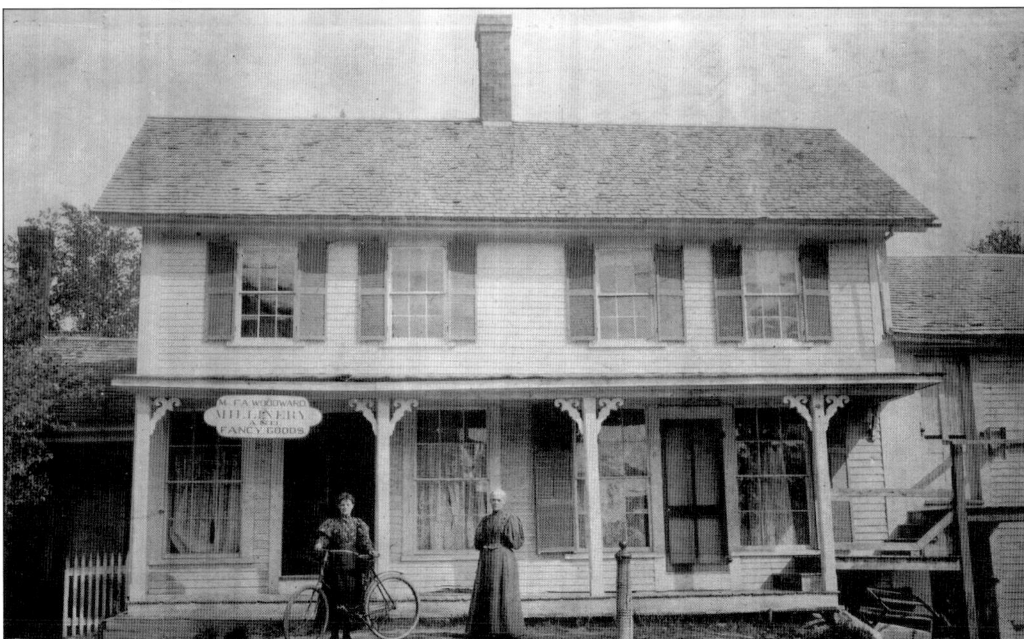

There were several millinery shops in Warner owned by women. Almira Morgan (left) rented space for her shop, and after her 1888 marriage to Frank Woodward, continued her millinery career. Her marriage proved to be unhappy, and she divorced Woodward and married John Yuill, a local housepainter. Grace Pierson was her assistant for many years. A 1909 advertisement showed shirtwaists costing 98¢. (WHS.)

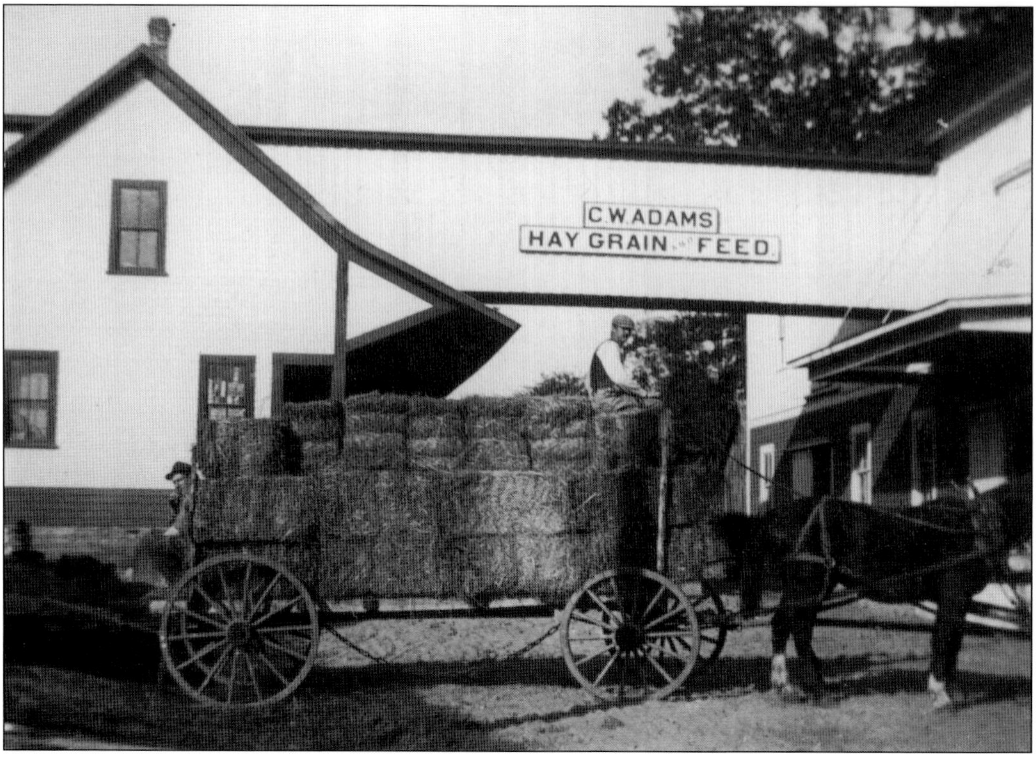

Jacob Adams built his store on land purchased from the railroad in 1898. His son Clarence operated the hay, grain, and feed store until it was sold to Lewis Shaw and Fred Courser Sr. in 1911. In April 1928, the store was destroyed by fire along with an electric gristmill, grains of all kinds, roofing, two new mowing machines, tedders, and planters. In November 1929, it became the Merrimack Farmers Exchange. (WHS.)

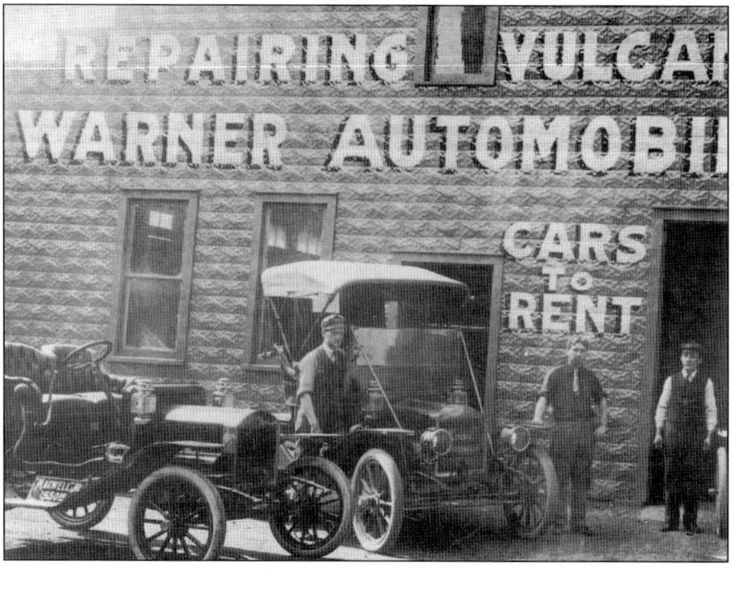

The Warner Garage was built for Alvin Jepson and John Everett Jewell in 1915. They sold Socony gasoline, repaired tires, and rented automobiles. The garage was used as the headquarters for the police while organizing a manhunt for the capture of two escapees from the infamous Sing Sing prison in New York in 1920. They were captured in an apple orchard on Tory Hill and brought here for charges. (WHS.)

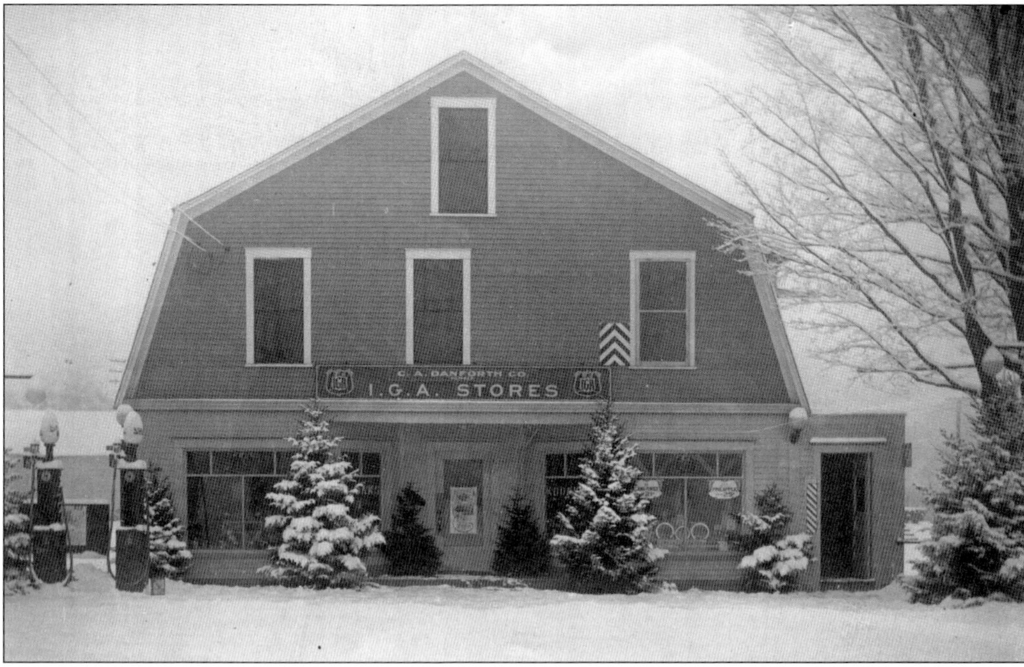

Brothers Carl and Scott Danforth opened the original Danforth's grocery in 1910. After the big fire of 1918, Carl continued the business across the street. He helped many farmers by granting them a line of credit. He sold foodstuffs, textiles, ready-to-wear clothing, and sundries, known as dry goods. The Independent Grocers Alliance (IGA), with its sloping floor and small-town charm, was one of the last local grocery stores. (Courtesy of Steven Hansen.)

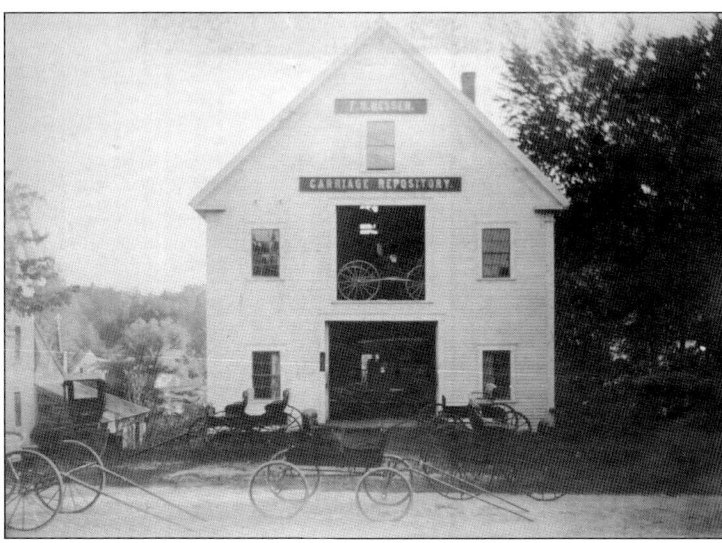

The three-story Messer Carriage Repository still sits along the Warner River. The ground floor originally held a horse barn. On the second floor, the Messers sold buggies, sleighs, two-seated pungs, and democrat wagons until they gradually switched to automobiles in the early 1900s. The third floor was the Grange Hall. This building was later converted into a craftsman's workshop. (BHS.)

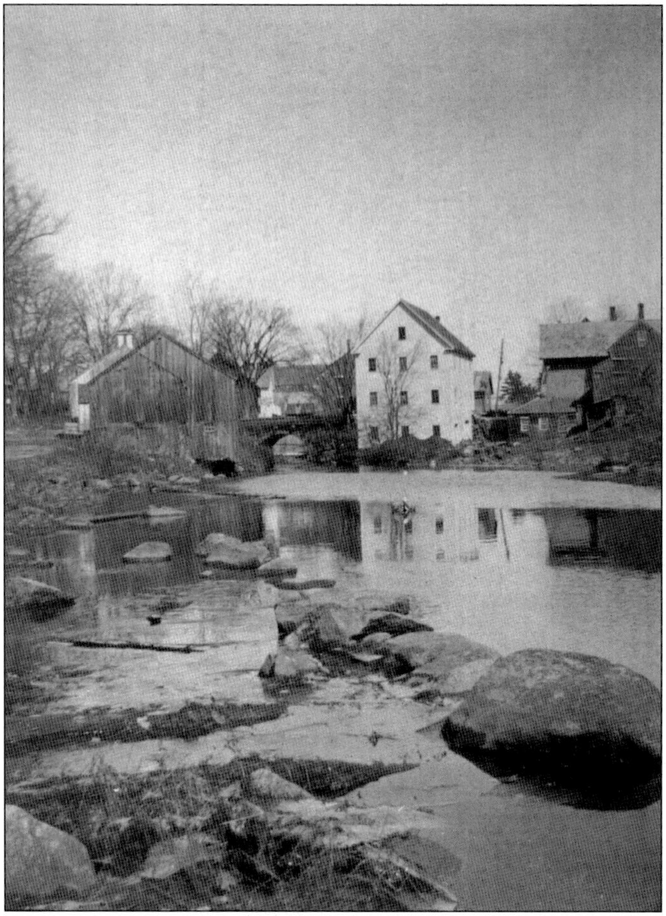

Looking upriver at the brick mill and carriage repository, one can see the original stone bridge, built in 1860, and the dam, built in 1928. Ed Hadley ran the Brick Mill where electricity was produced. At 6:00 p.m., the lights in town would dim while he was eating his supper. The 1938 hurricane cut the power for three weeks, but most people still had hand pumps, outhouses, woodstoves, and kerosene lamps. (Courtesy of Steven Hansen.)

The gristmill (left) and sawmill (right) were built by Capt. Nicholas Fowler in 1829. John Ela purchased them, and they were operated by various members of the family. Paul Shaw remembered "they had a sluiceway where fish gathered and a spot from which you could observe them just above water level. A sucker spear hung nearby, and many a fish met its fate as the result of a thrust of this weapon." (WHS–Pratt.)

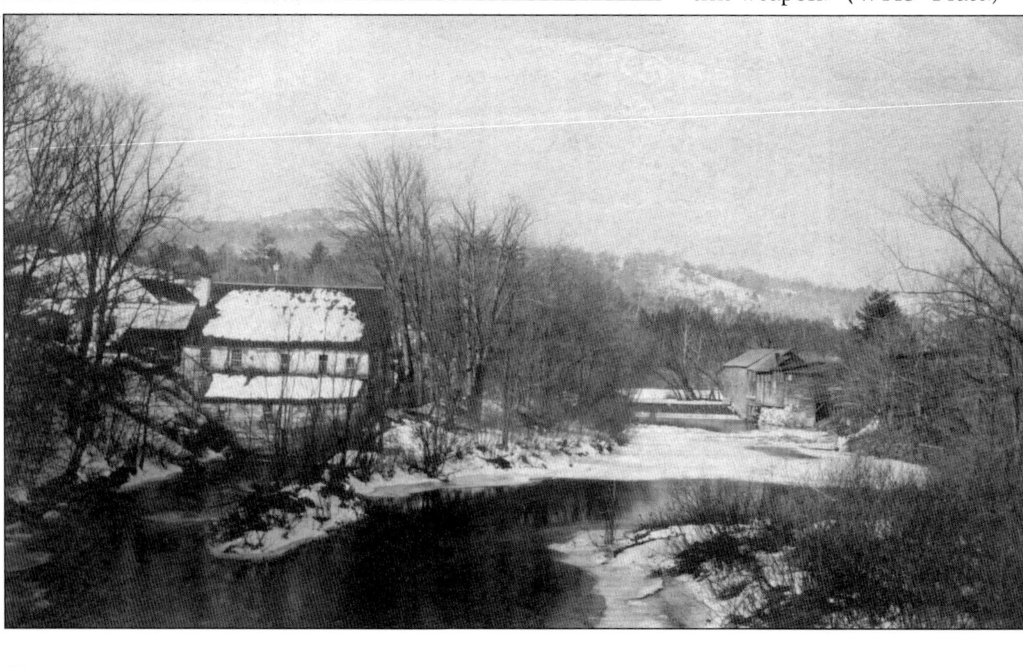

Stephen Chapin Pierce's obituary stated, "He was ingenious, mechanically inclined, and industrious, owning five dams and shops along the Warner River." He manufactured chairs and excelsior here having invented an original machine for shredding it. Coarse excelsior was used for packing fragile objects. Fine excelsior was used for stuffing furniture, mattresses, and baseball gloves. Pierce died penniless at the age of 81 in 1888. (WHS.)

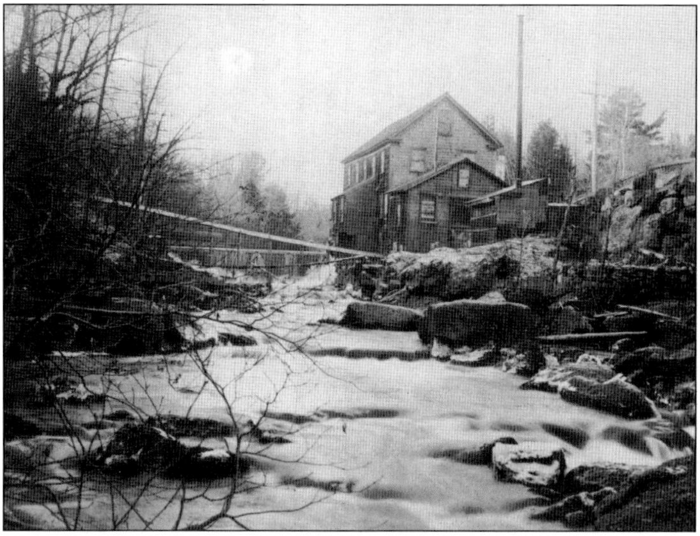

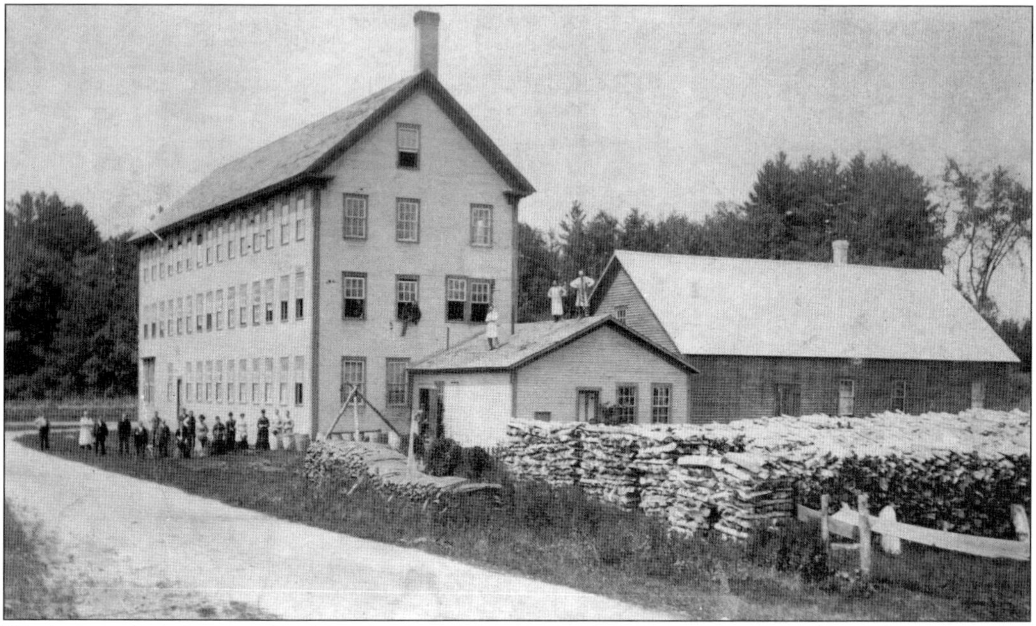

Workers at the Merrimack Glove Factory manufactured gloves and leather goods from 1880 until 1897, when fire destroyed their buildings. Irving Colby recalled the process of making gloves: "You cut two patterns from a skin with a cookie cutter gadget, sewed the two together, and turned them inside out. The boys did this by setting the fingertips on the points of upright spikes, then pulling the gloves down over them." (WHS.)

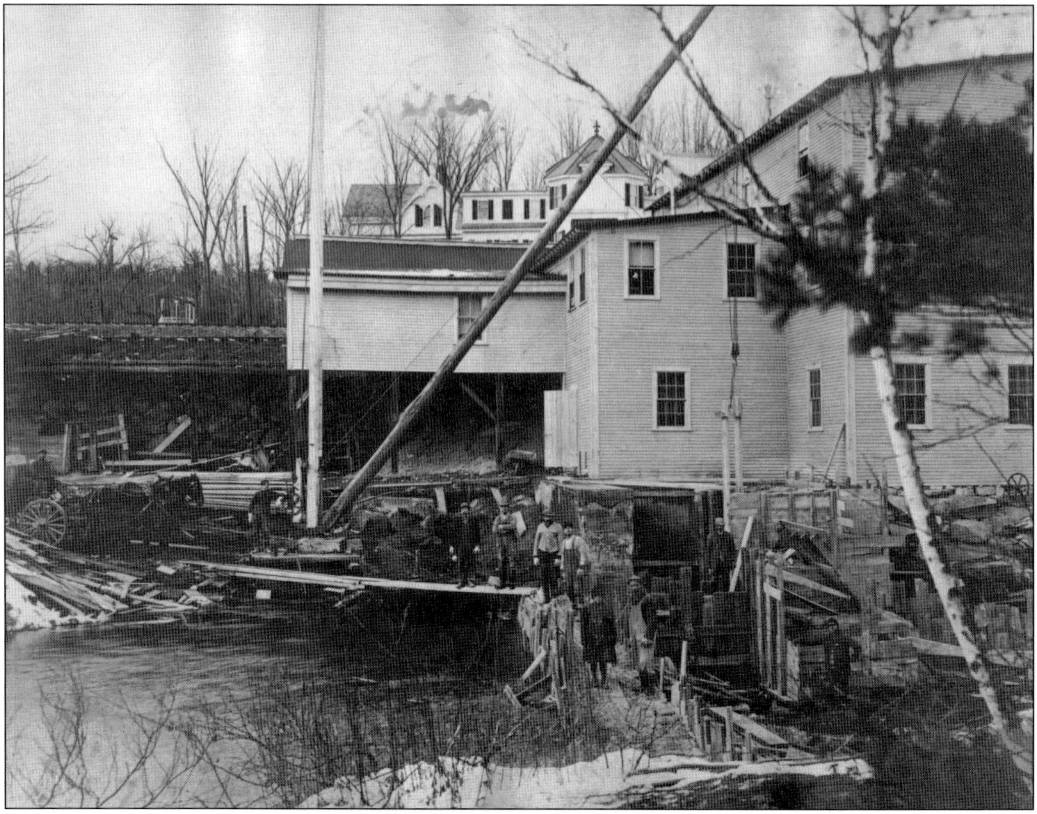

Men are working on the dam at the Redington Hub Company, located along the river between Roby and Melvin Mills. By 1890, the company was using a hundred carloads of elm logs for the manufacture of hubs. Four years later, they were selling 80,000 hubs and shipping them to various coach and wagon manufacturers including the Abbott & Downing Company, maker of the famous Concord stagecoaches. (WHS.)

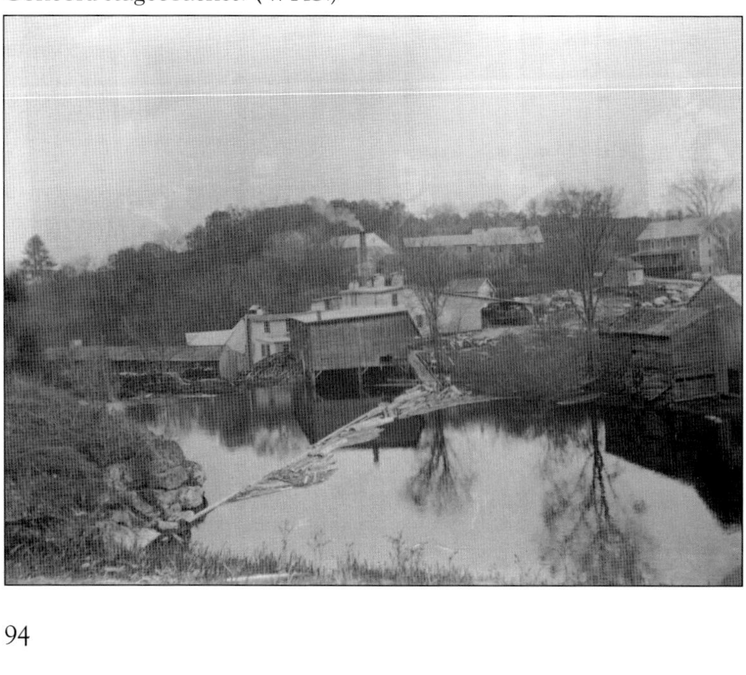

Waterpower at Davisville was first harnessed by Francis Davis, who built a gristmill and sawmill in 1768. By 1826, there was a woolen mill, a mill for grinding lead, an iron foundry, a tin yard, brickyard, plaster mill, and a blacksmith shop. All were destroyed in the flood of 1826. Many of the mills were rebuilt, and Walter and Henry Davis manufactured 600 tons of strawboard annually. (WHS.)

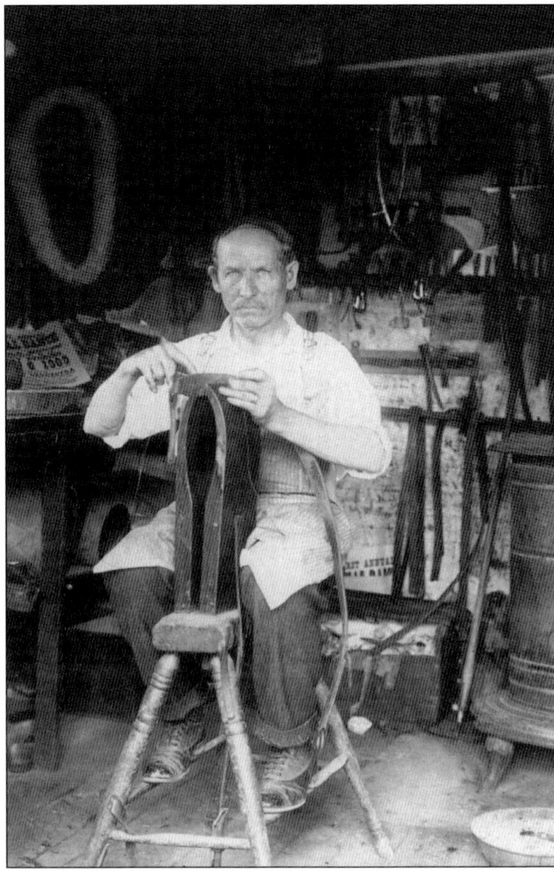

In the late 1880s, Silas Sawtell's Harness Shop was a fixture in downtown Bradford. He was always clad in a white frock coat and leather apron and spent his days seated here, eventually attracting tourists with cameras. He did his work by hand and used worn-out harnesses to make all types of handles. The building was razed in 1923 and replaced, briefly, by a railroad car diner. (Courtesy of Steven Hansen.)

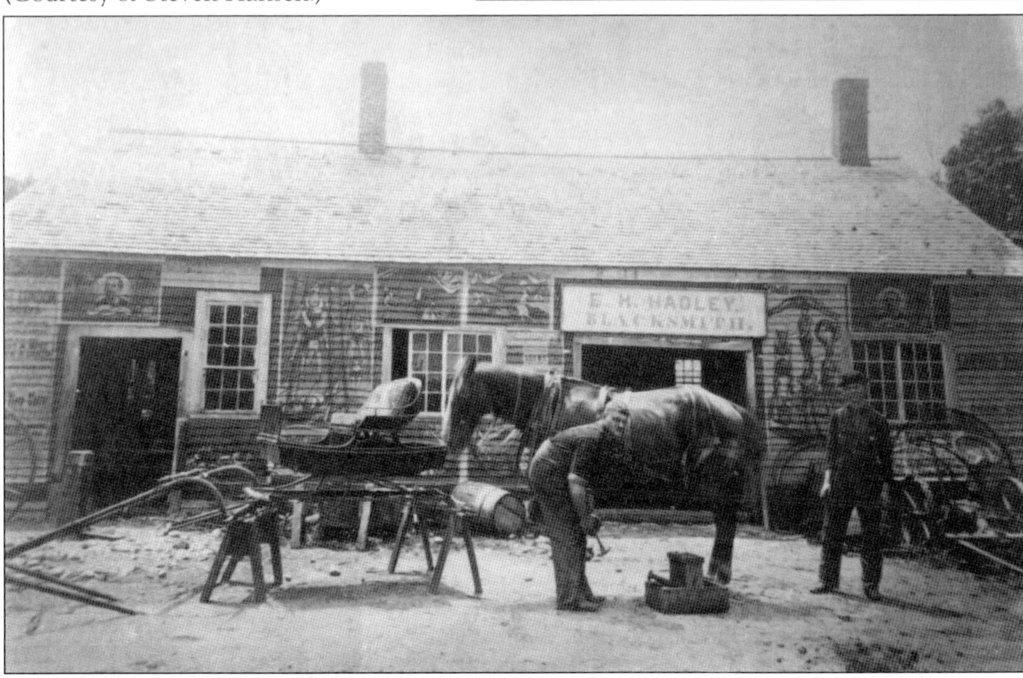

Blacksmiths provided a vital service in the early days, even acting as surgeons on occasion. In 1919, Archie Clement shod 141 horses and four pair of oxen in one week, but by 1923, he was mainly selling farm machinery. Other early blacksmiths were Leonard West, Benjamin Wiggins, and Ezekial Hadley, whose sign stated, "We work for those who pay us best, and then, if time, we work for the rest." (Courtesy of Steven Hansen.)

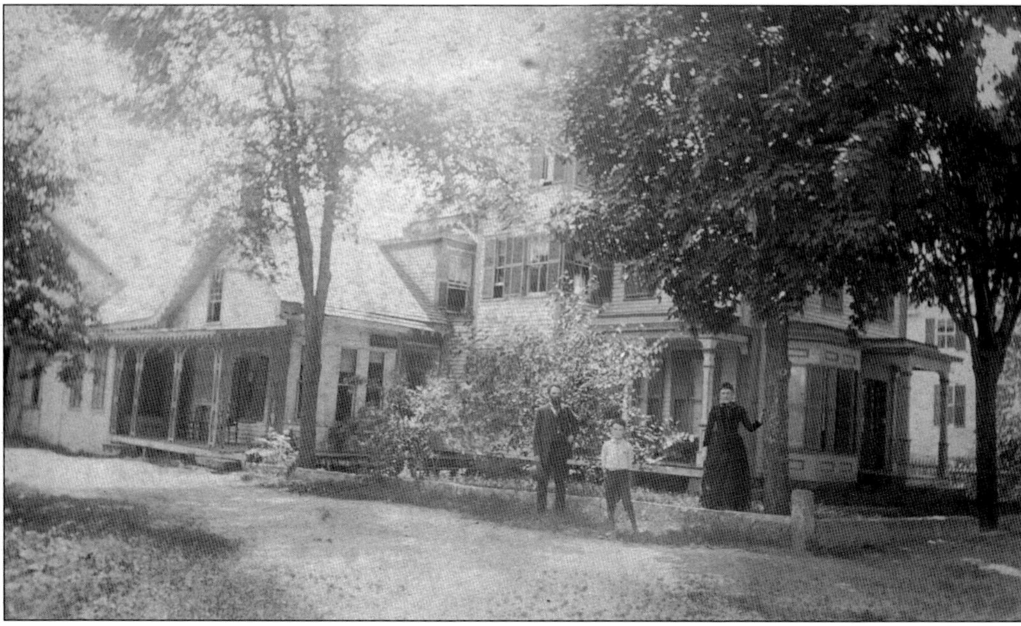

Dr. Frank Graves sold his business to his medical partner Dr. John Cogswell. Doctor Cogswell enlarged the house with a Victorian addition in 1880 and saw patients in the ell. Various doctors worked with him during the time of his practice until his son Dr. Lloyd Cogswell received his license to practice and came home to take over the business. (WHS.)

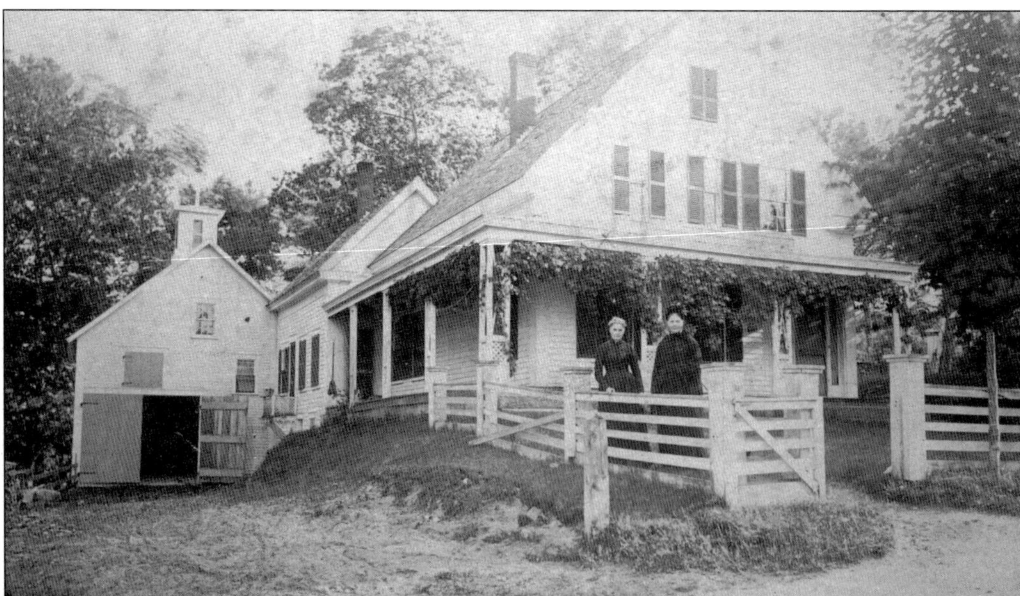

Many dedicated physicians used this as a home and clinic. The only hospital was a pesthouse for smallpox victims in 1848. One February, Doctor Carey "removed a large suspender button from the nose of Master Arthur Peaslee [who had] carried [it] in that receptacle since last November." In 1860, Doctor Fletcher became the town's first dentist, taking over the barber's role of tooth extractor. (BHS.)

Harrison Harris practiced law in Warner beginning in 1816 and constructed a small building in front of his house for an office. Although he had a lucrative career, his first love was farming. After the tragic death of his wife, Mary, from a carriage accident, daughter Amanda (age 18) took over the management of the household. Amanda went on to a successful writing career, and her sister Mary became the town's first librarian. (WHS.)

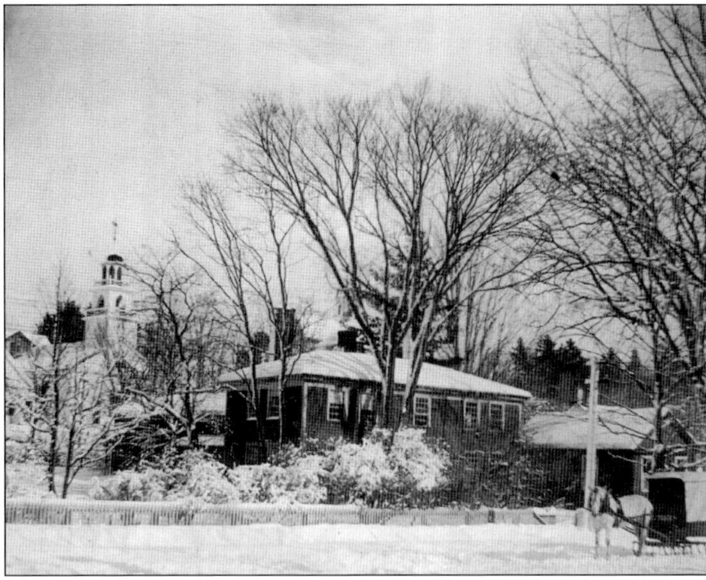

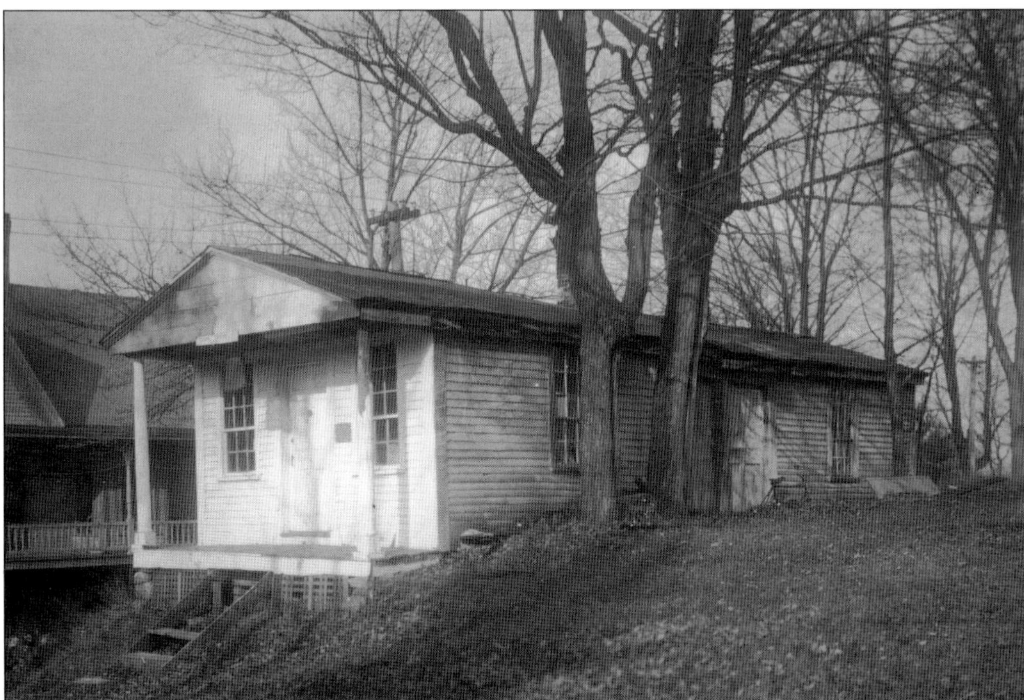

Col. Mason Weare Tappan formed the first New Hampshire Volunteer Regiment and became New Hampshire attorney general in 1876. He was a prominent businessman, lawyer, and politician. He worked energetically to promote the Bradford-Newbury Fair. This tiny building, which was used as his law office and later as a Boy Scout house, can still be seen on West Main Street. (Courtesy of Steven Hansen.)

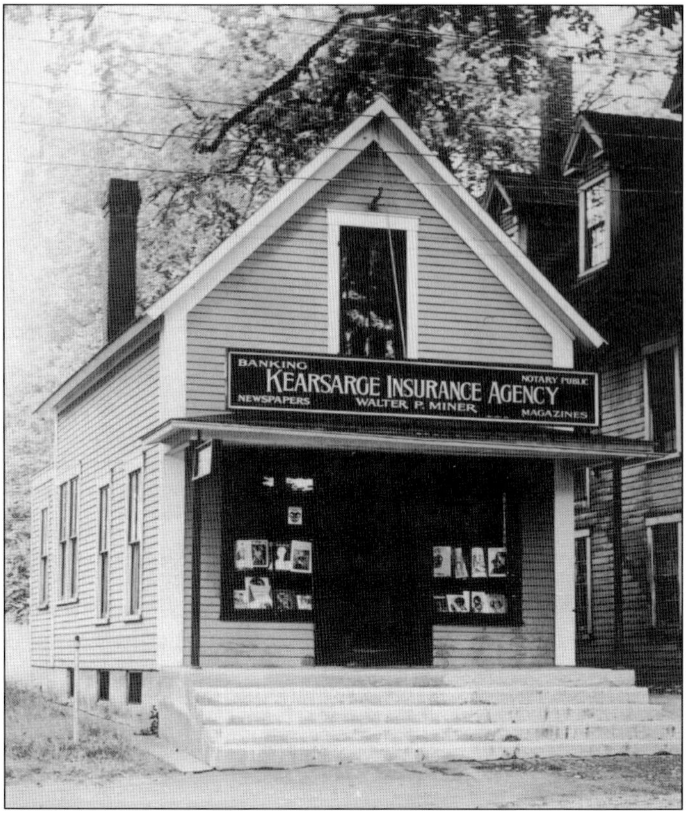

Lloyd Adams built this post office in 1885. Paine and Sarah Davis, Fred Myron Colby, and Andrew Hook kept the post office until 1916, when it was moved next door. Hook sold insurance, newspapers, magazines, and discounted railroad tickets. The Citizens National Bank and the Sugar River Savings Bank of Newport had a limited banking service at this location for decades. (Courtesy of John and Beverly Hill.)

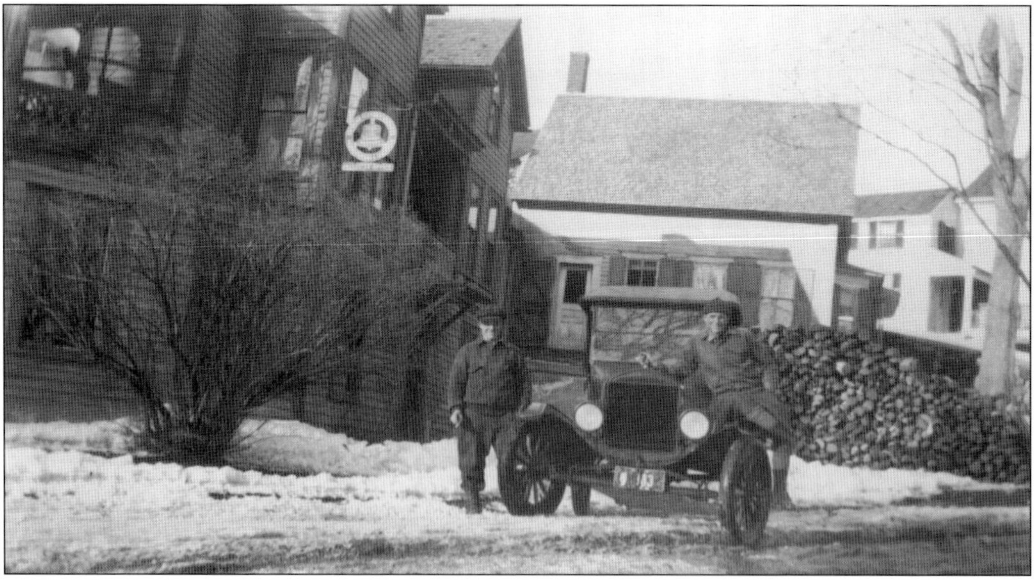

Pete Colby and Walter Ingalls, linemen for the Merrimack County Telephone Company, stand in front of a Model T Ford around 1926. The company was organized in 1896 "to construct and operate a telephone line in Bradford, Sutton, New London, Newbury and other towns within the County of Merrimack." On February 1, 1898, Orrin Sawyer agreed to take charge of the central station and switchboard in Warner. (WHS.)

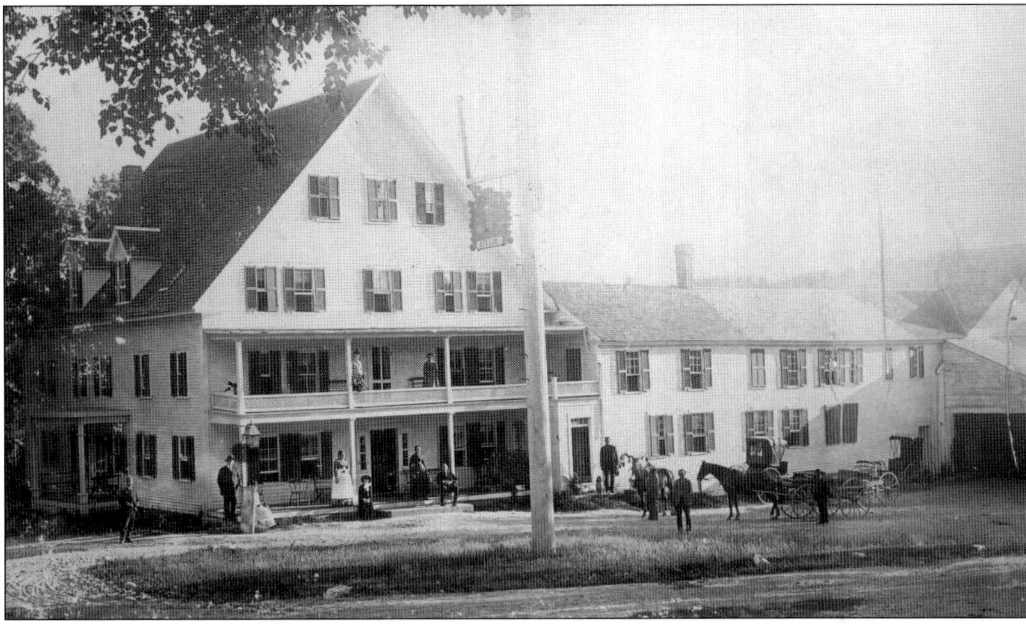

The Raymond House, built in 1804 by John Raymond and his wife, Hannah Presbury, was quite grand. At the time of its demise by fire in 1897, it was reputed to be the oldest continuously run hostelry in New England. Revolutionary War hero General Lafayette visited this site on his momentous tour of the country in 1825. (BHS.)

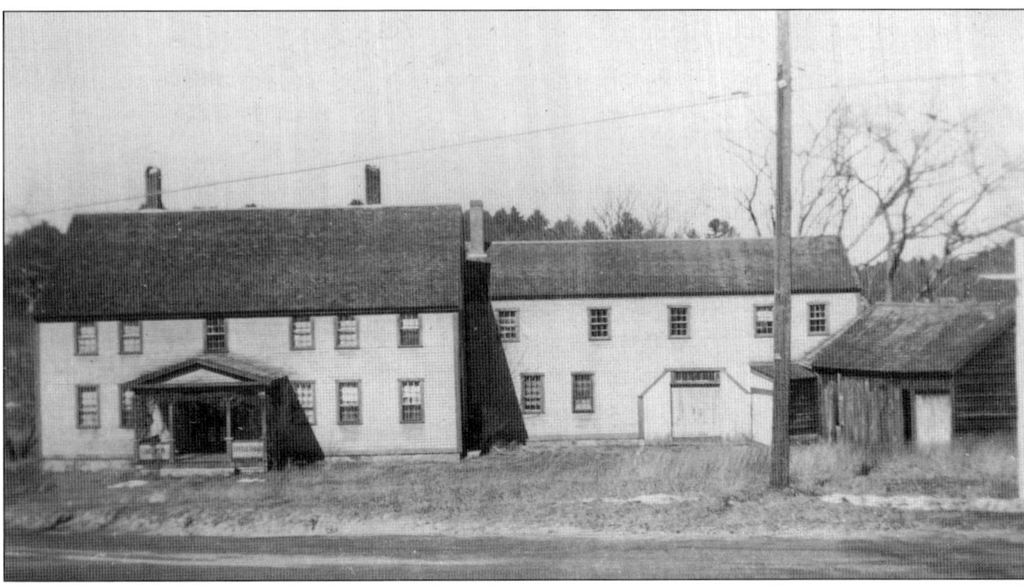

The Davis Tavern was built by Capt. Francis Davis in the 1770s. He made the trip to Portsmouth asking for the town's incorporation in September 1774. Stagecoaches stopped here on the route from Boston to Windsor, Vermont. There was a dance hall with a spring floor, an arched ceiling, and a musicians' platform in the ell. African American and Revolutionary War veteran Anthony Clark played his fiddle and taught dance classes here. (WHS.)

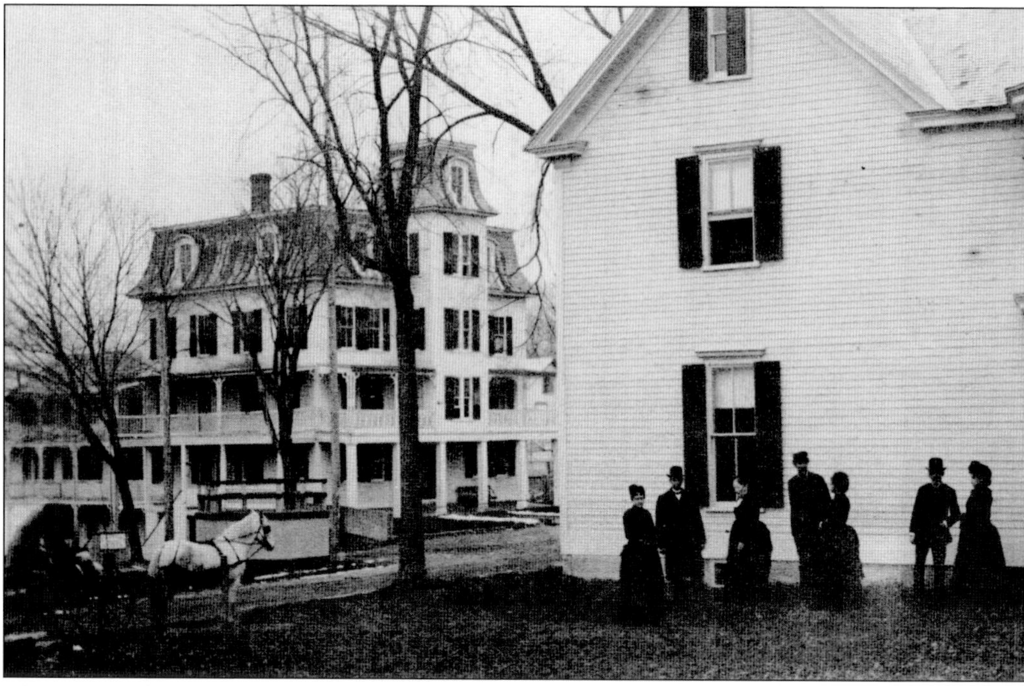

The original hotel, built by Nathan Colby in 1832, also served as a stop on the stagecoach route to Vermont. Nehemiah Ordway purchased it in 1872 and remodeled it with a distinctive French gambrel roof and rooms to accommodate 100 guests. Ordway worked hard to promote tourism. Unfortunately, the majestic hotel succumbed to a terrible fire in the winter of 1885. The Pillsbury Free Library was built here. (WHS.)

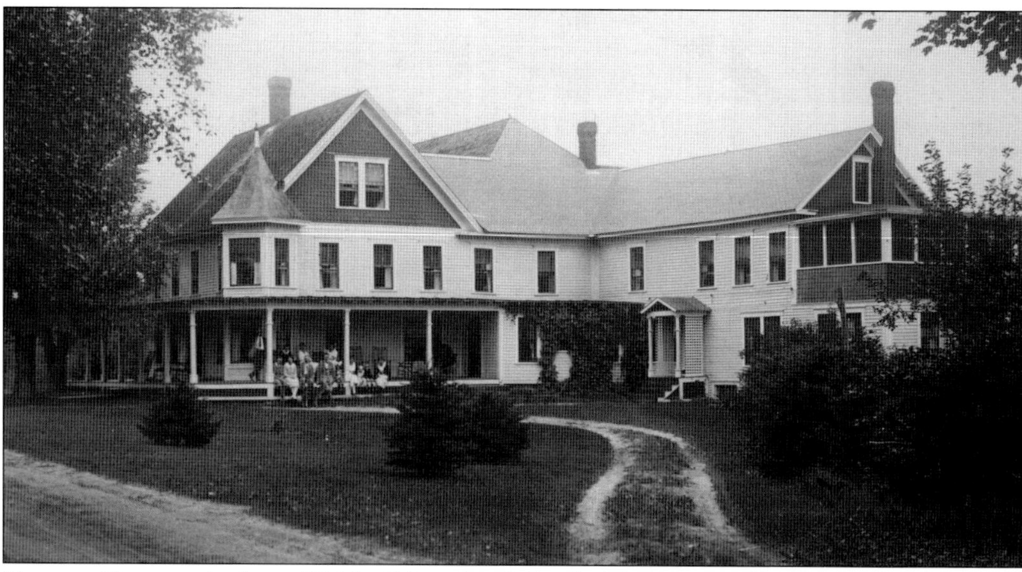

Pleasant View was built in 1896 by Edward and Estella Messer. Initially, they offered rooms for six guests with references. Their business increased to accommodate 85 guests, who for $6 a week bought lodging and homegrown vittles. Cottages, a bowling alley, a dance hall, a golf course, and a casino were added and the business stayed in the Messer family for many years. It is now the lovely Rosewood Country Inn. (BHS.)

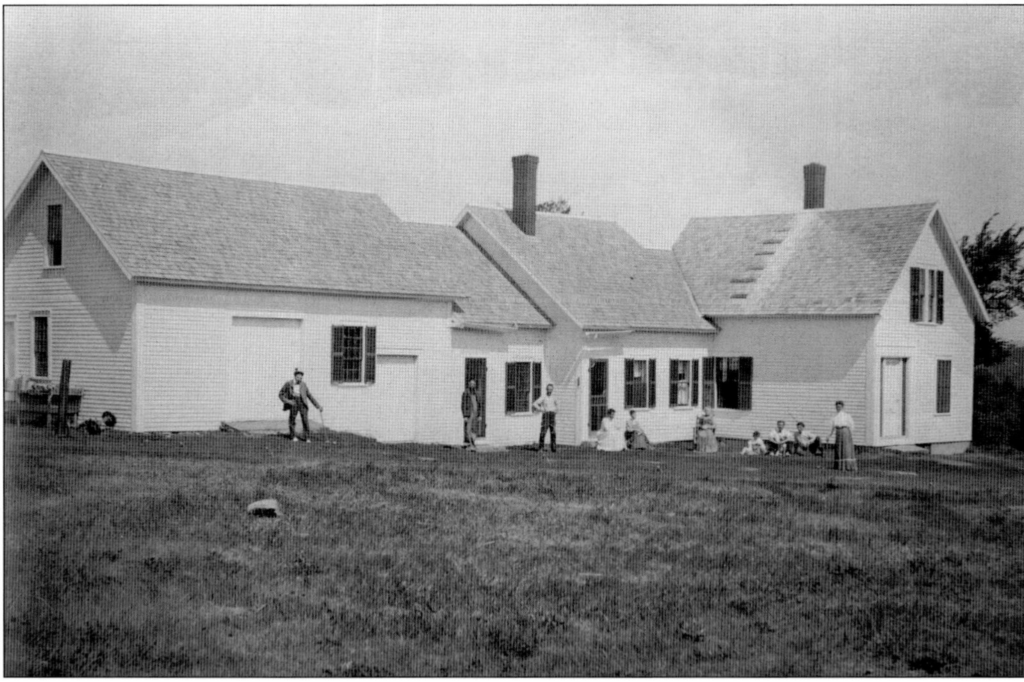

In 1903, Herbert Larkin paid John Hoyt in gold to build a large hotel near this home in Bradford Center. Everyone went to the fair, leaving one woman home to tend the fires lit to dry the wet plaster. Flames broke out, and she was unable to control the blaze. Luckily, the building was insured, and Larkin later built Indian Head Cottage, a fishing camp on Lake Massasecum. (Courtesy of Steve Hansen.)

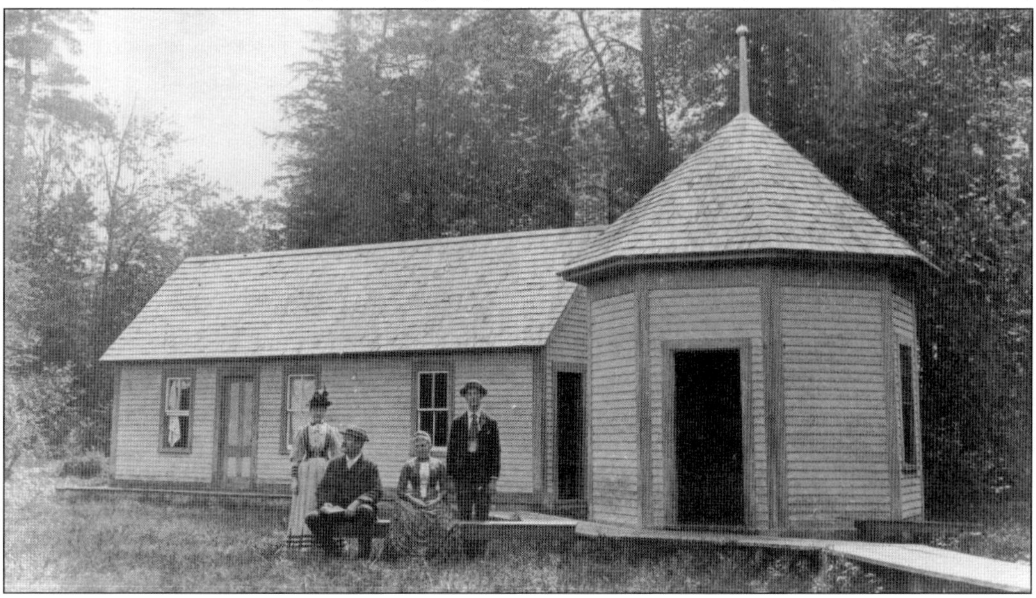

Sam Andrews built a hotel called the Hermitage in 1840 at this site known as "big medicine waters." In 1858, the enlarged Bradford Springs Hotel gained a bowling alley and a store. A tanneries dam created Lovewell Lake, which was fished by guests, although its odor challenged that of the sulfur springs. The restored springhouse resides at Sutton's Musterfield Farm. The hotel was rebuilt as Antrim's Maplehurst Inn. An easement preserves the site and nearby bog. (BHS.)

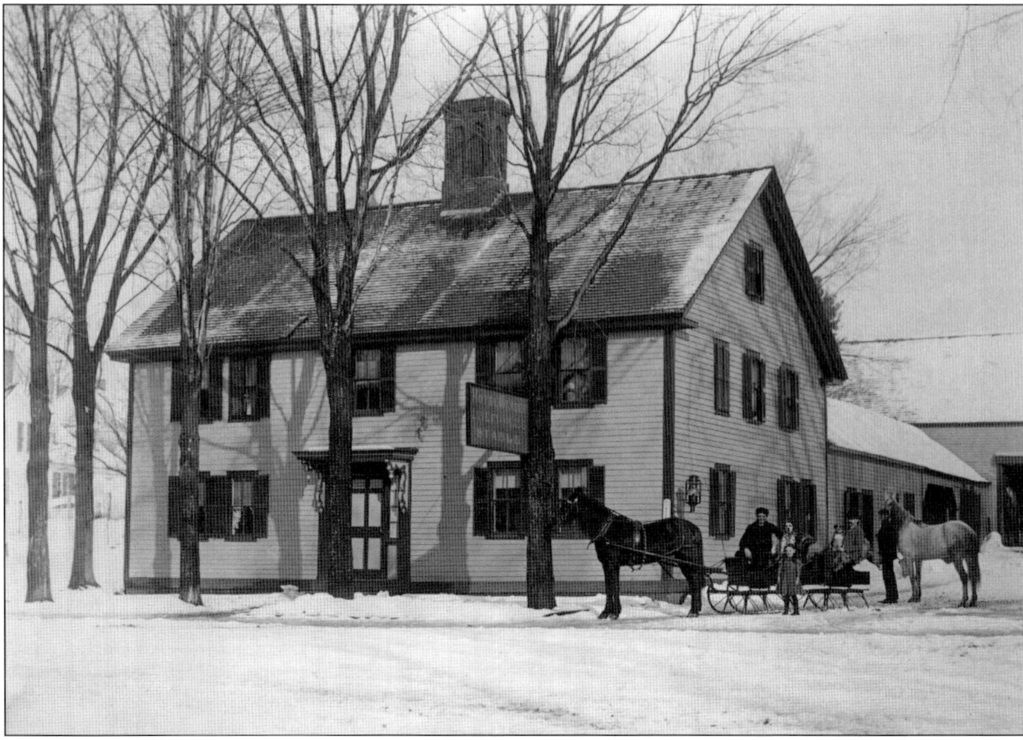

Pattee's Tavern and Hall was the first frame house built in the Main Village in 1785. Capt. Joseph Smith converted it to a private residence in 1811 and rented out the hall on the second floor for meetings. An 1828 advertisement displayed two mummies from Egypt. By the 1890s, it returned to its original use and was known as Hotel Warner and was managed by Lydia Cutting. (WHS.)

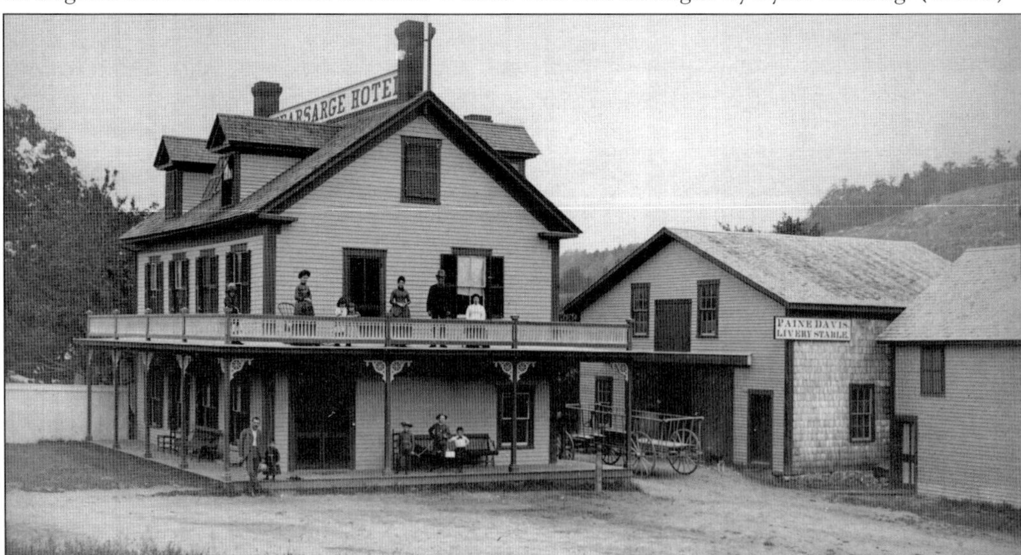

Following the destruction of Nehemiah Ordway's Warner & Kearsarge Mountain Hotel in 1885, Ordway converted the laundry building to accommodate guests. Dormer windows, chimneys, and piazzas embellished the 12 sleeping quarters. Postmaster Paine Davis and his family were the first proprietors. Over the years, it was known as the Adams House and later the Kearsarge Inn. (WHS.)

The Kearsarge Inn advertised "reasonable rates, clean and light rooms with comfortable beds. In our dining room we serve an abundance of well-prepared, good food. During the cold weather each room is steam heated. Daily, weekly, or longer term rates available upon application." The inn was a popular place for area teachers to board while teaching at local schools. (WHS–Pratt.)

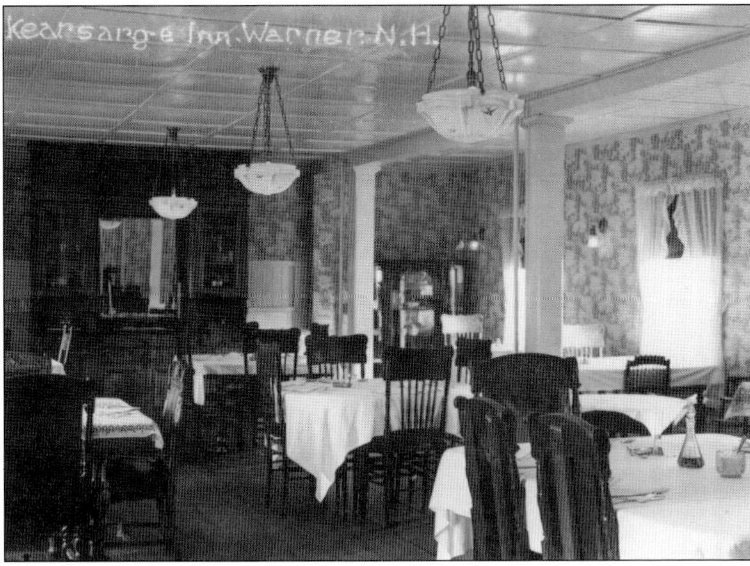

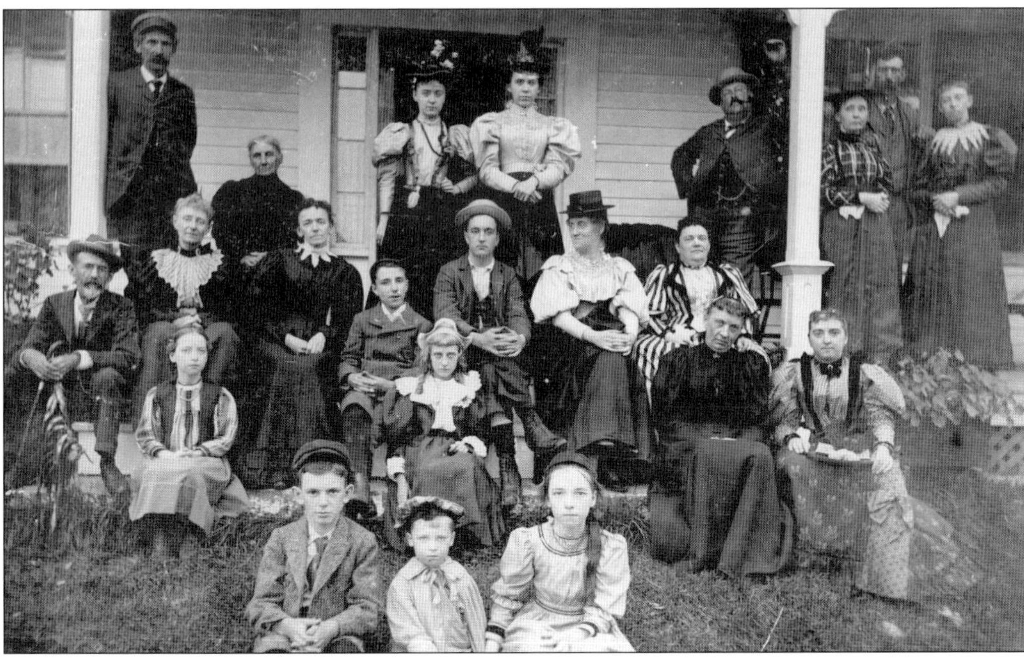

The Butman House (now St. Peter's Masonic Lodge) catered to well-dressed, middle-class tourists in the late 1800s. These men are wearing caps, fedoras, and straw boaters. The dresses feature mutton-chop sleeves and high necklines. "Fashionable Hairdresser, Fred Fitzgerald, Tonsorial Artist" advertised a pool table and fine tobacco for men in 1895. Harriet Stratton opened the first beauty shop on High Street in 1926, when short hair became fashionable for women. (BHS.)

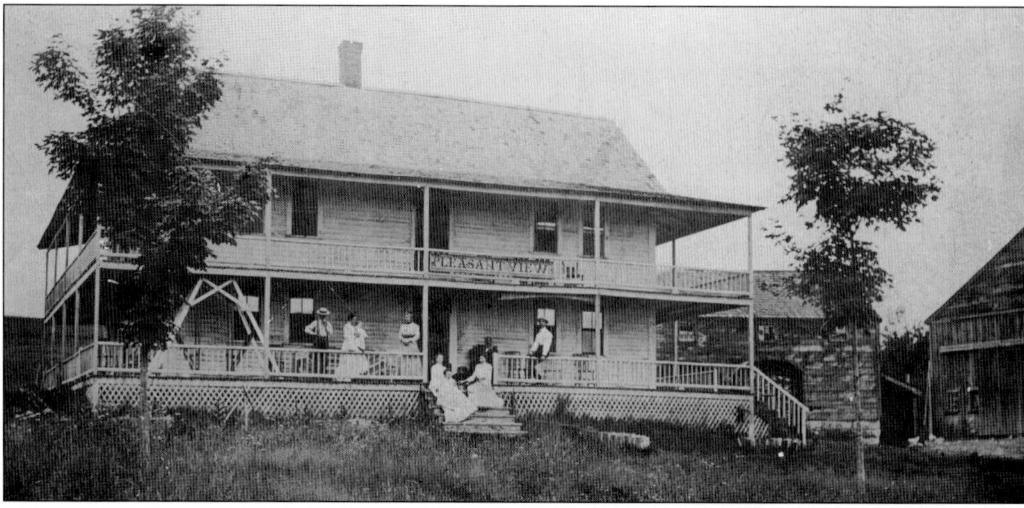

Fred Chase purchased this two-story Colonial on Pumpkin Hill in 1892 for $3,300. He added the two-story piazza, named it Pleasant View, and took in summer boarders. Warner had several boardinghouses scattered throughout the town over the years, including Maple Ridge in the North Village, the Clough's Burnt Hill Farm, the Amesbury, Glendon, Hillcrest, and Riverside in Davisville. (WHS.)

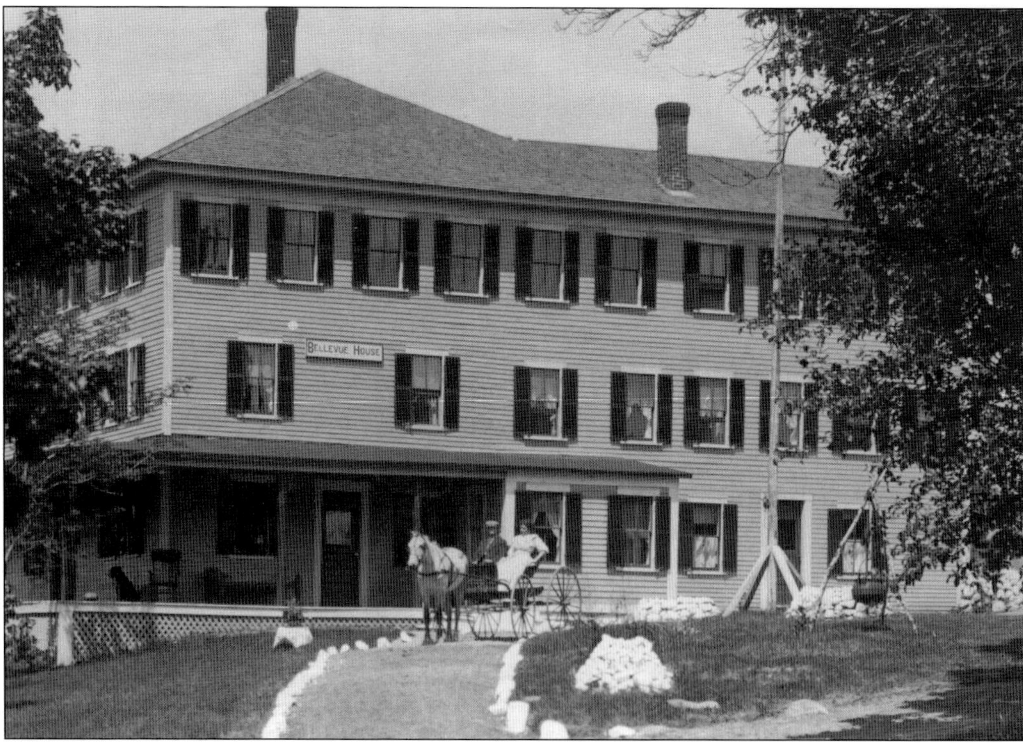

The Bellevue Hotel was run by Henry and Kitty Woods on Cochran Hill. When it burned in the early 1900s, the barn survived and became Fortune's Dance Hall. In the 1940s, advertisements appeared on trees all over town. Dancers would come to hear Frank Fortune's calls, then go to Evie's Snack Bar for refreshments. Eventually, the dances moved to Trow Farm on Fairgrounds Road, which also offered roller-skating. (Courtesy of Steven Hansen.)

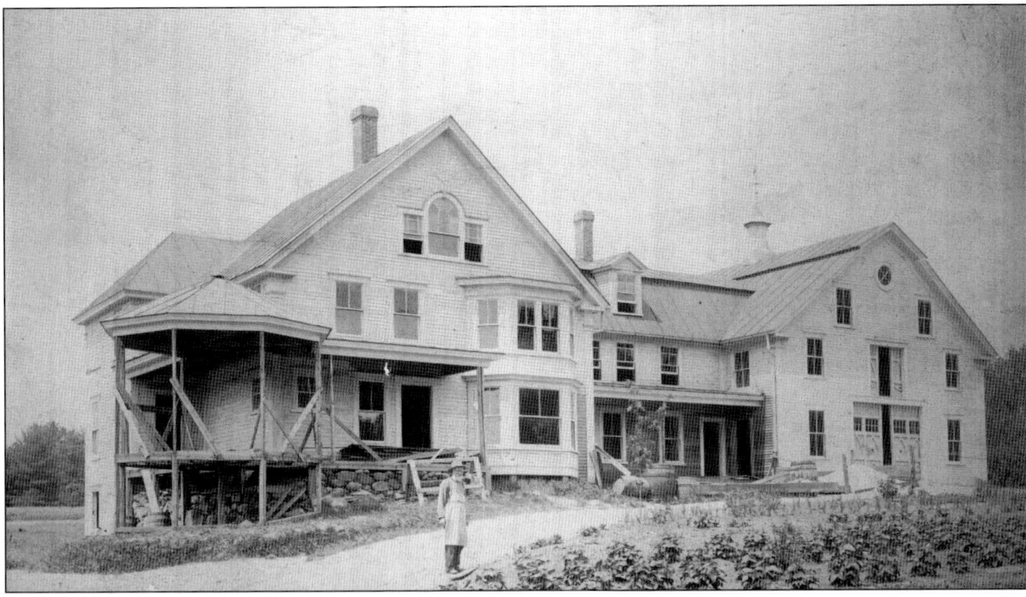

The Charles Gillis House opened in 1897 near the site of the historic Raymond House. The proprietors entertained only summer boarders until 1907 when they stayed open year-round. The business had many names over the years, including Acokaka, Hitching Post Inn, and Green Shutters. The Candlelite Inn, built in 1954, still lights up Lafayette Square with its sparkling presence as a retreat for city-worn travelers. (BHS.)

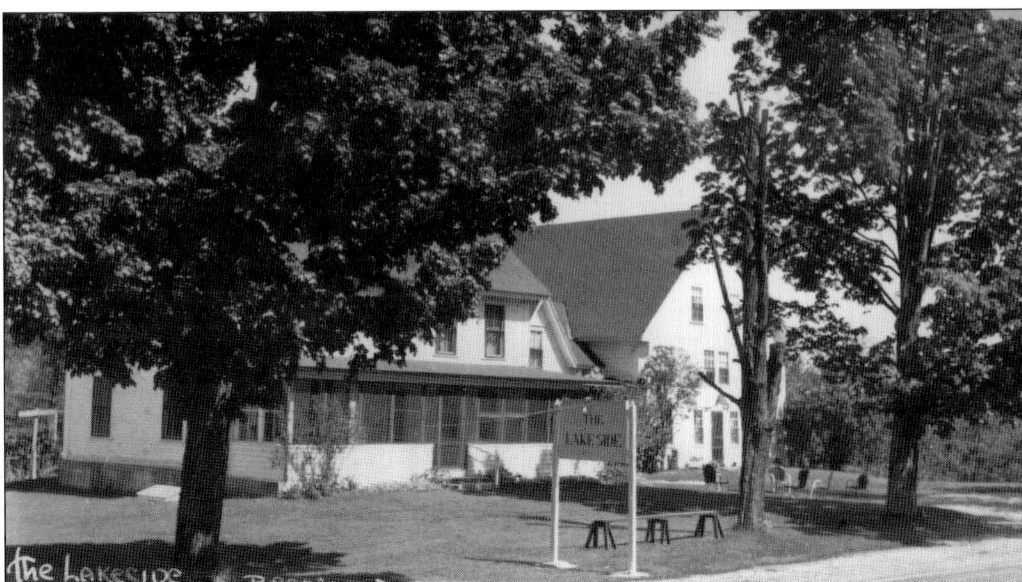

Lakeside has been serving guests at Lake Todd for a century. It is now known as the Appleseed Inn, a popular restaurant and modern-day tavern for locals and visitors alike. In 1945, there was a huge victory celebration with dancing in the streets, a speech by Gov. Charles Dale, and a parade featuring a patriotic float built by the Lakeside staff. Town parades still culminate at this spot today. (Courtesy of Steven Hansen.)

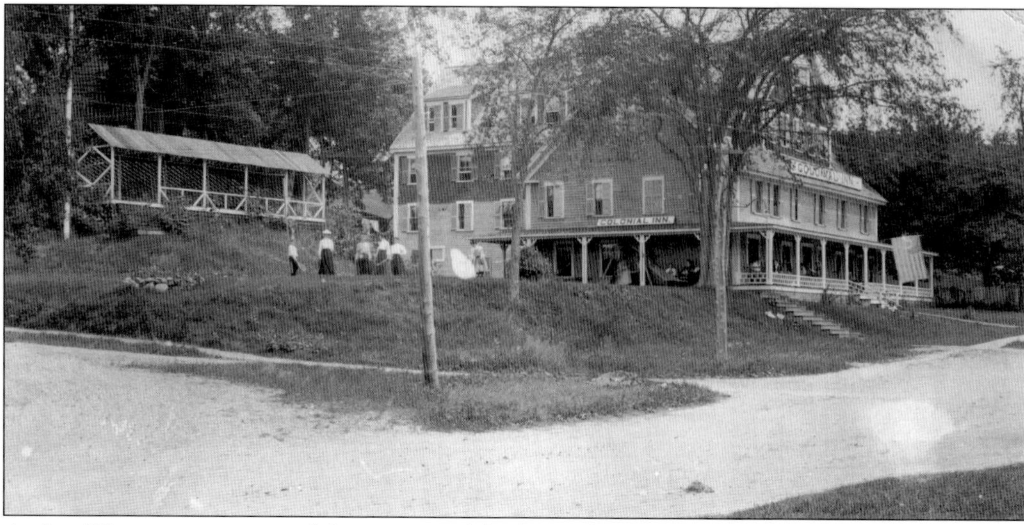

Arthur Thompson renovated the grain and feed store located across from the Main Depot into the Colonial Inn. He added an ell, third floor, bathrooms, and electric lights to accommodate 75 guests. Responding to requests, he added a covered pavilion, golf course, lawn tennis court, croquet grounds, and boat rentals. His hotel was strategically located across from the railroad station. (WHS.)

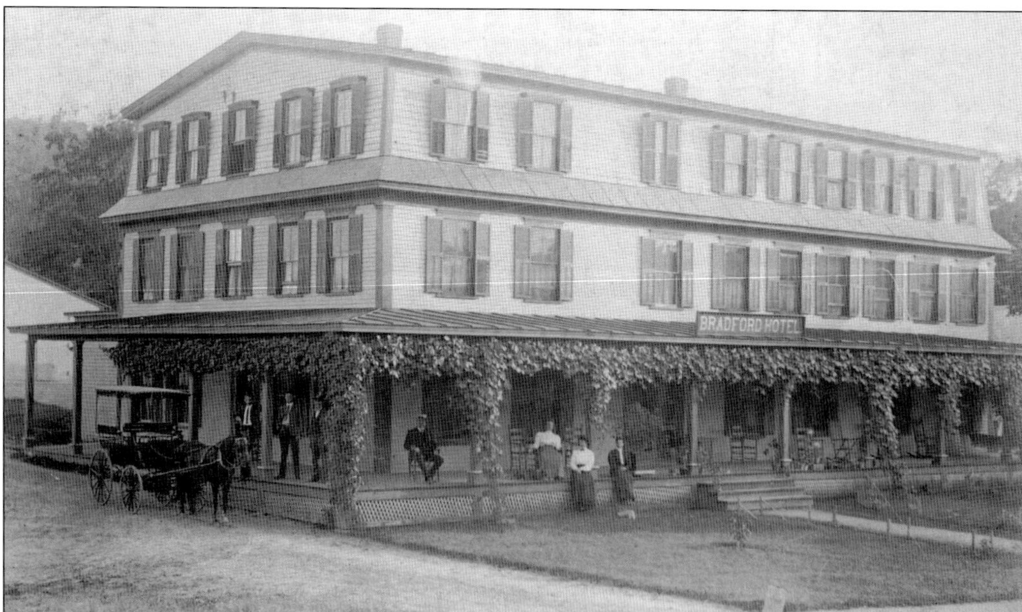

New Bradford Hotel was built in 1815 by Bradford's first postmaster, Samuel Jones. Later, housekeeper Elizabeth Page initiated suppers featuring venison and other game. In 1938, *New York Times* sportswriter Jack Reardon operated it as a sport-lover's paradise. It boasted a raft on Lake Todd, two large barns for dancing and indoor sports, weekly outings, and Sunday afternoon baseball games. "Visitor's comfort is the only house rule." (BHS.)

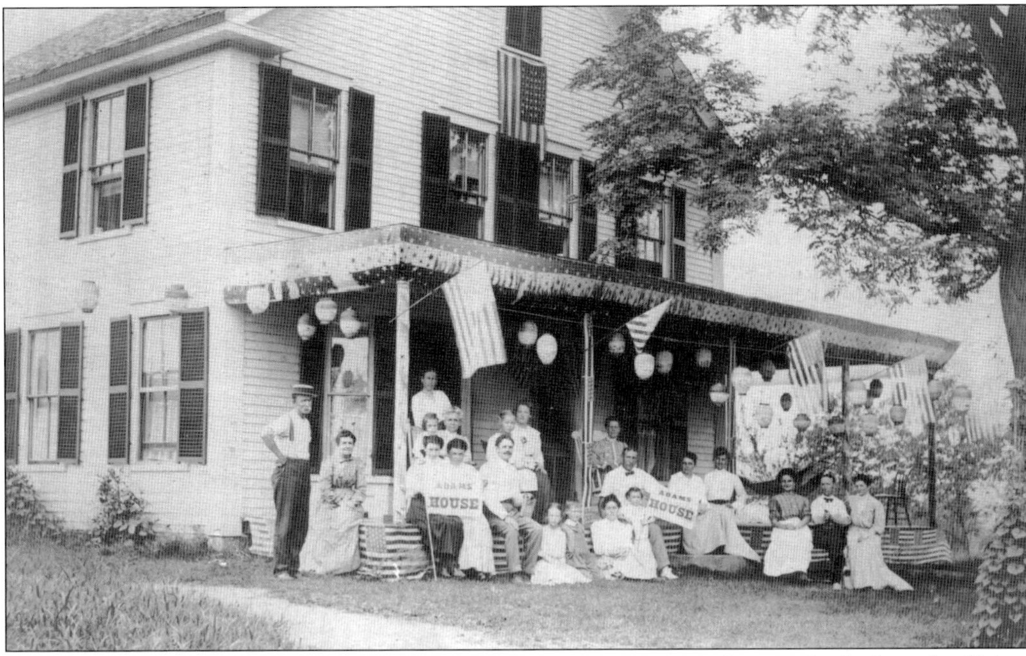

Warner celebrated Fourth of July with speeches, picnics, music, and a parade the length of Main Street. Civil War veterans marched or rode in a decorated stagecoach. Homes and businesses outdid each other with decorations. The Adams House guests enjoy the view of the parade from the porch. After the festivities, a rowdy baseball game was played, followed by fireworks in the evening. (WHS.)

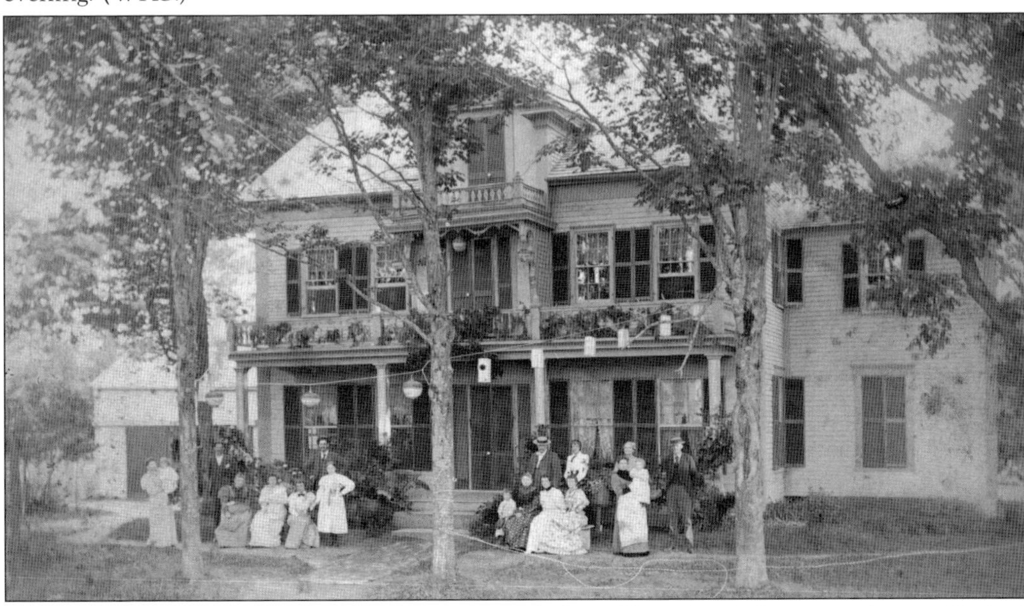

In 1878, Roswell Cummings bought Tappan's Woodside and later, handed it over to his son Gaylord. In 1912, this charming guesthouse accommodated a total of 1,500 guests. The accompanying farm consisted of 75 acres with a magnificent growth of pines that have since been preserved as the Tall Pines. The lanterns lend an extra-festive ambiance to the scene, but one wonders how the guests liked the mosquitoes. (BHS.)

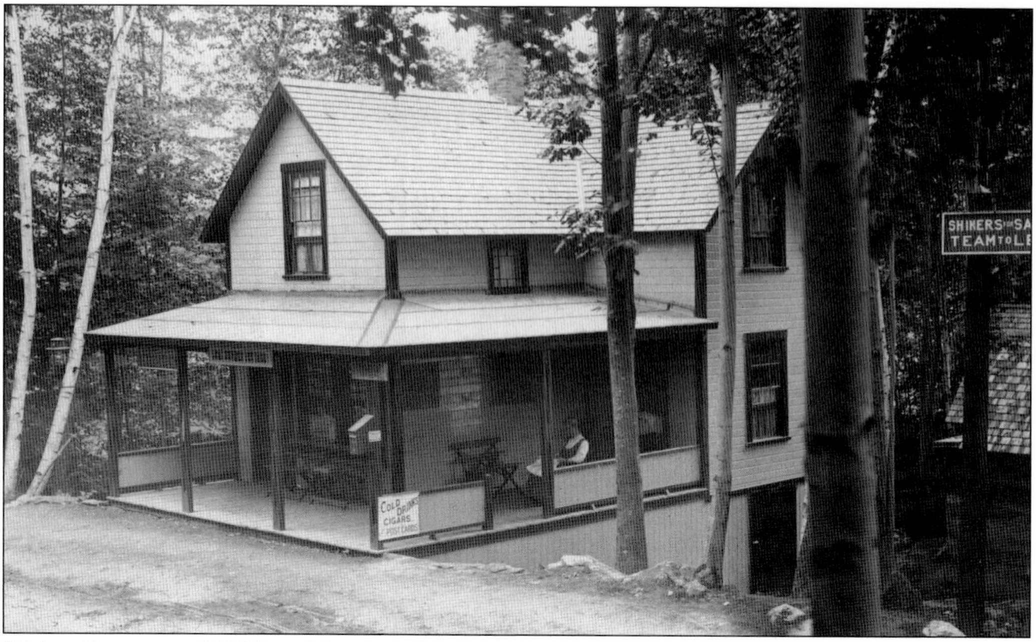

Walter Stevens and William Hart ran this enterprise in the 1930s, when cottages and businesses were springing up around Lake Massasecum. This beautiful body of water attracted many travelers over the years. Tom Cheney Tavern, built in 1790, served as a halfway house between White River Junction and Manchester. It later became Lake Massasecum Inn. Likewise, the original home of early settler Isaac Davis became Massasecum Lodge. (BHS.)

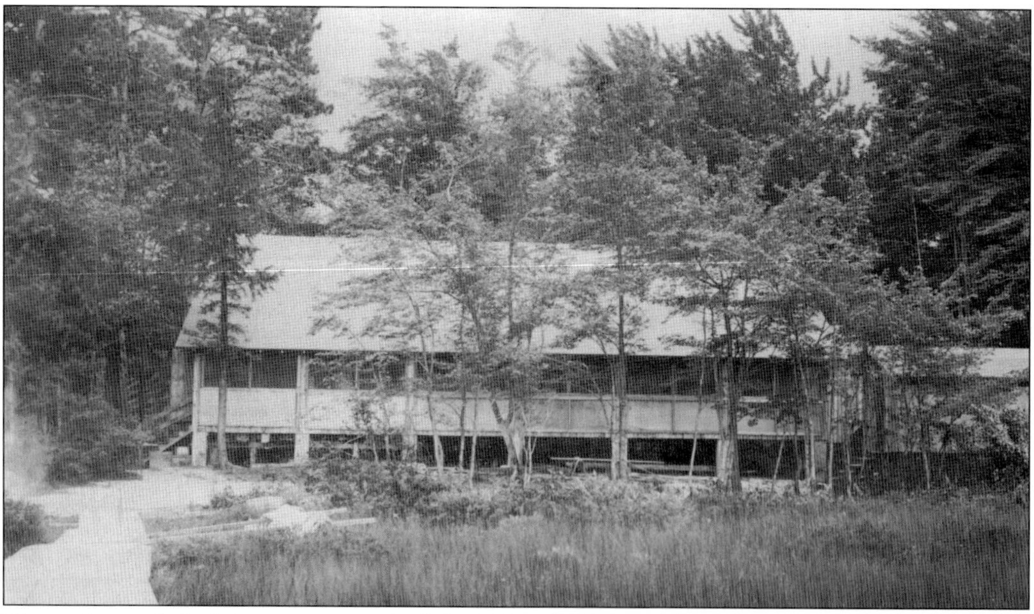

The casino on Lake Massasecum was built by Ralph Gilchrist and partners in 1919. They generated electricity in their own power plant. A stone boat was used to clear the pickerel grass where the beach is now located. Movies, dances, and concerts were held regularly. One Sunday in 1920, young Marshall Gilchrist scooped 75 gallons of ice cream. Guests continue to flock to the casino for this delicious summer treat. (Courtesy of Steven Hansen.)

Six

Pastimes

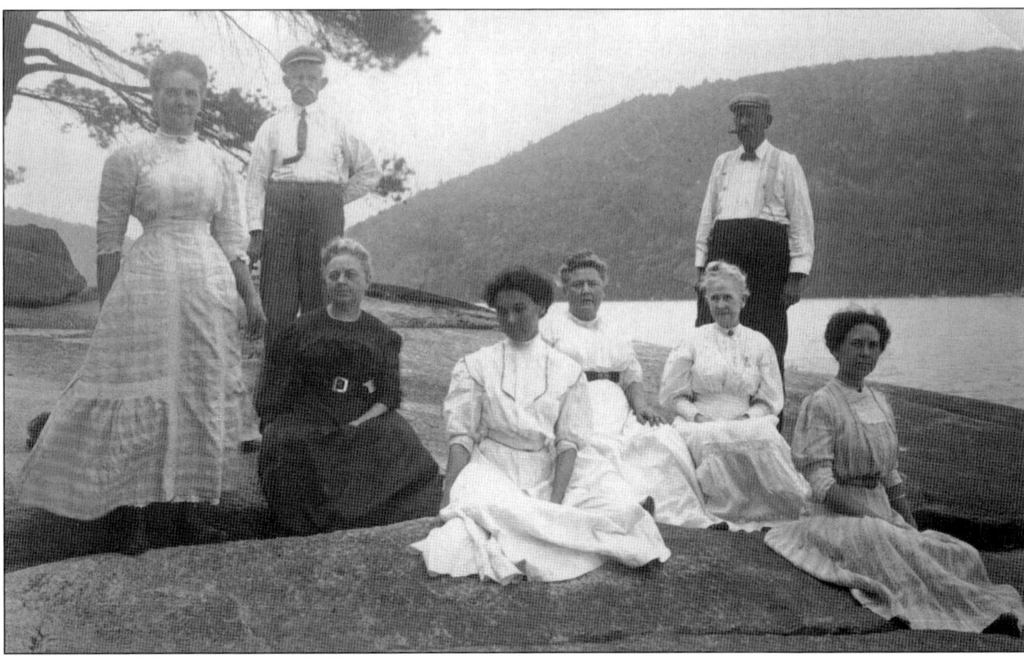

French's Park was willed to the town by John and Emma French in 1929 for "the inhabitants of Bradford and their friends." It was a treat for locals to travel the back roads by carriage and to picnic here. On any hot summer's day, laughter still resounds in this picturesque spot that has changed little over the years. Beach attire, however, has changed a bit. (BHS.)

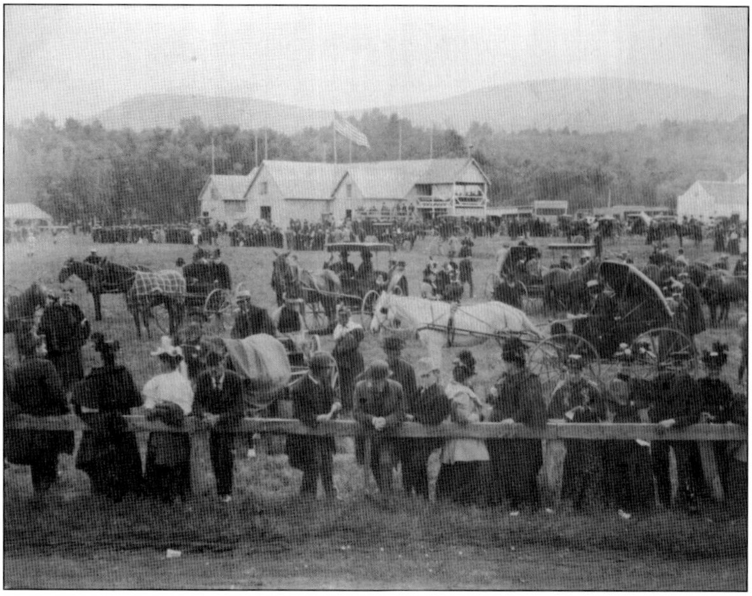

The first street fair was organized in 1871 by Stephen Pattee. Due to its success, Nehemiah Ordway laid out River Bow Park on land he owned along the Warner River. He had pavilions, exhibition halls, and a racetrack built. The fair was organized by the Kearsarge Agricultural and Mechanic Association. One year, 428 teams of oxen participated in the annual parade around the racetrack. (WHS.)

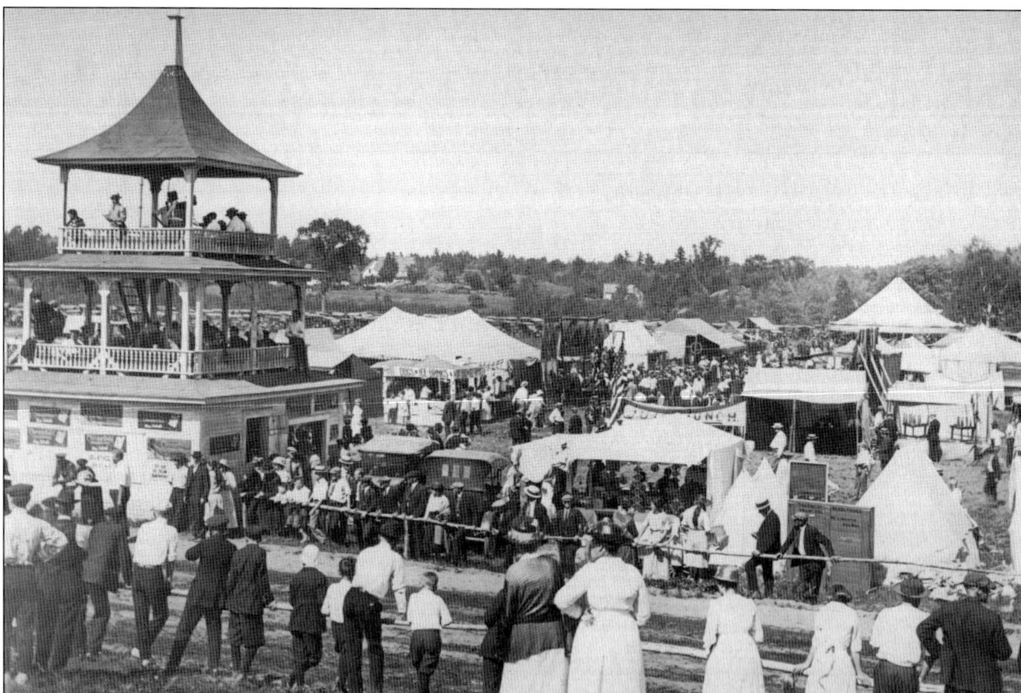

Established in 1875, the Annual Fair of Bradford and Newbury Agricultural and Mechanics Society became a smashing success that continued into the 1920s. Farm families came from miles around to exhibit produce, animals, and crafts. The Mile of Midway, Ferris wheel, sky divers (including the dog "Gyp"), an 80-oxen parade, horse pulling, hot-air balloon ascensions, racing cyclists, baseball games, and band music added to the agricultural and machinery displays. (Courtesy of Steven Hansen.)

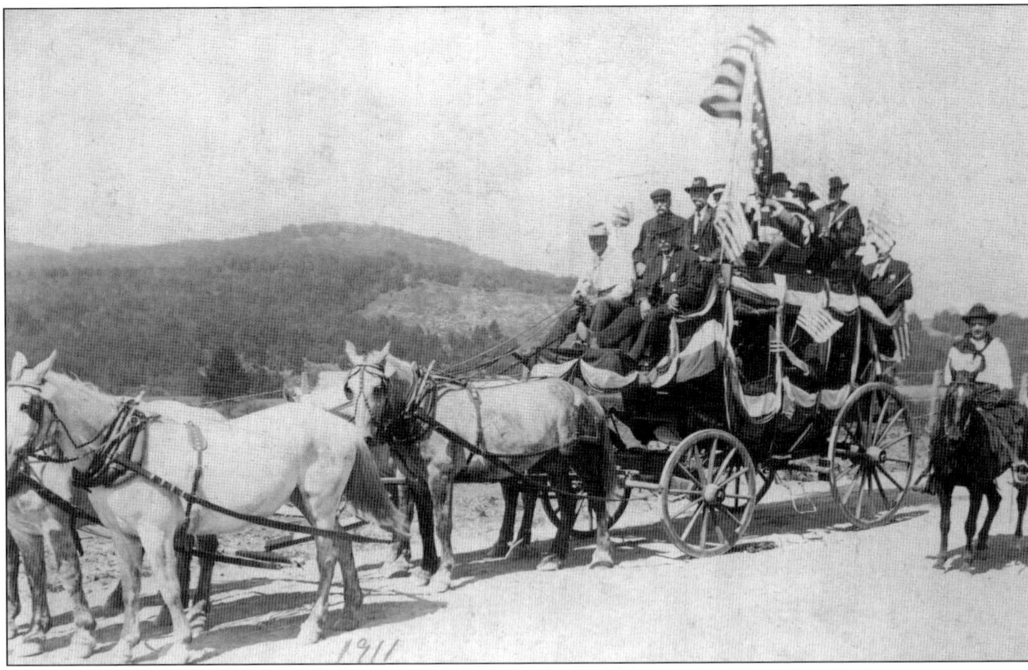

Col. Arthur Thompson sits with the stagecoach driver during this Fourth of July parade. Many of Warner's Civil War veterans are riding in and on top of this gaily decorated coach, making its way along the Plains section of Main Street. On Memorial Day in 1892, a dinner was served at the town hall to more than 800 people in honor the Grand Army of the Republic. (WHS.)

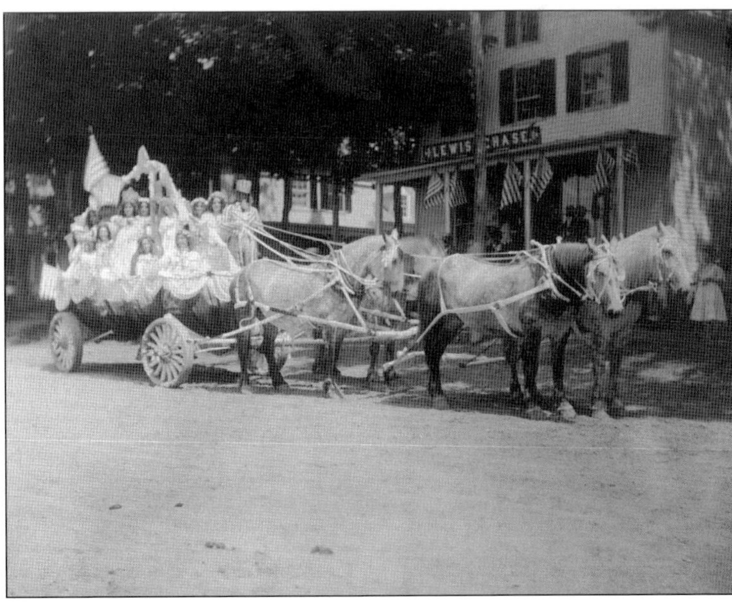

Several young ladies, dressed in white, rode in a tastefully trimmed hayrack driven by Uncle Sam in the Fourth of July parade of 1906. Several masqueraders on foot and horseback accompanied a variety of floats. About 400 people attended the rival baseball game between Henniker and Warner after a brief shower. Unfortunately, Warner lost 2 to 0. (WHS.)

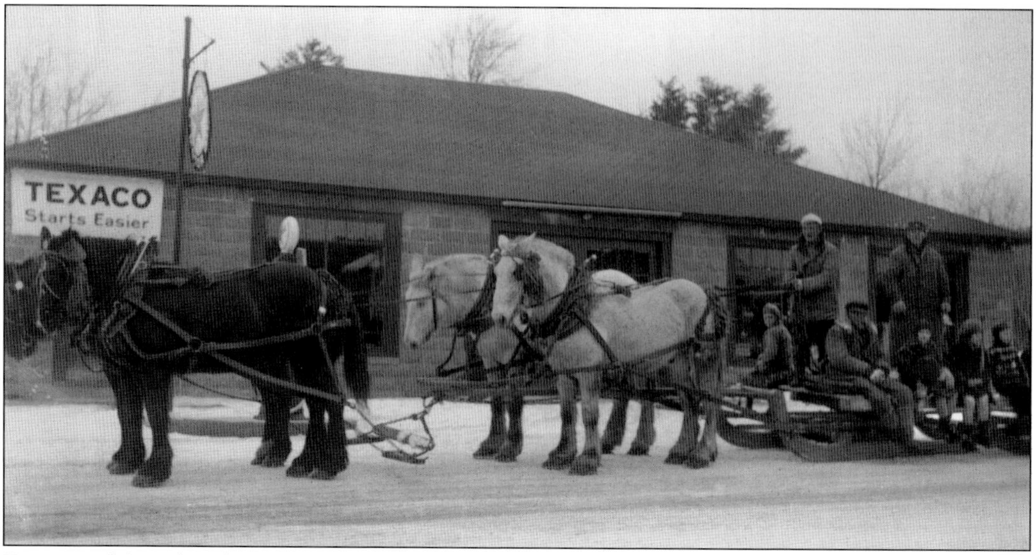

For several decades, the town held a winter carnival featuring a full weekend of entertainment. In 1934, there was a 57-float parade, plus skating, ski jumping, and snowshoe competitions, as well as a queen crowned at the Carnival Ball. In the background, a familiar structure stands on Main Street. It has housed many businesses over the years, including a general store, a soda fountain, a hardware store, and a garage. (BHS.)

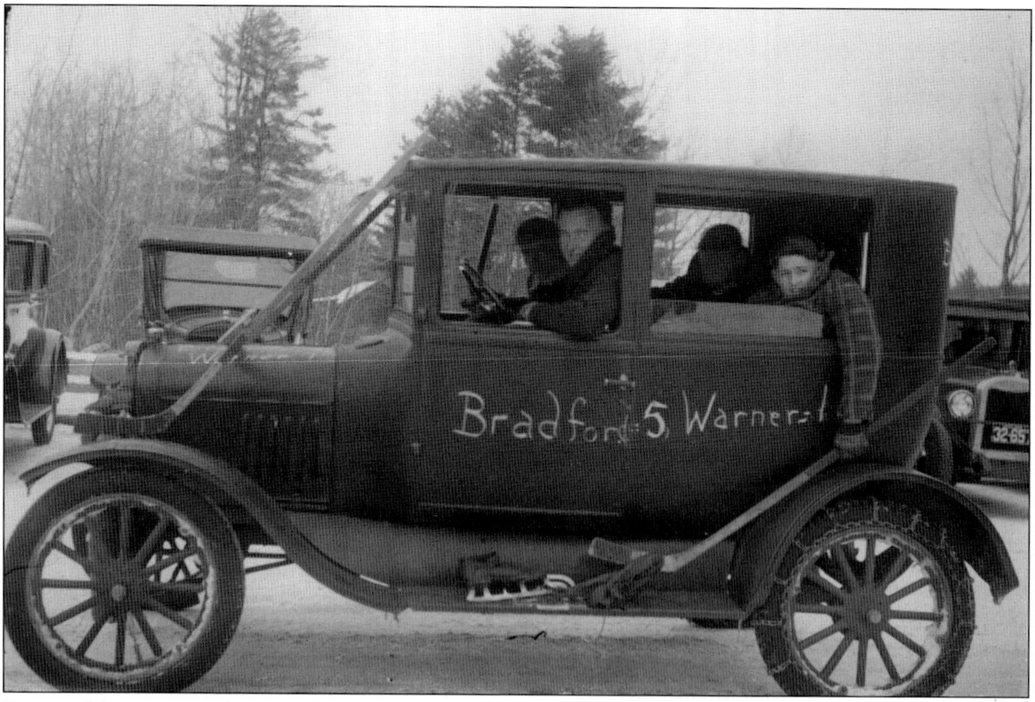

Pictured here around 1920, these happy victors most likely played their hockey game on Todd Pond. Carnivals were held near the dam on ice cleared by Doodlebugs, or tractor contraptions. Hay bale–sized blocks of ice were harvested to build an icehouse from which the Woman's Club would serve hot dogs. Scrub hockey was also played on the fish-rearing pool during those rare winters when ice froze deep before the first significant snowfall. (Courtesy of Steven Hansen.)

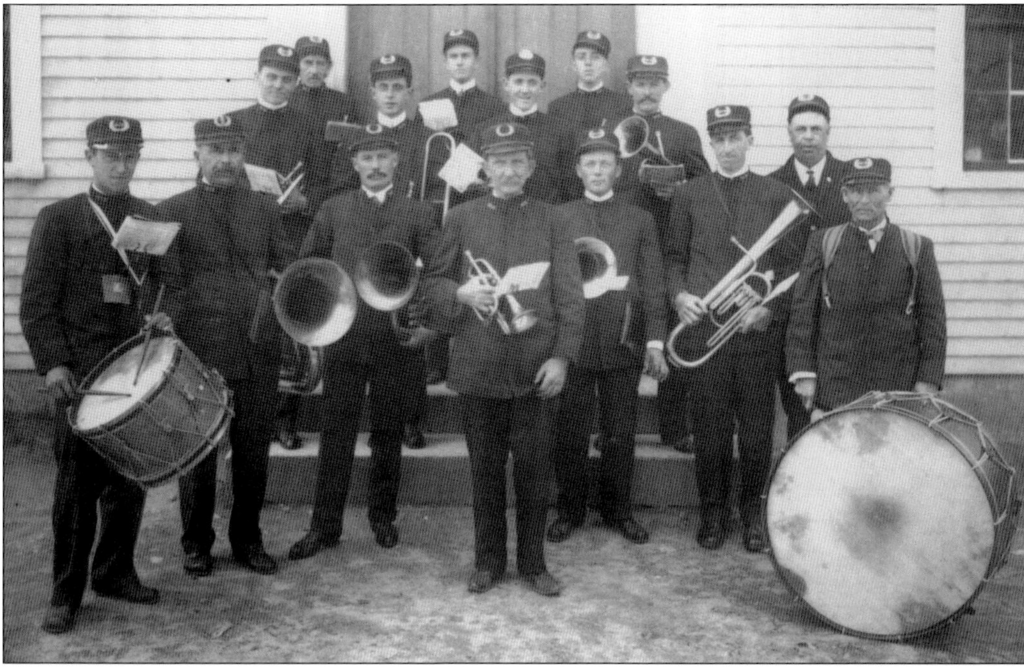

The Bradford Band members, proudly wearing their new uniforms, stand in front of town hall on Memorial Day in 1913 with leader Elbridge Hoyt (center). The Bradford Band began in the early 1880s and featured some of the town's finest musicians. They played at most dedications, dances, and parades in both Bradford and neighboring towns. In 1933, Warren Smith established a fund that continues today to support musical events in town. (BHS.)

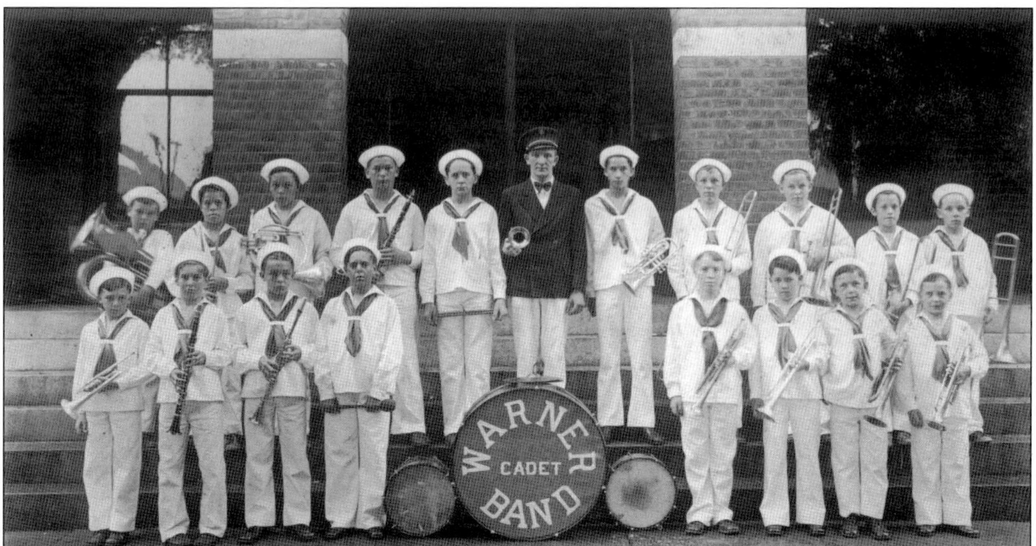

The Warner Cadet Band made its first appearance at the 1930 class day exercises at Simonds Free High School. The youngsters in new uniforms were directed by Hugh Flanders. Flanders, a mail carrier and hotel owner of Maple Ridge with his wife, Lib, was also known as a bandleader. His group played in Warner and surrounding towns as happy crowds swirled and danced to the Big Band sound. (WH –Pratt.)

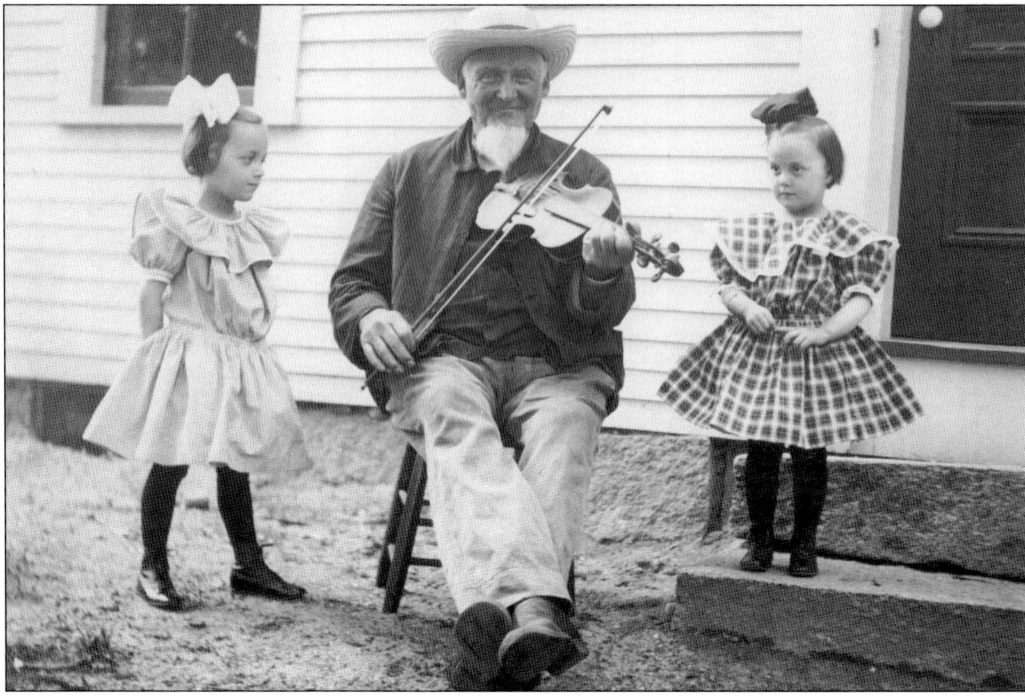

Ezekial Hadley is pictured here with his granddaughters Earline and Carolyn. Fiddles were featured at everything from fancy dress balls to kitchen junkets. Hadley's Ideal Orchestra, with Laura Sanborn on piano, played at the Grand Calico Ball in 1900. An original bass viol is on display at Bradford Center. It was made by the musical Hoyts to play selections from Watt's hymns at the meetinghouse dedication in 1838 and, later, at dances. (BHS.)

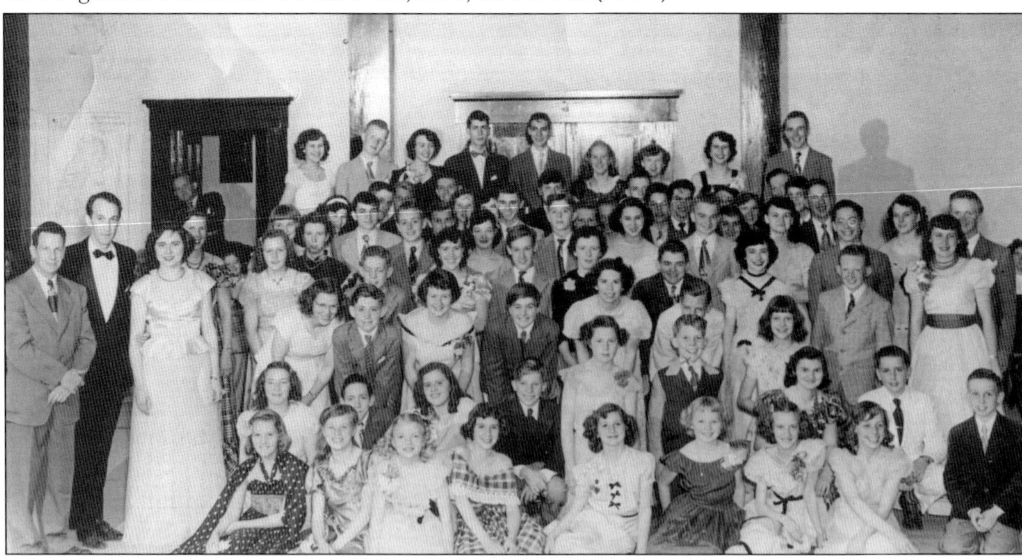

Charles Ballard's Dancing Class, pictured here in the 1940s, invited young people to attend sessions in both Bradford and Warner. This photograph, taken upstairs in the Bradford Town Hall, shows the ticket booth in the background. Ballard and teacher Marion Humphrey kept a tight rein on etiquette and attire. There was a receiving line at every session, a Grand Ball with evening gowns, and a Grand March every spring. (Courtesy of Steven Hansen.)

This curious sight of an outdoor organ features Mabel Gardner at the keyboard at a local fair. Organs were common in meetinghouses because they required little tuning and could withstand temperature changes better than pianos. Hymns were familiar and uplifting for everyone and were relatively easy to learn by rote. Shape notes (triangular, square, round) were introduced in New England in 1801 to facilitate congregational and community singing. (BHS.)

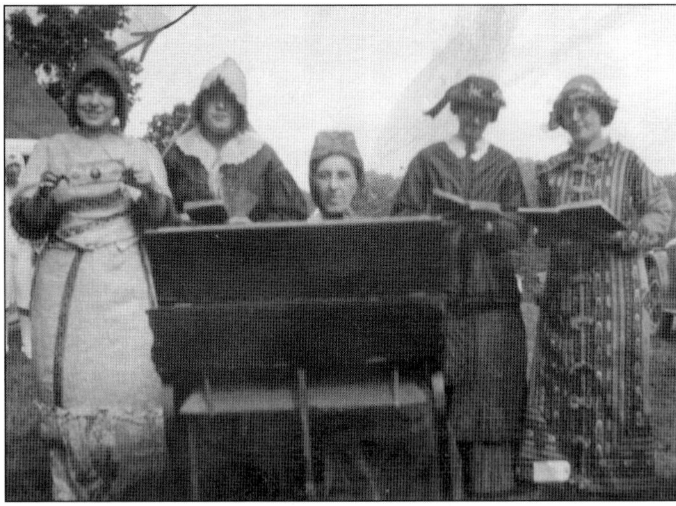

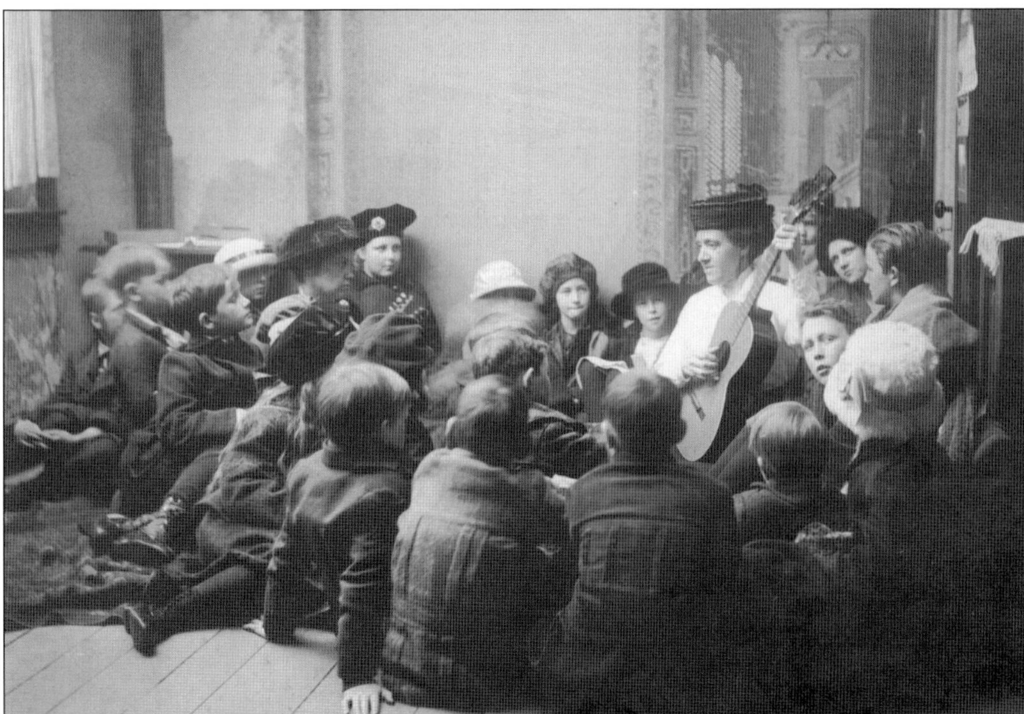

These teachers are leading the children in song with their guitars. Many women taught voice and music in town. Susie Carroll, wife of a successful merchant, chose to continue her musical career by teaching piano to adults and children. Recitals were given every year to an enthusiastic crowd at the town hall. She also performed at weddings and funerals, as well as taught at the high school. (WHS–Hardy.)

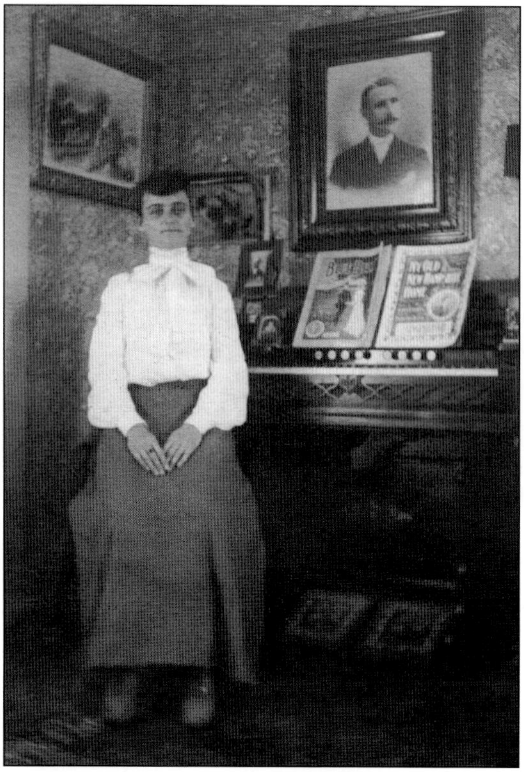

Mary Lizzie Wilson, seen at left, was one of several women who taught piano in town, along with Helen Felch and Clara Blanchard. Schoolteacher Martha Cilley was also a fine pianist who accompanied her students in operettas, such as *Cinderella in Flowerland*, performed in the town hall opera house in 1916. When Ed Hadley started showing silent motion pictures in the town hall in 1910, a pianist was also employed to play the musical score. (BHS.)

Bradford-born Will Cressy and his wife, Blanche Dayne, were world-renowned vaudeville performers who played here in 1919. Amateur productions included *Ye Olde Deestrict Skule* (1899), an all-female cast in *Samantha Allen at the Court of Fame* (1908), and *Cranberry Corners* (1915). Bradford also owns a theatrical backdrop painted by Charles Washington Henry, a famous 19th-century artist who traveled from town to town, presenting vaudeville performances. (BHS.)

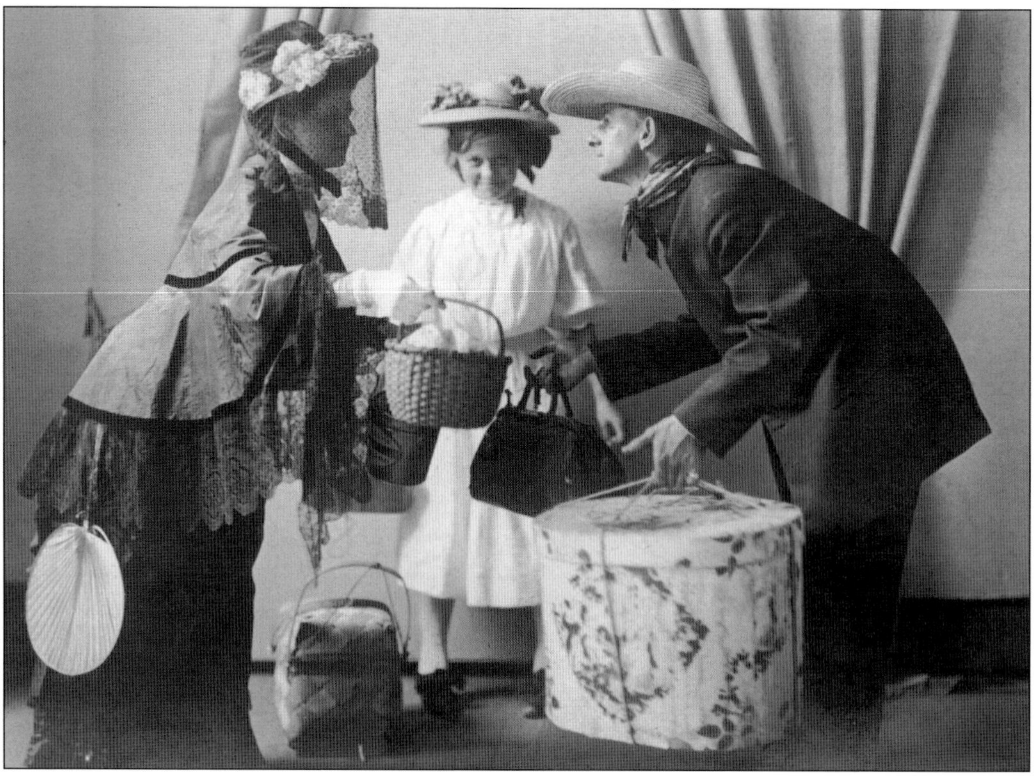

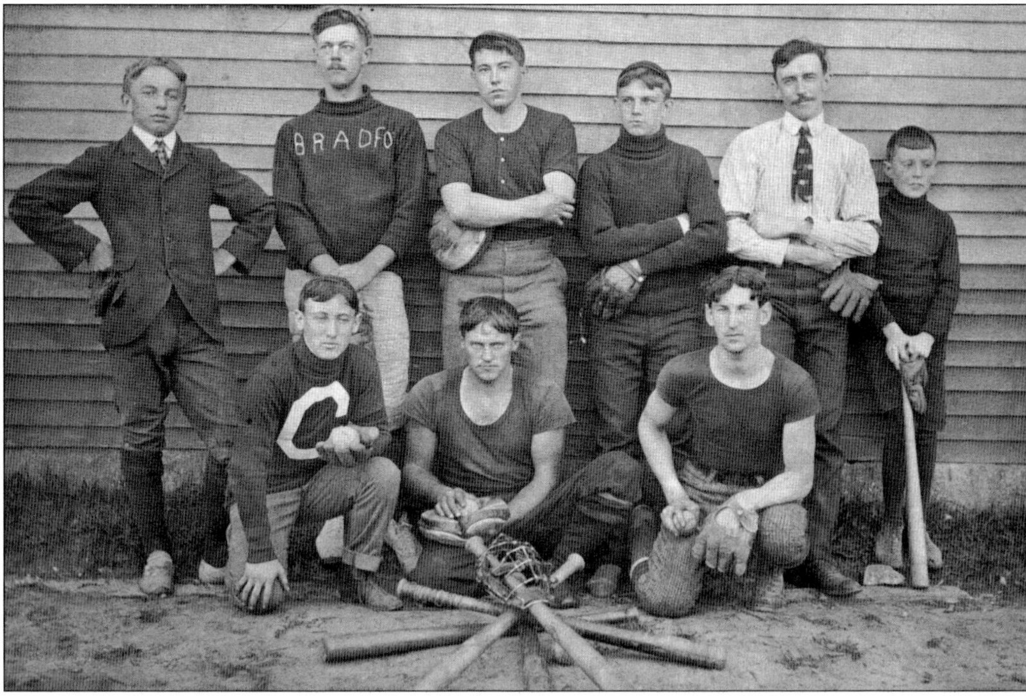

Bradford has boasted many baseball teams over the years, and America's favorite pastime remains vital today in its youth sports programs. In 1947, Brown-Shattuck Field was designated as a memorial to two local veterans. Baseball games were also played on Sunny Plain, the town green, and on the railroad grounds. The Indians and the Squaws, two basketball teams, played upstairs in the town hall in the 1930s. (Everett Kittredge.)

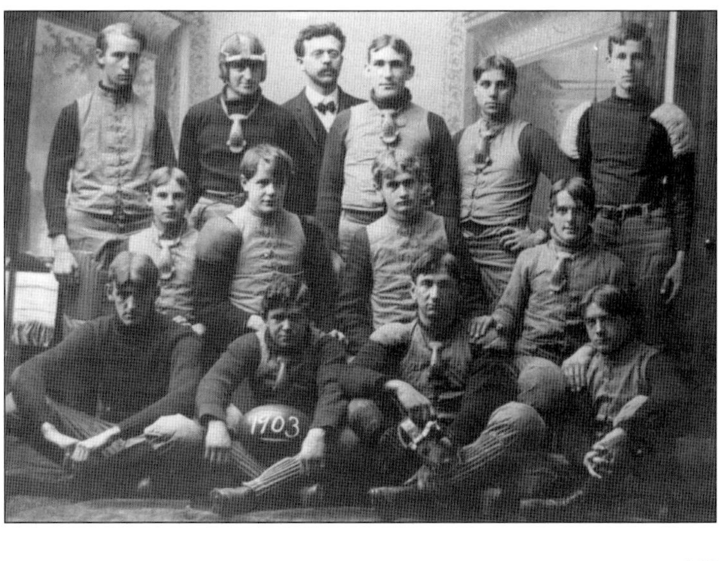

The first Simonds Free High School football game was held in October 1903. Despite the rain, 200 spectators attended. Newport's high school team had more experience and outplayed the newly formed squad by a score of 30-0. The Dartmouth coach had only four days of practice with the inexperienced squad. Despite the thumping, the town and the team were looking forward to the next match-up. (WHS.)

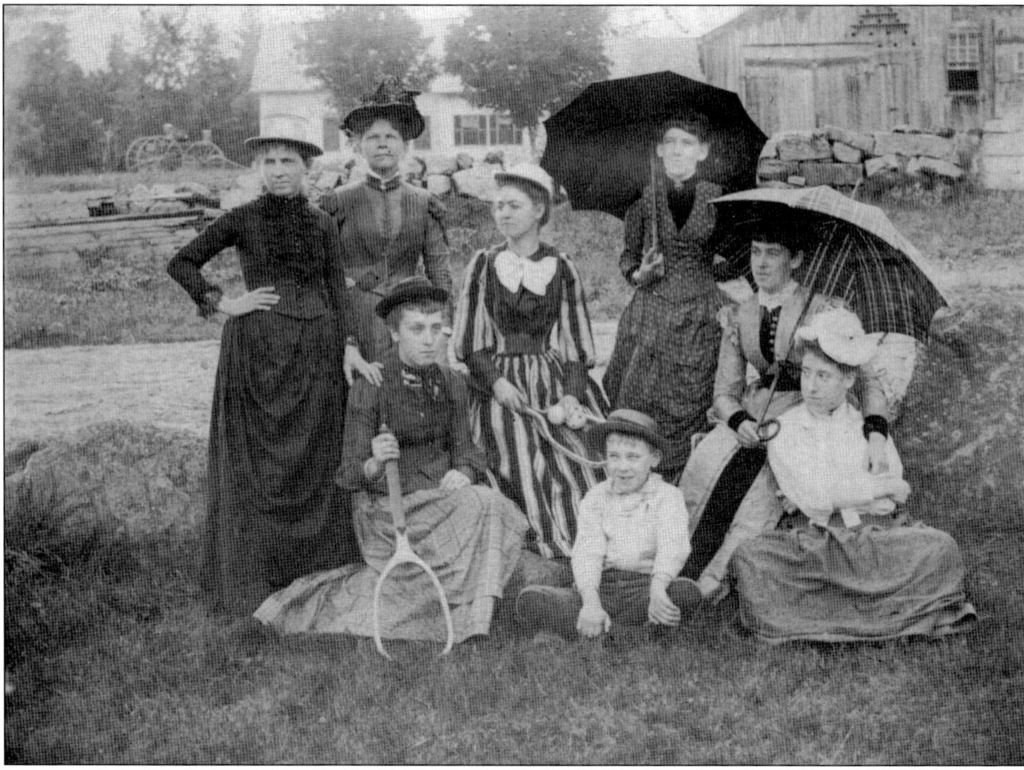

These women are getting ready to play a dainty game of badminton on the Baptist church lawn. Perhaps they are waiting for a band concert or a parade. Over the decades, various groups, such as the Un-Named Club and Bradford Fish and Game, organized diversions in town. The popular tradition of Fourth of July fireworks began in the 1950s when the town allocated $15 for the event. (Courtesy of Steven Hansen.)

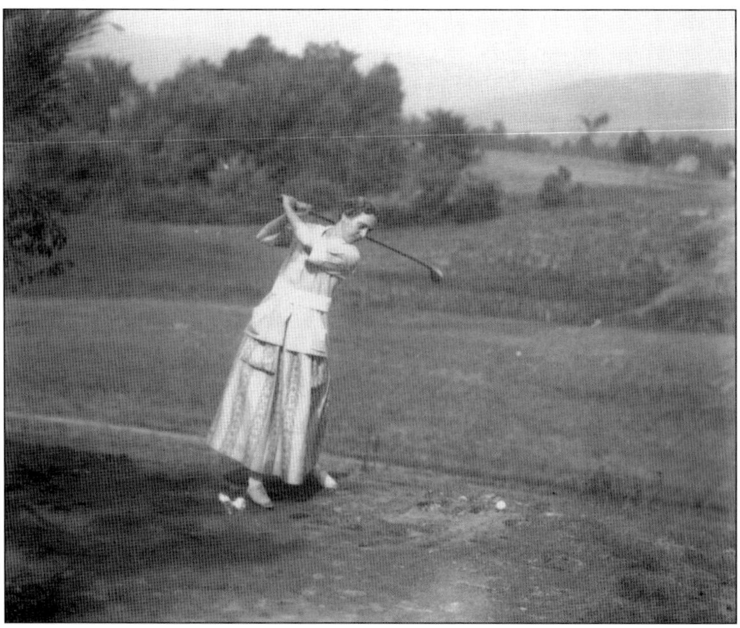

As the Industrial Age progressed, physical labor demands were mitigated and recreational sports came into fashion. This c. 1920 image shows a female golfer in a modest calf-length dress playing on the nine-hole Pleasant View course. Elsewhere in town, Bald Sunapee Country Club offered one of the area's first 18-hole courses. In later years, the Loch Lyndon golf course thrived here. (Courtesy of Steven Hansen.)

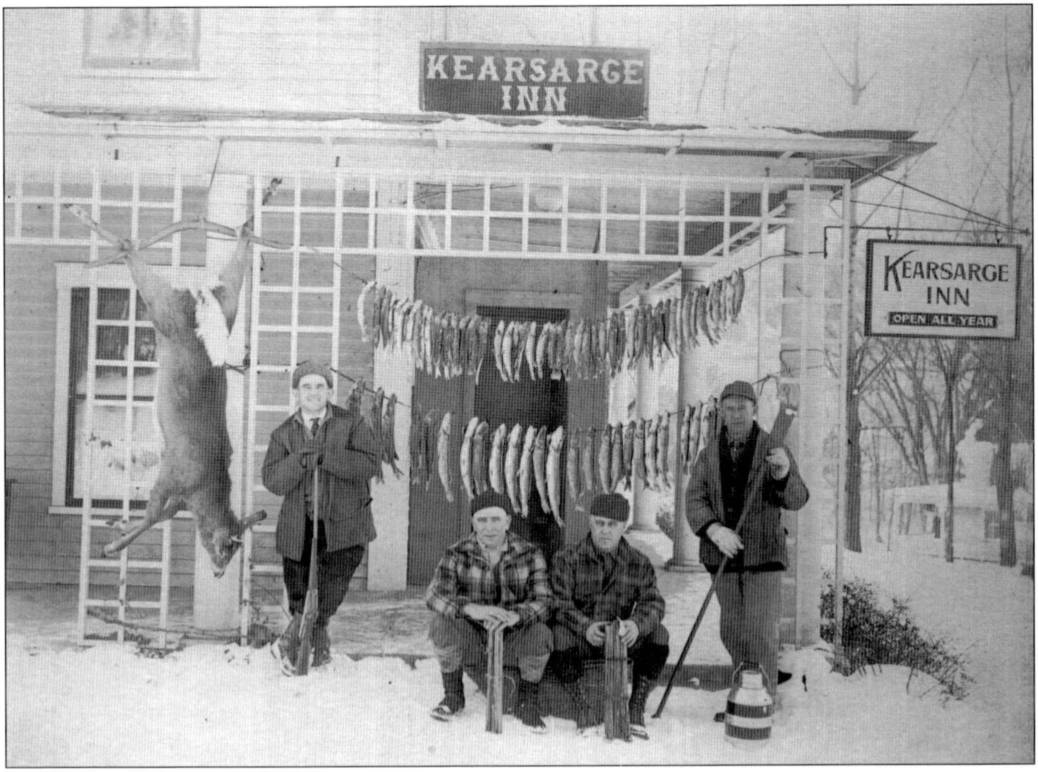

Elizabeth and Charles Malchow operated the Kearsarge Inn from 1915 to the 1940s. Charles supplemented their income by working as a deputy for the New Hampshire Fish and Game Department. He often served as a guide to the sportsmen who stayed at the inn. He escorted them to secret hunting and fishing spots. These men, with their rifle and tip-ups, show off their catch on the front porch. (WHS.)

Joseph Sanborn may have caught these fish on the West Branch, but no self-respecting fisherman would reveal his favorite spot. Fishing was done for sustenance, sale, and fun. Bert Hall peddled fish by horse and wagon throughout surrounding towns. His fish stock would arrive by train the night before. He would rise at 3:00 a.m. to clean the fish by lantern light and would continue on his rounds until 8:00 p.m. (BHS.)

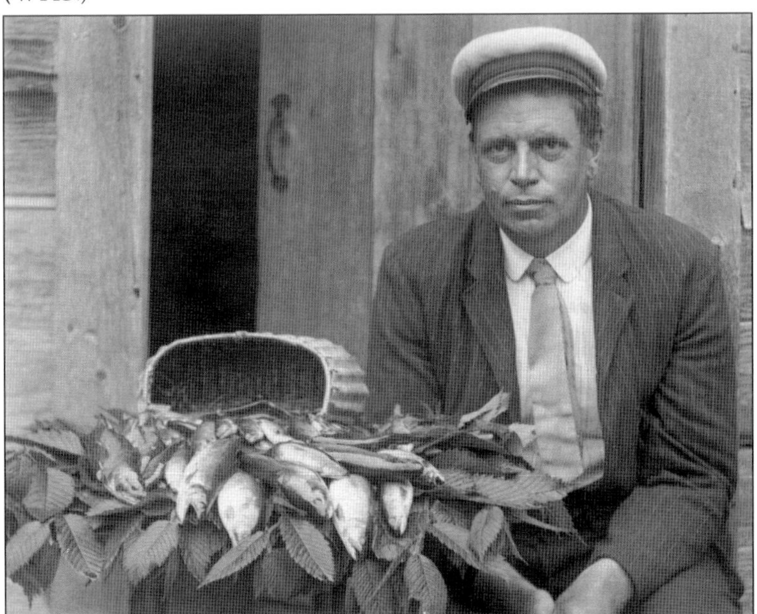

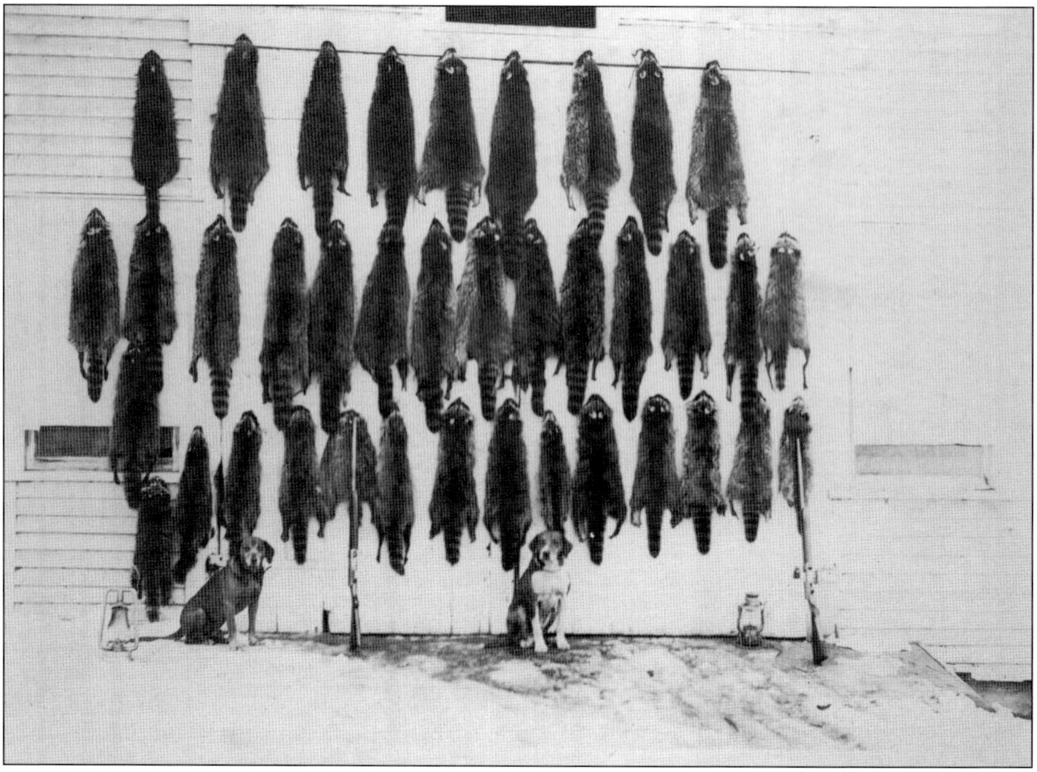

Raccoon hunting was a popular pastime, and hunters had to have a good coon dog to lead the chase. Herb Martin and Oliver Harris shot these raccoons in the 1920s. The dog on the right was Herb's dog named Ring, and Harris had borrowed a dog. Several men and boys ran trap lines in the winter for beaver, mink, otter, and an occasional bobcat. (WHS.)

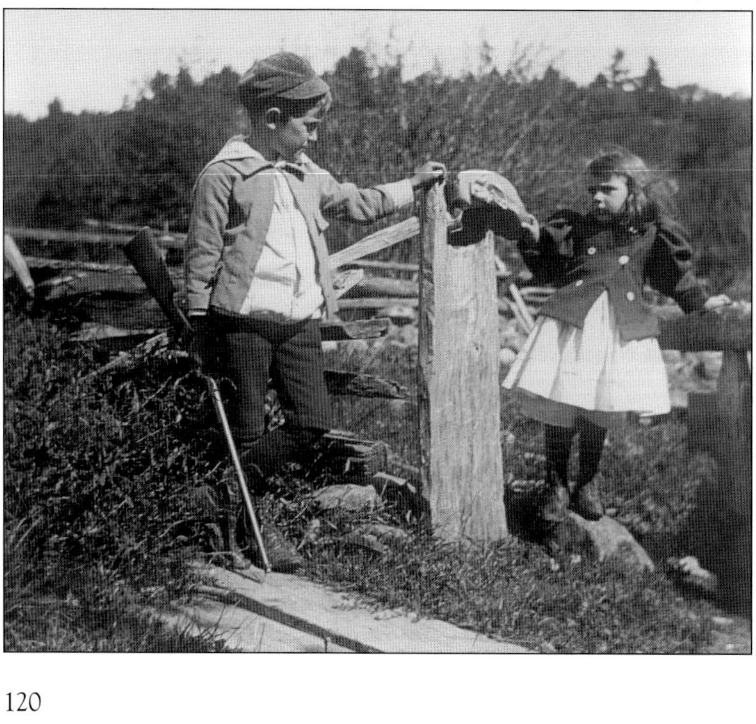

Ralph and Helen Badger, residents of Lowell, Massachusetts, are visiting their relatives, Herman and Sophronia Badger, in the Minks. Ralph holds his gun and Helen places her straw hat on the fence post. Over the course of four years, their mother, Jennie, compiled photograph albums of their visits to Warner with images of the children fishing, helping with chores, and playing on the farm. (WHS.)

Nine-year-old Theron Jameson stands for his formal portrait in 1915. He is displaying his corn, which won first prize at the Grange Fair. That year, he sold $5 worth of golden bantam sweet corn, which he raised on 1/32 of an acre. (BHS.)

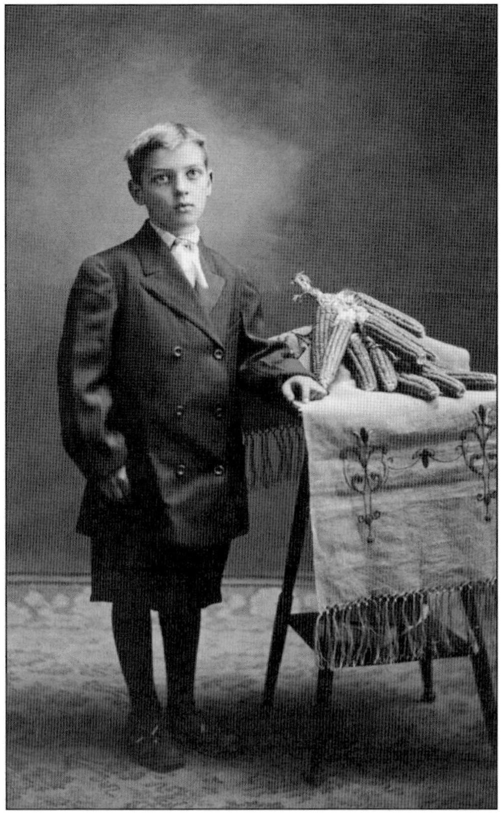

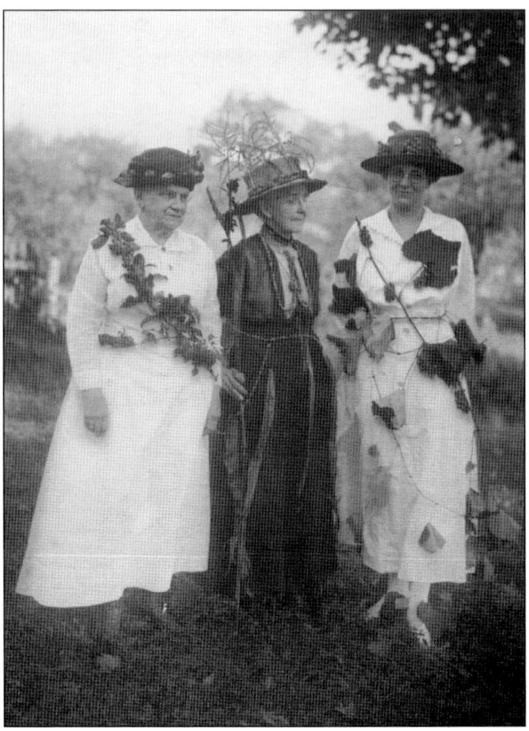

Isabelle Greeley, known as the founder of the Mercy Hathaway White Chapter of the Daughters of the American Revolution, is pictured here on the left with two other members of the local Grange. They are dressed in costumes to represent the Worthy Patrons of Husbandry, Flora, Ceres, and Pomona (or Flowers, Grain, and Fruit). Established in 1875 for the promotion of agriculture, the Bradford Grange continued until 1958. (BHS.)

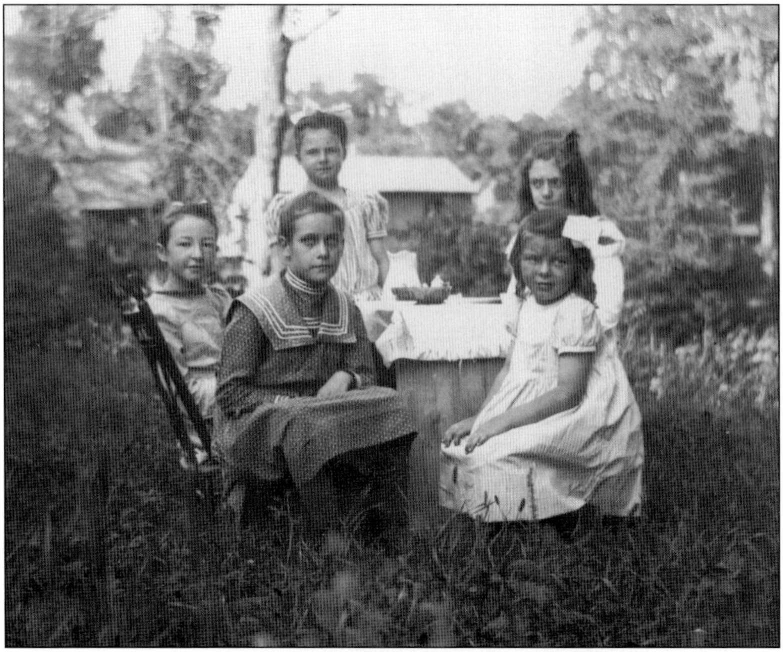

Abby Cilley (seated far left) and her playmates in Waterloo are dressed in their Sunday best and enjoying a summertime tea party. Abby and her sister Ruth attended the Waterloo schoolhouse, and their family boarded the schoolteacher. Abby became the mother of the "Belles of Melvin" after her marriage to Elmer Bartlett in 1912. (WHS.)

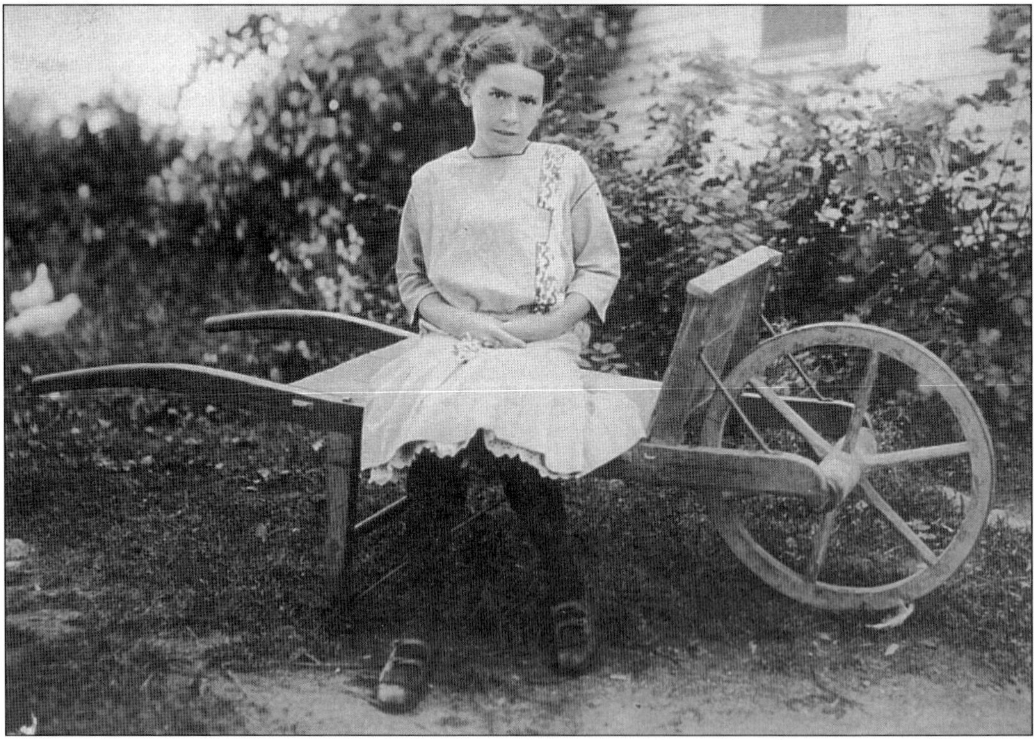

Geraldine Adams is sitting pretty on an open wheelbarrow in her family's dooryard around 1900. Itinerant photographers would take family photographs to sell. Real-photo postcards were a convenient mode of communication and became a craze that appealed to all social classes. For a penny, a person could send an invitation up or down the railroad track and be sure of its exact delivery time. (Courtesy of Sonny Harris.)

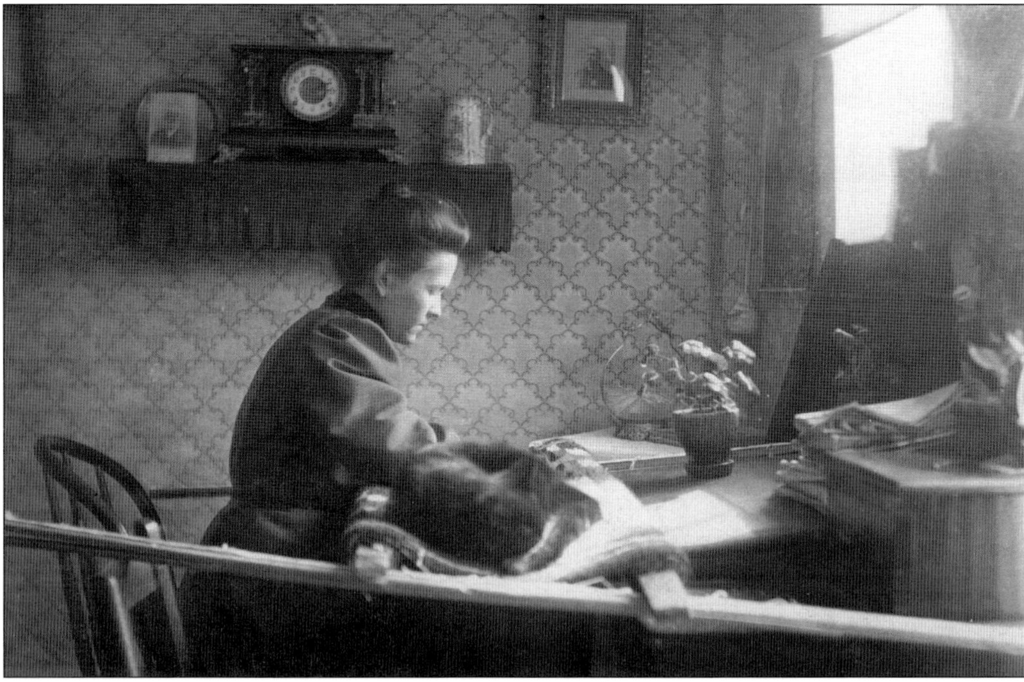

Laura Sanborn shares a quiet hour with her cat around 1900. She lived in this house, which is still located in Bradford Center, until she was nearly 100 years old. Her copious notes and collection of photographs and artifacts have proved to be valuable assets to the Bradford Historical Society. She is hooking a rug from wool remnants to grace her home. Nothing was wasted a century ago, as recycling was a necessary practice. (BHS.)

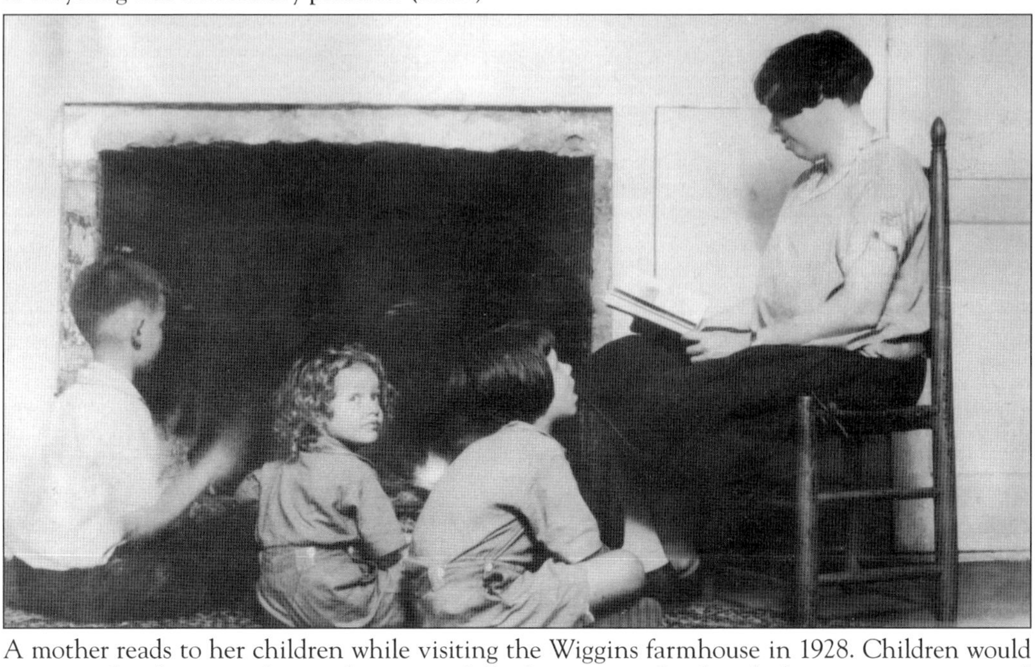

A mother reads to her children while visiting the Wiggins farmhouse in 1928. Children would continue their lessons at home when it was difficult to get to school, and education was recognized as a means of advancing a family's prospects. (Courtesy of Connie Dayton.)

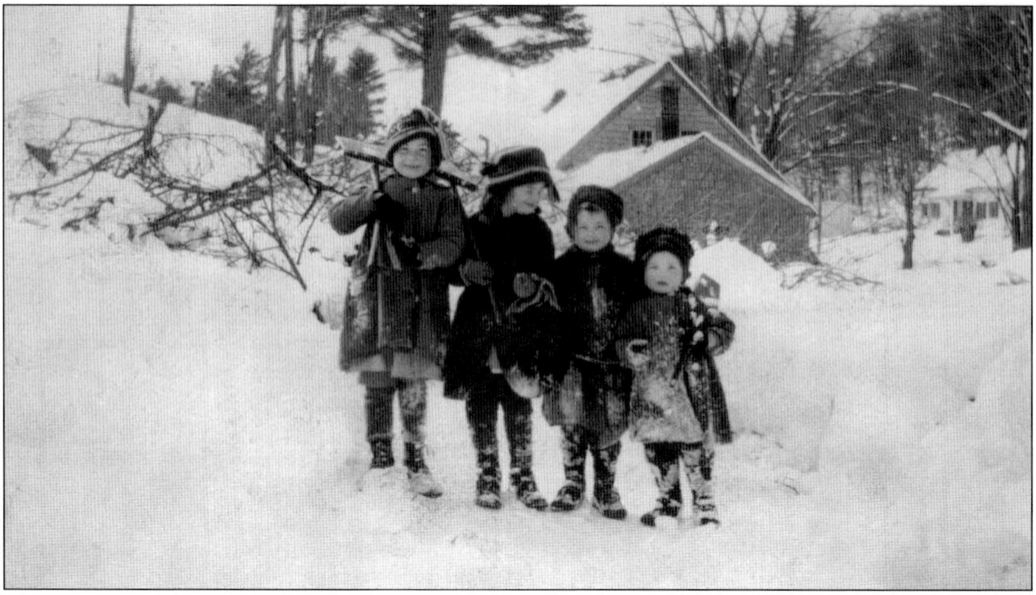

Margaret, Louise, Alice, and Helen Bartlett (pictured from left to right) were affectionately known as the "Belles of Melvin." They are assisting their father, Elmer, with the chore of shoveling snow. Growing up without any brothers, the girls took on many tasks usually relegated to boys. They hauled wood from the excelsior mill for heating, assisted with barn chores, and planted the garden. They were forbidden to walk on the railroad tracks to school. (WHS.)

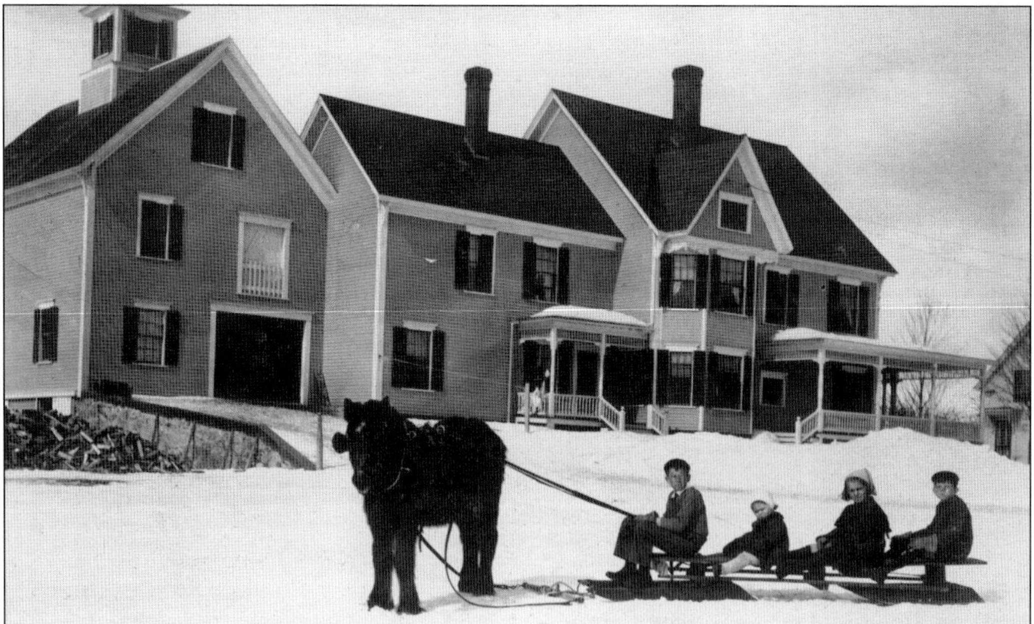

Horace, Lawrence, Mary, and Herbert Martin (pictured from left to right) pose with their pony and double-runner sled in front of their home on Kearsarge Street. These sleds were used for coasting on the rolled or plowed roads in winter. Tory, Pumpkin, and Burnt Hills were popular spots with steep grades and long runoffs. Then it was a long trudge back up the hill, unless one had a pony. (WHS.)

This boy, thought to be Nelson Spaulding, poses with his trusty collie. Cats and dogs were considered working animals in the earliest days, catching rodents and herding sheep. Scotsman Sam Stoddard trained border collies on Hogg Hill in Bradford. He took many honors for their performances at agricultural fairs and spent the winter months with his dogs in western states, working them on the range. (Courtesy of Steven Hansen.)

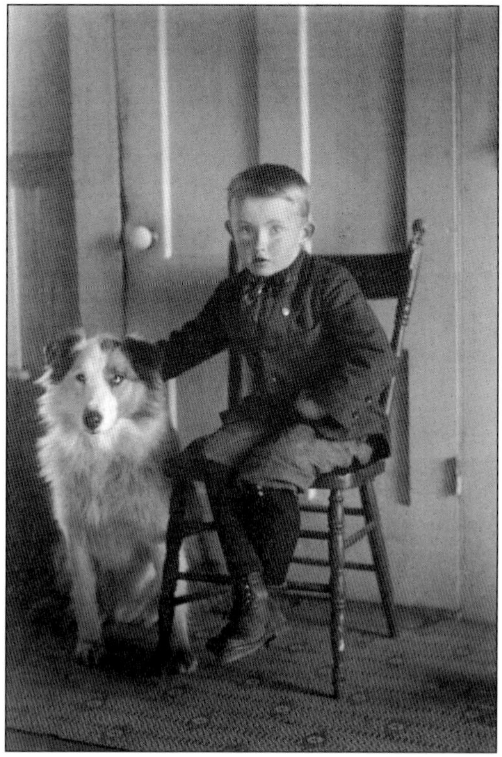

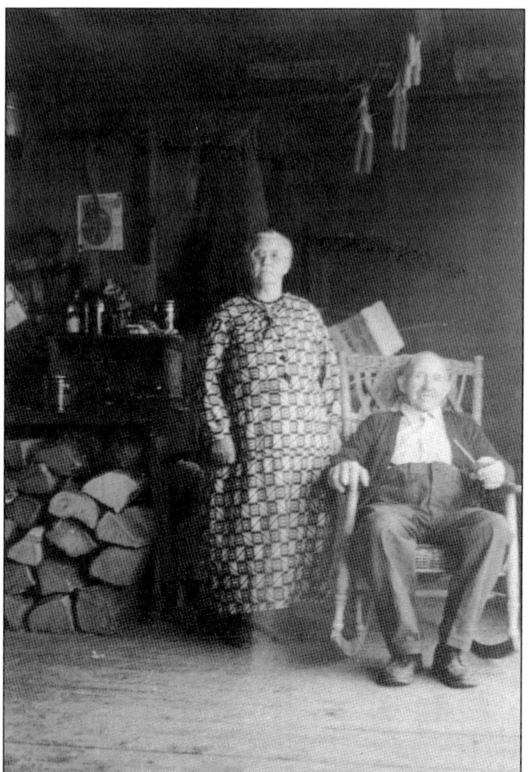

This unidentified elderly couple takes a rest at day's end. Resident Will Cressy's diary reads: "When the cows are in the stanchions / And the horses had their hay / When the evenin' chores are tended, And things are put away . . . / Well it ain't quite heaven maybe / But it's mighty close to it / When the day dies in the country / And the evenin' lamp is lit." (BHS.)

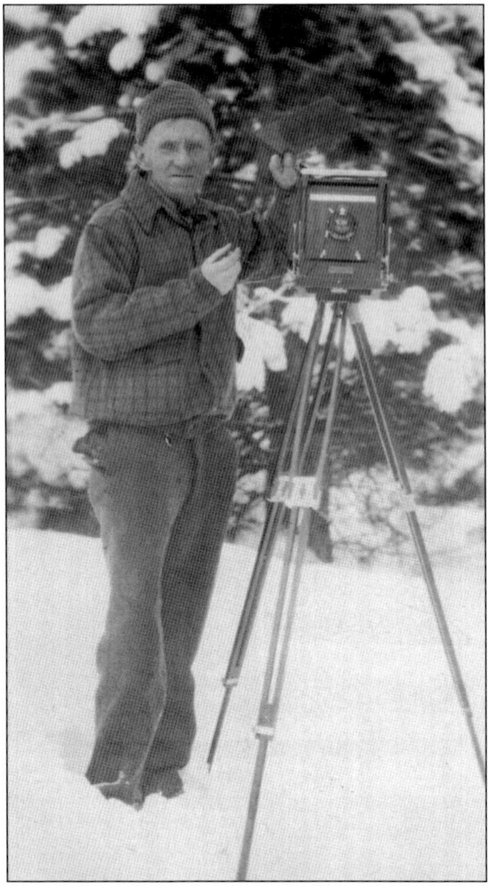

This is a portrait of Ralph Pratt with his camera. Pratt was responsible for taking hundreds of photographs of Warner through the years, ranging from primly lined schoolchildren in front of the Warner Graded School to businesses and homes along Warner's streets to images of his beloved Mink Hills and Mount Kearsarge. He attended art school in Boston and taught art in Warner's one-room schoolhouses. (WHS.)

Alice (second from left) and Charles Hardy (far right) are shown playing cards with friends in the studio of their home. Alice probably learned photography from her father, Moses Harriman. Charles managed the telephone company and operated a jewelry store in their home. The Hardys took several unique photographs in the street outside of their studio, including this book's cover image. (WHS–Hardy.)

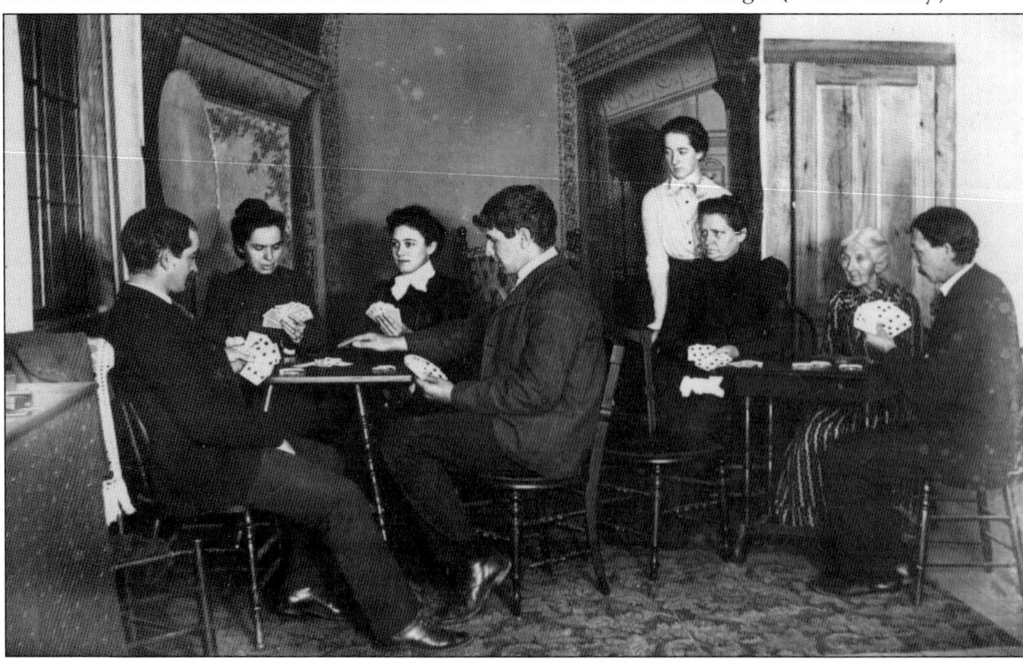

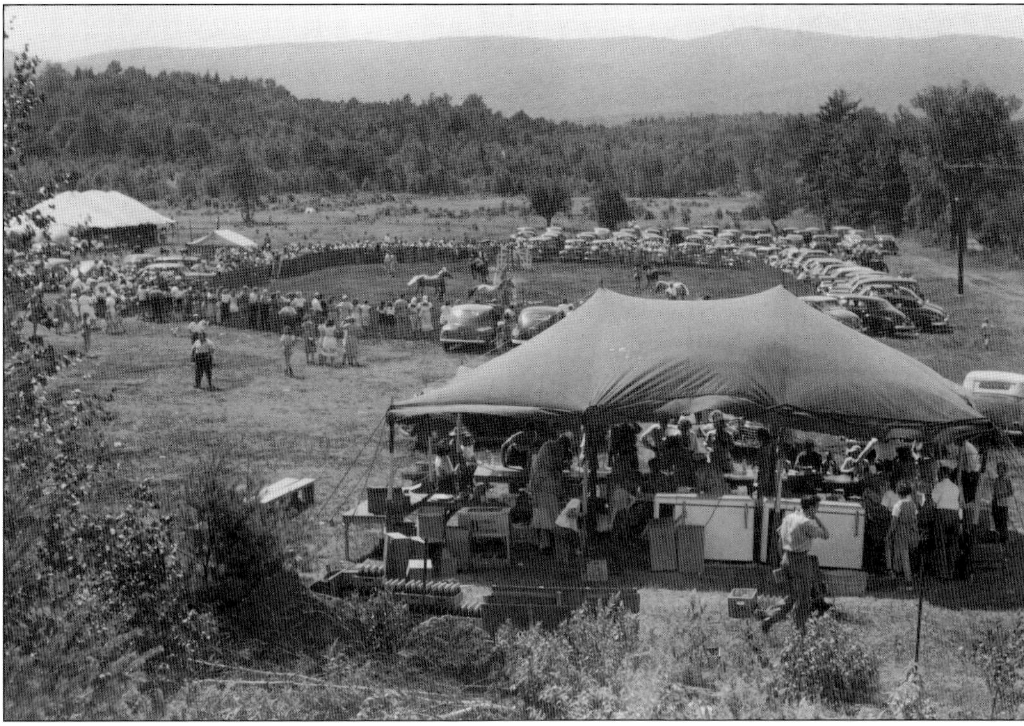

The Bradford Horse Show, which began as an addition to the annual Woman's Club Fair, was a resounding success in 1947–1948. Ideal weather helped to draw thousands of participants and spectators from neighboring states. The event featured a 4-H Field Day, a mile-long parade, a chuck wagon supper, and a play. The show eventually moved to Mount Sunapee State Park. (BHS.)

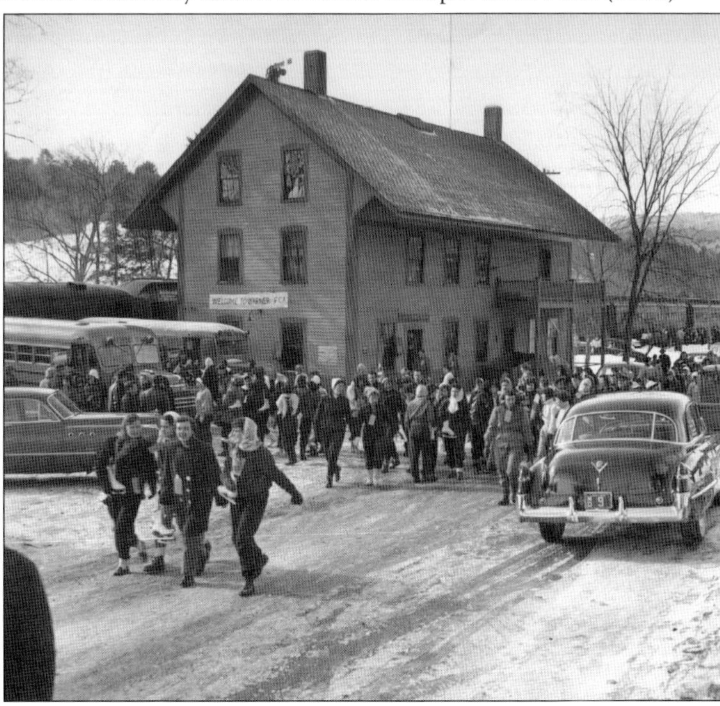

Warner is famous for having the first snow train in 1931. The rope tow was not installed until after World War II, so skiers trudged up Tory and Burnt Hills and skied down. The Warner Planning & Development Committee organized events with many Boston businesses including the John Hancock Co., which arrived 1,500 strong to ski, skate, toboggan, and consume a delicious turkey shortcake dinner before returning home. (WHS.)

Discover Thousands of Local History Books Featuring Millions of Vintage Images

Arcadia Publishing, the leading local history publisher in the United States, is committed to making history accessible and meaningful through publishing books that celebrate and preserve the heritage of America's people and places.

Find more books like this at
www.arcadiapublishing.com

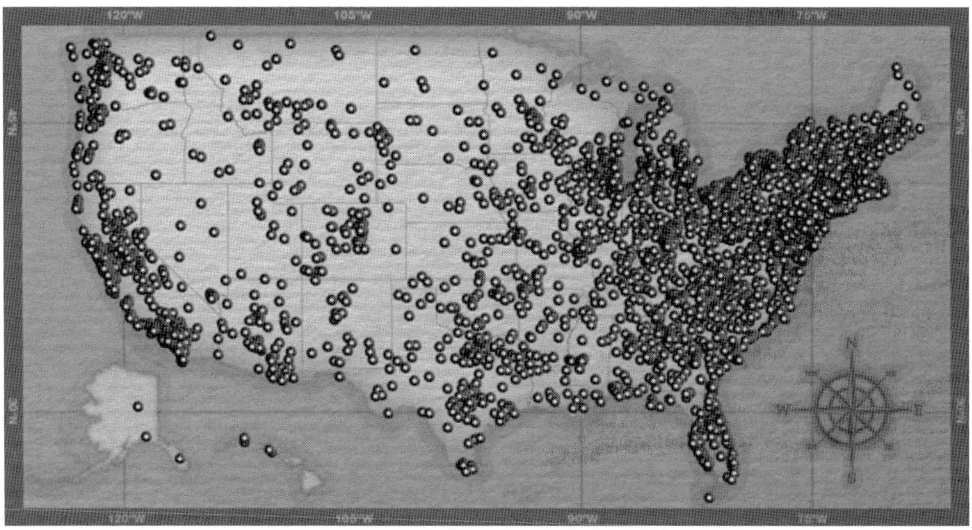

Search for your hometown history, your old stomping grounds, and even your favorite sports team.

Consistent with our mission to preserve history on a local level, this book was printed in South Carolina on American-made paper and manufactured entirely in the United States. Products carrying the accredited Forest Stewardship Council (FSC) label are printed on 100 percent FSC-certified paper.

MADE IN THE USA